Website Design and Development with HTML5 and CSS3

Series Editor
Jean-Charles Pomerol

Website Design and Development with HTML5 and CSS3

Hassen Ben Rebah
Hafedh Boukthir
Antoine Chédebois

WILEY

First published 2021 in Great Britain and the United States by ISTE Ltd and John Wiley & Sons, Inc.

ISTE Ltd
27-37 St George's Road
London SW19 4EU
UK

www.iste.co.uk

John Wiley & Sons, Inc.
111 River Street
Hoboken, NJ 07030
USA

www.wiley.com

Library of Congress Control Number: 2021940275

British Library Cataloguing-in-Publication Data
A CIP record for this book is available from the British Library
ISBN 978-1-78630-696-8

Contents

Foreword

When Hassen Ben Rebah contacted me to write the foreword to his new book on HTML5 and CSS3 in collaboration with his colleagues, I was surprised by the invitation. One can only accept such an honor. Hassen Ben Rebah is a university teacher recognized for his know-how and knowledge of web programming (HTML5, CSS3, JavaScript, etc.). He is excellent at passing his knowledge on to others. Two people have embarked on this new adventure with him: Antoine, a lead developer at Amazon, and Hafedh, a fellow teacher. The collaboration of these three authors promises to culminate in a fine work.

It is also worth remembering that 2020 is the 10th year that HTML5 has been creating a stir in the world for web designers! What better time to produce this new opus on HTML5? Of course, the first official version was released in 2014, but we had all been eagerly awaiting it since 2010. The HTML5 specifications are the longest of all the major versions of HTML to be written since it came into existence. This just shows the power of this version!

Today, we cannot talk about HTML5 without associating it with CSS3. This version of stylesheets has existed for 20 years, yet it has only been effectively integrated into modern navigators for a quarter of its life. Modernity, indeed, as CSS3 offers a veritable arsenal of selectors, use of web fonts, gradients, shadows and animations without a single line of JavaScript! The only limit to your creativity will be your own imagination.

Who better than two teachers and a lead developer to explain the magic of these two computer languages? Hassen, Antoine and Hafedh will accompany you throughout this book in your understanding and mastery of the indissociable pairing that is HTML5 and CSS3. In it you will find a whole repository for each language, as well as concrete examples of their use. This book will become your new bedside reading.

Teddy PAYET
Lead Developer CTO Freelance
July 2021

Preface

Book objectives and structure

This book discusses website programming through the study of the HTML5 and CSS3 web development languages. The first is used for the structuring and content of a site, and the second for graphic design and formatting.

The book begins by focusing on studying the HTML5 and CSS3 languages; it then presents the procedure for creating a website (choice of architecture, hosting, updating, referencing, etc.) as well as the key rules to be applied in order to ensure the success of the project, in particular by better meeting user needs.

In addition, there are examples illustrating the majority of the chapters in the book. This work also features corrected practical exercises, structured according to an expanding logic: from designing a simple HTML5 page to creating a professional website. These exercises serve to teach readers the basic concepts they need to master if they wish to create a website: page structure, element positioning, insertion of forms, tables, images, videos, audios, etc.

All the source codes of the practical exercises presented in this book are available on GitHub.

Target readership

This book is intended for both students and academics starting out in the field of web page development and creation, and also for website designers and web designers wishing to develop their creations.

July 2021

1

The Web and its Future

At the turn of the 21st century, information, including access to the Internet, became the basis for personal, economic and political progress. A popular name for the Internet is the "information highway", and it became the place where one goes to find the latest financial news, to browse library catalogs, to exchange information with colleagues or to participate in a lively political debate. The Internet is the tool that will lead you, beyond telephones, faxes and isolated computers, to a rapidly growing network of information without borders.

The Internet complements the traditional tools you use to collect information, graphical data, view the news and connect with others. The Internet is shrinking the world; bringing information, skills and knowledge on almost all subjects imaginable directly to your computer.

The Internet is what we call a meta network, that is a network of networks that covers the entire world. It is impossible to give an exact number of the amount of networks or users that make up the Internet, but it easily exceeds several billion (4.57 billion Internet users in the first quarter of 2020 according to the site blogdumoderateur[1]).

1.1. Background

The Internet was first designed by the Department of Defense, as a means of protecting US government communications systems in the event of a military attack. The original network, baptized ARPANET (after the Advanced Research Projects

For a color version of all the figures in this chapter, see: www.iste.co.uk/benrebah/website.zip.

1 BDM is a medium launched in 2007 by HelloWork, aimed at web workers and connected professionals: https://www.blogdumoderateur.com.

Agency that developed it), evolved into a communication channel between the entrepreneurs, military personnel and academic researchers who contribute to ARPA projects.

1.1.1. *The 1960s: context of the Cold War*

In 1957, the Advanced Research Project Agency (ARPA) was created in the United States to lead a small number of projects aimed at ensuring scientific and technical predominance over the Russians. Making up this organization was some of the United States' most valued scientists.

In 1967, Lawrence G. Roberts, who had recently chaired the ARPA computer network project, presented these scenarios for the ARPANET (Advanced Research Projects Agency NETwork). Meanwhile, that same year, Donald Davies and Robert Scantlebury of the National Physical Laboratory (NPL) in the United Kingdom announced the design of a packet-switching network.

1.1.2. *The 1970s and 1980s: birth of the TCP/IP protocol*

In 1969, the ARPANET began to operate, initially linking up four universities. Using this connection, four facilities were able to transfer data and perform lengthy calculations, remotely, on multiple computers.

During the 1970s, research laboratories gradually linked up to the ARPANET.

In 1970, the Network Control Protocol (NCP) was used on ARPANET with the aim of linking heterogeneous devices (IBM, Unix, etc.).

In 1983, the NCP was definitively cast aside in favor of the Transmission Control Protocol/Internet Protocol (TCP/IP), which is still in use now and represents the main protocol of the Internet. The TCP is responsible for segmenting a message into packets and rearranging the packets after they are received, while the role of IP is to ensure that packets pass from one computer to another until they reach their destination.

1.1.3. *The 1980s, 1990s and 2000s: evolution of the Internet to the WWW*

In 1977, the TCP/IP was effectively used to link several networks to the ARPANET. More than a hundred computers were connected, and from this point, the number would continue to increase year after year.

In March 1989, Tim Berners-Lee, a computer scientist at the CERN (European Council for Nuclear Research), advised putting documents on the CERN website that were linked by hyperlinks, with the aim of helping physicists searching for information. The origin of the Web dates back to this point in time.

In the early 1990s, the birth of the Internet as we know it today was announced: the Web was defined by a collection of HTML (HyperText Markup Language) pages combining text, images and links that can be reached via a URL (Uniform Resource Locator), based on HTTP (HyperText Transfer Protocol).

In 1991, in Geneva, Tim Berners-Lee developed the Internet interface known as the World Wide Web (WWW), allowing the network to be opened up to the general public by facilitating website consultation instructions.

In 1991, 300,000 computers were connected, with this figure reaching 1,000,000 by 1992.

In 1992, the first link (*known as a hyperlink*), enabling access to the CERN's Internet site, was built on the Fermilab server in the United States: this was the beginning of the weaving of the WWW. The Net continued to expand at an exponential rate during the 1990s under the impetus of the Web.

The year 1993 saw the birth of the first web browser, designed by Netscape, which supported text and images. That same year, the National Science Foundation (NSF) founded a company to enable the registration of domain names.

In 1993, there were 600 sites, with this figure exceeding 15,000 by 1995. Today, the WWW has come to be the most valued service on the Internet.

As of 2008, there were 1.5 billion Internet users worldwide, 1.3 billion email users, 210 billion emails sent daily, 186.7 million websites and 133 million blogs.

E-commerce revenues exceeded $2,300 billion in 2017 and are expected to reach $4,500 billion in 2021.

1.2. Phases of evolution of the Web

The World Wide Web, commonly known as the Web, and sometimes as the Net, presents a hypertext system running on the Internet. The Web is used to consult accessible pages on websites using a browser. The image of the spiderweb originates from the hyperlinks that interconnect web pages.

1.2.1. *1991–1999: Web 1.0, static or passive?*

Web 1.0 functioned in a strictly linear manner: a producer would offer content that was displayed on a website, and Internet users would consult this site. This generation of the Web favored product-oriented sites, which had little influence on user influx. This period was marked by the birth of the first e-commerce sites. Proprietary programs and software were extremely costly.

Figure 1.1. *Web 1.0: diffusion*

1.2.2. *2000–2010: Web 2.0, collaborative or social?*

Web 2.0 offered a completely new outlook. It promoted the sharing and exchange of information and data (text, videos, images and more), and witnessed the upsurge of social media, blogs, wikis and smartphones. The Web was becoming more popular and stimulating. The customer's opinion was constantly coveted and users developed a taste for this virtual collectivization. However, the reproduction of content of disproportionate quality led to an overabundance of information that was difficult to verify.

Figure 1.2. *Web 2.0: collaboration*

1.2.3. *2010–2020: Web 3.0, semantic or smart?*

Web 3.0 aimed to classify the vast mass of usable information according to the conditions and requirements of each user, according to their positioning, preferences, etc. Websites evolved (and continue to evolve) into online applications that can automatically analyze written and pictorial data, that are able to understand, interpret and classify them, and rediffuse them to new Internet users.

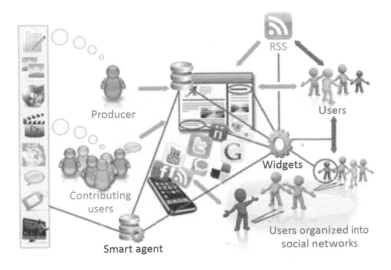

Figure 1.3. *Web 3.0: semantic*

1.2.4. *Since 2020: Web 4.0, intelligent*

It is very difficult to predict what the Web will become. Some believe that the future of Web 3.0 is Web 4.0, or the artificial intelligence-based Web. The purpose of this Web is to introduce people into a steadfastly remarkable environment (*strong and robust*). Nova Spivack[2], founder of Radar Networks, gives the definition of Web 4.0 as "the ability to work with tools online only". Similarly, Joël de Rosnay[3], consultant to the president of the Cité des sciences et de l'industrie (a science museum whose name means "City of Science and Industry") at La Villette, Paris, indicates that this version of the Web is synonymous with cloud computing.

---

2 Nova Spivack is an American entrepreneur: https://en.wikipedia.org/wiki/Nova_Spivack.
3 Joël de Rosnay is a French writer: https://fr.wikipedia.org/wiki/Joël_de_Rosnay.

NOTE.– Wikipedia[4] defines cloud computing as a concept referring to the use of memory and computing skills of devices and servers shared all over the world, and interconnected by an international network: the Internet.

EXAMPLE.–

There are now clothes that are available that include electronic chips using biosensors to detect information on the body. This information can then be sent to calculators connected to the Internet via wireless networks such as WiFi. This information can be used to identify the wearer of the clothes in the event of an accident, for example. The individual can be recovered by utilizing the information transmitted between the different technologies in use (*biosensor, WiFi network, Internet and satellites*).

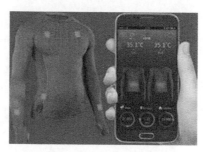

Figure 1.4. *Connected textiles*

EXAMPLE.–

Certain refrigerators can automatically detect missing ingredients, and with a single click and without the need to open it, the refrigerator gives you a description of the missing ingredients as well as the nearest supermarkets that sell this product.

Figure 1.5. *LCD screen of a Samsung smart refrigerator[5]*

---

4 https://www.wikipedia.com.
5 www.francoischarron.com.

1.3. Web application architecture

1.3.1. *The three levels of abstraction of an application*

In general, we can divide a computer application into three different levels of abstraction:

– *Presentation*, also known as HMI, promotes interaction between the user and the application. This layer governs keyboard and mouse input, and presents information on the screen. It is strongly recommended that this aspect be ergonomic and pleasant.

– *Processing* represents the tasks to be performed by the application. They are divided into two categories:

- local processing, assembling the checks performed on the conversation with the HMI (e.g. checking and input assistance);

- global processing, essentially forming the application. This is what is known as the *business logic* layer.

Data, more precisely access to data, which involves assembling the tools for managing data stored by the software.

Presentation		Presentation management	
		Presentation logic	Core of the application
Processing	Local	Processing logic	
	Global	Processing management	
Data		Data logic	
		Data management	

Table 1.1. *The three levels of abstraction of an application*[6]

NOTE.– These three levels can be nested or distributed in several possible ways between multiple computers.

---

6 http://www.info.univ-angers.fr/pub/gh/internet/ntiers.pdf.

1.3.2. *One-tier architecture*

In the case of a one-tier application, the three layers are connected and run on the same device: it is a centralized architecture. In this situation, users access applications running on the primary server (the mainframe) through passive terminals, which are slaves. The primary server handles all processing, in addition to the presentation that is easily relayed back onto client devices.

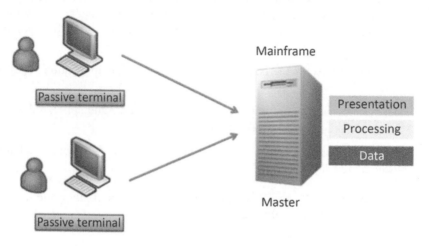

Figure 1.6. *Architecture of an application on a central server*

Benefits	Disadvantages
Meets the needs of a single user	Mainframe overload
Easy to deploy	Maintenance is difficult

Table 1.2. *Benefits and disadvantages of one-tier architecture*

1.3.3. *Two-tier architecture*

In the case of two-tier architecture, also known as a client-data server, or first-generation client-server, the client device is satisfied with assigning data management to another service. A specific example of this architecture is a management application that runs on a Windows or Linux operating system and accesses a central DataBase Management System (DBMS). This application makes it possible to benefit from the power of calculators deployed in a network in order to provide a user-friendly interface, while ensuring consistency of the data, which are always managed centrally.

A centralized DBMS handles data management and runs frequently on a dedicated server. This server is queried using a query language, usually Structured Query Language (SQL). The conversation between the client and the server can therefore be summarized as the sending of requests and, in response, data matching the requests.

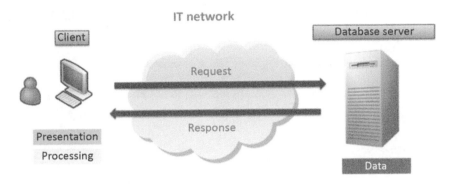

Figure 1.7. *Two-tier architecture (client-data server)*

NOTE.– The exchange of messages between the client and the server is accomplished via a network by means of a middleware (*the network layers and software services promoting conversation between the components of a distributed application*).

Benefits	Disadvantages
User-friendly interface Centralized data Powerful architecture for a reduced number of users (< 50)	Fat client: the client supports most application processing Application updates must be deployed for all clients Limited number of clients: changes in the number of clients cause a degradation in server performance

Table 1.3. *Benefits and disadvantages of two-tier architecture*

1.3.4. *Three-tier architecture*

Three-tier architecture, also known as the client-distributed server, or the second-generation client-server, subdivides the application into three different service levels:

– first level: presentation and local processing (*data formatting, input checks,* etc.) are accomplished by the client device;

– second level: global processing of the application is accomplished by a web server equipped with application extensions;

– third level: the data are accomplished by a database server (*centralized DBMS*).

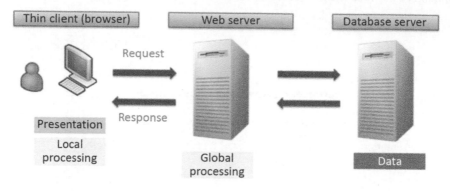

Figure 1.8. *Three-tier architecture*

Benefits	Disadvantages
Thin client Easier deployment Centralized DBMS	All of the complexity lies in the intermediate tier (the web server)

Table 1.4. *Benefits and disadvantages of three-tier architecture*

1.3.5. n-*tier architecture*

n-tier architecture was created to address the limitations of three-party architectures and to create robust, easy-to-maintain applications. In reality, *n*-tier architecture confirms the distribution of the application layer between different services and not the reproduction of the layers. The application layer consists of "business" components that are independent and specialized. They communicate with each other and can collaborate, and are installed on different workstations.

This architecture promotes the free distribution of business logic to facilitate the distribution of the load on all levels.

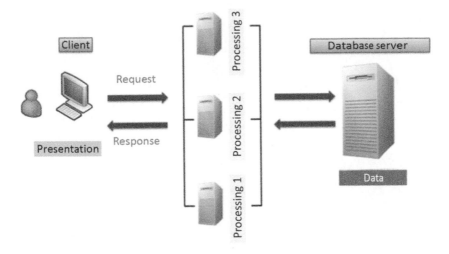

Figure 1.9. n-*tier architecture*

2

The Language of the Web: HTML5

An Internet site is formed by a set of connected resources or web pages, generally associated with a well-defined topic, which are made available to Internet users through a web address.

Today, an Internet site represents the most modern means of publication and communication. Creating a web page requires the use of a specific language, called HTML (Hyper Text Markup Language).

HTML is a "markup" language that is used for the creation, representation and structuring of the content of a web page by means of formatting elements or tags.

These tags have well-defined meanings, such as inserting an image, creating a link or a paragraph, etc., and are generally inserted into the text of a document before being interpreted and displayed by the web browser.

HTML is a standard published by W3C (World Wide Web Consortium).

2.1. Overview

2.1.1. *Origins of HTML5*

– 1986: Creation of the first ever SGML (Standard Generalized Markup Language) for structuring various types of content. This language was considered very complex in order to be applied to the Web, hence the need to introduce a new, more lightweight language based on the same concepts.

– 1991: Creation of the first version of the HTML language (HTML 1.0) by Tim Berners-Lee, in the form of a personal invention.

– 1994: Appearance of the second version of the HTML language (HTML 2.0); this version was the cornerstone of subsequent generations of HTML. HTML 2.0 is a W3C recommendation.

– 1996: Appearance of the third version of the HTML language (HTML 3.0). This version was characterized by the integration of several new features in the language, namely, tables, text positioning and applets.

– 1998: Appearance of the most commonly used HTML version on the Web (HTML 4.01). This version provided developers with the possibility of using frames (splitting a web page into multiple areas), tables and more advanced forms. Similarly, with this version it was possible, for the first time, to use CSSs (Cascading Styles Sheets) to format the content of a web page.

– 2000: The XHTML (EXtensible HyperText Markup Language) language was defined by the W3C: this was a new presentation of the HTML language as an XML application.

– 2012: The WHATWG (Web Hypertext Application Technology Working Group), launched by Ian Hickon (at Google since 2017), began the development of the HTML 5.0 language. This new version brought several improvements to the language, namely, the ability to easily integrate audio and video media, better arrangement of the content of the web page and new options for forms.

2.1.2. Syntax and lexicon of the HTML5 language

The HTML5 language was created to structure and give meaning to the content of the web page. Its lexicon essentially revolves around three basic terms: element, tag and attribute.

2.1.2.1. Elements

Elements refer to the identifiers describing objects (text, image or multimedia object) within a web page, including the structure and content.

EXAMPLE.–

```
<p></p>: to designate a paragraph
<a></a>: to designate a link
```

2.1.2.2. Tags

The term "tag" is one of the basic concepts of the HTML language. The elements in HTML are often made up of several sets of tags. These tags are not displayed as such on the web page, but it is thanks to the browser installed on the user's computer that their effect will be displayed correctly.

There are two types of tags:

– Paired tags: made up of two tags, one opening and one closing. The opening tag is marked at the beginning with the "<" sign and at the end with the ">" sign. The closing tag follows the same principle, but the element name is preceded by the slash character (/).

EXAMPLE.–

```
<strong>display a text in bold</strong>
```

– Singular tags: these tags are most often used to insert an element in a well-defined location on the web page. For this type of tag, it is not necessary to mark the beginning and end of this element.

EXAMPLE.–

```
<img />
```

NOTE.– In order to not confuse the concepts of "tag" and "element", consider the following example: `<p>The element P comprises terms in <em>emphasis</em>.</p>`.

In addition to the text, the <p> element contains other tags (in this case <em> as an example), while the <em> tag only contains text.

2.1.2.3. *Attributes*

Attributes are properties used to add additional statements to a given element (*an identifier (id), a source (src)*, etc.). They are always embedded in the opening tag and must be distanced from each other by at least one space. Each attribute generally accepts a value placed in quotation marks.

An element with attributes can accept the following syntax:

```
<element attribute_1="value_1" attribute_2="value_2"> Content of the
element</element>
```

EXAMPLE.– Case of a singular tag.

```
<imgsrc="http:/logo.jpg" alt="Logo"/>
```

2.1.3. *Basic rules of HTML5*

2.1.3.1. *A well-formed document*

An HTML5 document is said to be well formed if it observes the following basic rules:

– the elements and attributes are case insensitive. For example: <div> and <DIV> are acceptable;

– pair elements must contain two tags, one opening and one closing, which simplify the browser's task. For example, instead of writing:

```
<ul>
    <li>theme 1
    <li>theme 2
```

it is advisable to present the following code:

```
<ul>
    <li>theme 1</li>
    <li>theme 2</li>
</ul>
```

– singular tags contain only one tag, which ends with the characters "/>", preceded by a space. For example, instead of writing:

```
<imgsrc="logo.jpg">
```

it is recommended to present the following code:

```
<imgsrc="logo.jpg"/>
```

– the elements in an HTML document must not overlap and thus observe the principle of first open, last closed. For example, the following code is said to be incorrect:

```
<p>the student achieved a high<strong>average</p></strong>
```

and must be corrected to the following:

```
<p>the student achieved a high<strong>average</strong></p>
```

– all attributes must accept a value enclosed in quotes ("). Attributes belonging to the same element must be separated from each other by at least one space. For example, instead of writing:

```
<div class=C1 title=T1>This is a text</div>
```

it is recommended to present the following code:

```
<div class="C1" title="T1">This is a text</div>
```

– a value must be assigned to all attributes embedded within an element, even those that can have a unique value. For example, instead of writing:

```
<input type="radio" checked disabled/>
```

it is advisable to present the following code:

```
<input type="radio" checked="checked" disabled="disabled"/>
```

It should be noted that exceptions exist for attributes that accept Boolean values, i.e. the presence of only the name of an attribute means that the latter's value is true, whereas its absence implies that the value is false.

2.1.3.2. A compliant document

An HTML5 document must also observe inclusion rules, i.e. a well-defined element can only contain one of its child elements and can only be included in one of its parent elements. For example, instead of writing:

```
<div>
    <body></body>
</div>
```

it is advisable to present the following code:

```
<body>
    <div>
        <!-- Content of the division -->
    </div>
</body>
```

2.1.4. Working environment

To create a web page with HTML5, the most appropriate working environment needs to be used. Table 2.1 contains a non-exhaustive list of editors.

NOTE.– To test a web page that has already been created using a standard or visual editor, the user must have a web browser (Google Chrome, Opera or Mozilla Firefox).

Editor	Logo
Notepad++ is an open-source text editor developed in C++, running on Windows and integrates the syntax highlighting of the source code.	
Visual Studio Code is an extensible code editor developed by Microsoft, running on Windows, Linux and macOS.	
Brackets is an OpenSource code editor developed by the Adobe Systems teams for developing and designing web pages in HTML, CSS or JavaScript formats.	
Atom is an open-source text editor developed by GitHub, running on macOS, GNU/Linux and Windows. It supports plug-ins written in Node.js and Git Control.	

Table 2.1. *Examples of web development editors. For a color version of this table, see www.iste.co.uk/benrebah/website.zip*

2.2. Structure of an HTML5 document

An HTML5 document can accept the following structure:

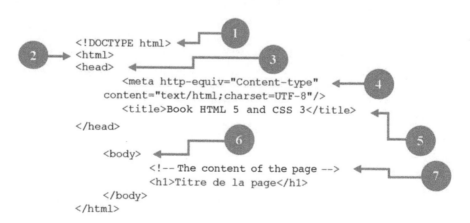

Table 2.2 describes the elements shown in the previous example.

No.	Meaning
1	DOCTYPE declaration This is a mandatory declaration that specifies the type of document that will be created.
2	Root element \<html\> – This is the root of the document. – It has two child elements: \<head\> and \<body\>. – It has attributes such as: - lang: its value is a standardized code that corresponds to the default language used at web-page level; - dir: designates the reading direction of the text at page level. It can have the value "ltr" (*text reads from left to right, as in English*) or "rtl" (*text reads from right to left, as in Arabic*). EXAMPLE.– \<html lang="ar" dir="rtl"\>…\</html\>
3	Header of a document: the \<head\> element This contains information that is essential for the web page to display correctly. This information, called metadata, is represented by the following elements: – \<base /\>: an empty element containing the list of the following attributes: - id: the identifier of the element; - href: a mandatory attribute whose content is presented in the form of a URL that defines the address of all files embedded in the web page. EXAMPLE.– If we write the following code: \<base id="d1" href="http://www.site.com/"/\> the browser will try to find an image whose URL is indicated on the server by:/site/images/image.jpg at the address: http://www.site.com/lesson/images/image.jpg – \<link /\>: an empty element whose information is represented by its attributes. It is used to define a link between the current web page and another external file required by the HTML5 page. The most important attributes of this element are: - rel: determines the name of the relation to be defined with the external document; - type: determines the content of the external document; - href: contains the absolute or relative address of the associated external resource as the value. EXAMPLE.– \<link rel="stylesheet" type="text/css" href="file.css"/\> where: – rel="stylesheet": the external document is a style sheet (CSS); – type="text/css": the document is a style sheet (CSS); – href="file.css": the document path.

No.	Meaning
4	Meta-information: the <meta /> element – This is an empty element whose information is represented by its attributes. – The information for this element is invisible on the web page, but is generally aimed at browsers, the web server and search engines. – Each piece of information is represented by a name/content pair: - the name is specified in the name or http-equiv attributes, whose roles are similar; - the value is associated with the content in the content attribute. SYNTAX.– <metaname="name_1" content="value_1"/> <meta http-equiv="name_2" content="value_2" /> Most of the values of the name and http-equiv attributes are keywords. EXAMPLE.– <meta name= "author" content="Hassen" /> <!-- designates the author of the web page --> EXAMPLE.– <meta http-equiv="Content-type" content="text/html;charset=UTF-8" /> <!--designates the type and encoding of the document -->
5	<title> element – This is the title of the web page. – Any web page must have a title to describe its content. – The title must be fairly short (fewer than 100 characters). – The title is displayed at the top of the web page.
6	Body of the document: the < body> element – This is the container of all of the textual and graphical elements of a web page. – It is the main area of the page; its full content will be displayed on the screen.

No.	Meaning
	Comments
7	– A comment in HTML is a simple text, most often used to explain a code, that will never be displayed on a web page: it is ignored by the browser. – A comment always observes the following syntax: <!-- this is an HTML 5 comment -->

Table 2.2. *Structure of an HTML5 page*

2.3. Structuring the content of a web page

2.3.1. *The <div> element*

The semantic structure of an HTML document of what is between <body> and </body> is essential for the presentation of the web page to Internet users. This allows a <div> element to be added directly into the <body> part of the document. It is used to create what is called a "page division" or "section". Such a division offers the possibility of grouping a very wide variety of HTML elements (i.e. text, form and image) within a single block. It is then possible to apply precise positions.

The most commonly used attributes with the <div> element are shown in Table 2.3.

Attribute	Value	Description
class	Name of class	Define a class to an element.
id	Id	Define an identifier – ID – to an element.
lang	Language of the content	Define the language used within the content of an element. For American English: lang="en-us".
title	Text	Additional information about an element.
dir	Ltr or rtl	Define the reading direction of the text of an element.
accesskey	Character	Define a keyboard shortcut to access an element.
hidden	Hidden	Used to hide or mask an element. Masked elements are not displayed at page level.

Table 2.3. *The attributes of the <div> element*

EXAMPLE.–

```
<!DOCTYPE html>
<html>
<head>
      <meta http-equiv="Content-type" content="text/html;
      charset=UTF-8"/>
      <title>The div tag</title>
</head>
<body>
<div id="banner">
      <imgsrc= "banner.jpg" height="100" width="500"/>
</div>
      <div id="menu">
      <imgsrc= "menu.jpg" height="100" width="500"/>
      </div>
</body>
</html>
```

Section 1

Section 2

Figure 2.1 shows the result obtained.

Figure 2.1. *The result of using the <div> tag. For a color version of this figure, see www.iste.co.uk/benrebah/website.zip*

2.3.2. *The <span> element*

<span> is an HTML element very close to the <div> element; it is essentially an online generic container that is used to group elements, in order to apply style properties to them using CSS rules. Unlike <div>, which is a block-type element, <span> is a line-type element.

EXAMPLE.–

```
<!-- HTML code -->
<p>This book is a <span class="m">good support</span>for web
developers</p>
/*CSS code that consists of marking the words "good support" in red*/
.m{color="red"}
```

NOTE.– The attributes used with the <span> element are id, class, title, dir and lang.

2.3.3. *The new elements of HTML5*

The HTML5 language paid great attention to the structures of existing websites and standardized their use through the definition of certain tags.

Previously, it was possible to organize the splitting of a web page into multiple parts through the use of the <div> tag, whereas now developers use particular elements that refer to the type of content to include.

This contribution has the advantage of improving the visibility of pages to search engines, which have become better at distinguishing the informative parts of the site from other parts, such as navigation or advertising areas.

2.3.3.1. *The <header> tag*

The majority of websites have a header, which can generally contain a logo, slogan, banner, etc.

It is preferable to put this type of information inside <header> </header>:

```
<header>
        <!-- the content of the header of the web page -->
</header>
```

Figure 2.2. *The <header> of the mes.tn[1] site. For a color version of this figure, see www.iste.co.uk/benrebah/website.zip*

NOTE.–

– A <header> can contain different types of objects: image, text, hyperlink, video, etc.

– A web page can contain multiple headers, if it is made up of several sections, with each section able to accept its own <header>.

2.3.3.2. The <footer> tag

The footer is generally located at the bottom of the HTML document. It can contain information such as legal notices and contact links.

```
<footer>
        <!-- the content of the web footer -->
</footer>
```

---

1 mes.tn: Website of the Ministry of Higher Education and Scientific Research of Tunisia.

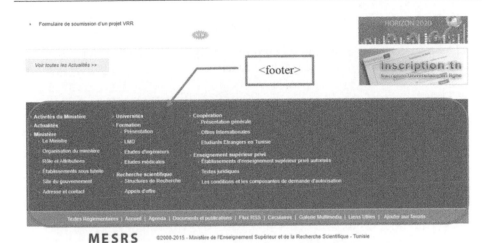

Figure 2.3. *The <footer> of the mes.tn site. For a color version of this figure, see www.iste.co.uk/benrebah/website.zip*

2.3.3.3 *The <nav> tag: main navigation links*

The <nav> tag must contain the main navigation links of a website. It can group the main menu of the site as an example. Typically, a menu can be presented as a bullet-point list placed between <nav></nav>:

```
<nav>
<ul>
<li><a href = "index.html">Ministry Activities</a></li>
<li><a href="latest news.html">Latest news</a></li>
<li><a href = "ministry.html">Ministry</a></li>
</ul>
</nav>
```

Figure 2.4 shows the main menu of the mes.tn site that could use the <nav> tag.

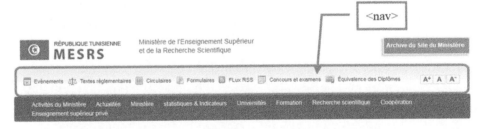

Figure 2.4. *The <nav> navigation links of the mes.tn site. For a color version of this figure, see www.iste.co.uk/benrebah/website.zip*

2.3.3.4. *The <section> tag: a section of the page*

The <section> tag is used to group different types of elements belonging to the same theme. It is most often used with a header:

```
<section>
        <h2>Title of the section</h2>
        <!-- Content of the section-->
</section>
```

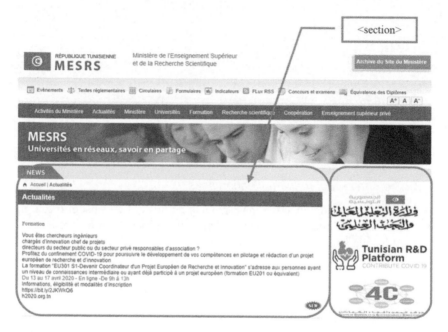

Figure 2.5. *<section> page section of the mes.tn site. For a color version of this figure, see www.iste.co.uk/benrebah/website.zip*

NOTE.– A section can contain an <h2> title, as well as the <header> element. In a single web page, it is possible to find more than one <h2> title, but it makes no sense to have more than one <h1> level 1 title.

2.3.3.5. *The <aside> tag: additional information*

The <aside> tag is used to define separate content that is complementary to the displayed document. This type of content is generally located on the side:

```
<aside>
        <!-- List of additional information -->
</aside>
```

NOTE.– A web page can contain multiple <aside> elements.

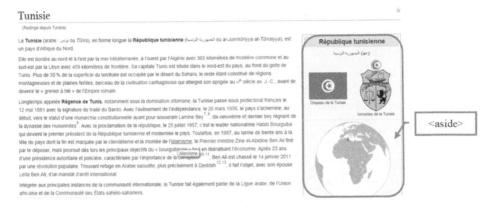

Figure 2.6. *<Aside> additional information block on wikipedia.org. For a color version of this figure, see www.iste.co.uk/benrebah/website.zip*

2.3.3.6. *The <article> tag: an independent article*

The <article> tag is generally used to wrap a standalone piece of content that is independent of the other elements of the web page.

This content may be reused on another site. For example: newspaper articles and gadgets.

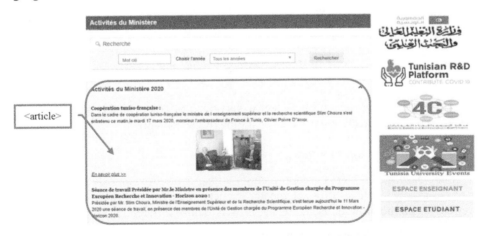

Figure 2.7. *An example of an <article> article from the MES.tn site. For a color version of this figure, see www.iste.co.uk/benrebah/website.zip*

2.4. Text organization

2.4.1. *Paragraphs and texts*

2.4.1.1. *The <p> tag*

A piece of text becomes more readable and easy to understand if it is divided into several paragraphs. In HTML, and in order to define a paragraph, it is recommended to use the <p></p> tag.

EXAMPLE.–

```
<body>
        <p>Welcome to ISET Mahdia!</p>
        <p>I wish you an excellent academic year 2019- 2020</p>
</body>
```

Figure 2.8 shows the result obtained.

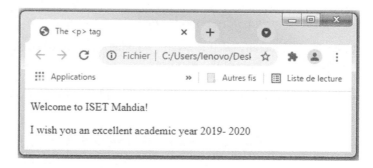

Figure 2.8. *Effect of the <p> tag*

NOTE.– When using the <p></p> tag, a paragraph is automatically preceded and followed by a line break to mark the separation of the content.

2.4.1.2. *The <blockquote> tag*

The <blockquote> tag is used to identify a long quote from an external source. It can essentially include flow elements, namely, paragraphs, titles and images. Depending on the browser used, this tag is used to have different effects:

– spacing from the document margin;

– a space before and after the content of the tag;

– etc.

The <blockquote> tag has the attribute shown in Table 2.4.

Attribute	Value	Description
cite	URL	Defines the source of the quote

Table 2.4. *Attribute of the <blockquote> tag*

EXAMPLE.–

```
<body>
A wise old man said:<blockquote>In life we do not do what we want but
we are responsible for what we are.</blockquote>
</body>
```

Figure 2.9 shows the result obtained.

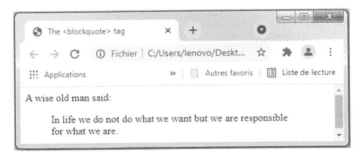

Figure 2.9. *Effect of the <blockquote> tag*

2.4.1.3. *The <q> tag*

The <q> tag is used to contain a short quotation. The result of its use displays a text surrounded by quotation marks in all browsers except Internet Explorer 7 and earlier versions.

EXAMPLE.–

```
<body>
A wise old man said:<q>Better late than ever.</q>
</body>
```

Figure 2.10 shows the result obtained.

Figure 2.10. *Effect of the <q> tag*

NOTE.– The <q></q> tag has the same "cite" attribute as the <blockquote> tag that defines the source of the quotation.

EXAMPLE.–

```
<body>
Jean-Paul Sartre said:<q cite="https://www.canva.com/fr_fr/citations/
anglaise/"> In life we do not do what we want but we are responsible
for what we are.</q>
</body>
```

2.4.1.4. The <strong> tag

The <strong> tag attributes high importance to a given text. In a web page, using this tag displays the text in bold.

EXAMPLE.–

```
<body>
    <p><strong>Decision making</strong>is a complex cognitive
process aimed at selecting a type of action from different
alternatives.</p>
</body>
```

Figure 2.11 shows the result obtained.

Figure 2.11. *Effect of the <strong> tag*

2.4.1.5. *The <em> tag*

The <em> tag is used in a paragraph to emphasize a portion of text.

The text framed by <em></em> is displayed in italics.

EXAMPLE.–

```
<body>
        <p> Hello and welcome!<br/>
        This is our last session<em>be careful</em>.</p>
</body>
```

Figure 2.12 shows the result obtained.

Figure 2.12. *Effect of the <em> tag*

2.4.1.6. *The <b> tag*

This is a historic tag that allows a text fragment to be displayed in bold.

In HTML5, it is preferable to replace it with the <strong> tag.

EXAMPLE.–

```
<body>
        <p>Hello Mr:<b>Hassen</b>, welcome</p>
</body>
```

Figure 2.13 shows the result obtained.

Figure 2.13. *Effect of the <b> tag*

NOTE.– Differences between <b> and <strong>:

– the <b> (for "bold") tag is used to frame a word or text fragment that the user wishes to display in bold: it is a style tag;

– the <strong> tag allows a word or text fragment that it frames to be attributed more contextual importance (a semantic value);

– in HTML5, the <strong> tag is defined as a structure tag and not as a style attribute. Its contribution to the <b> tag comes from its independence with respect to a given style.

2.4.1.7. The <i> tag

This is a historic tag used to display a portion of text in italics.

EXAMPLE.–

```
<body>
      <p>Hello Mr:<i>Hassen</i>, welcome</p>
</body>
```

Figure 2.14 shows the result obtained.

Figure 2.14. *Effect of the <i> tag*

NOTE.– Differences between <i> and <em>:

– the <i> tag is used to frame a word or text fragment that the user wishes to display in italics: it is a style tag;

– the <em> tag allows a word or text fragment that it frames to be attributed more contextual importance (a semantic value);

– in HTML5, the <em> tag is defined as a structure tag and not as a style attribute.

2.4.1.8. *The <small> tag*

The <small> tag is used to decrease the text size.

It is mainly used for secondary content: annotations and legal notices (copyright, etc.).

EXAMPLE.–

```
<body>
        <p>This course material is designed for students in their first
year of ISETS higher education<br/> specializing in information
technology.</p>
        <p>We hope that this material offers you a great degree of help
and information on "Web programming".<br/> We would be grateful if
you could share with us your comments and suggestions.</p>
        <small>Hassen BEN REBAH ©</small>
</body>
```

Figure 2.15 shows the result obtained.

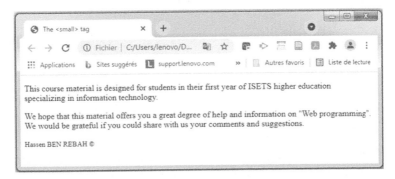

Figure 2.15. *Effect of the <small> tag*

2.4.1.9. *The <dfn> tag*

The <dfn> tag is used to indicate a word or expression to be defined in a text block. It only contains the term to be defined.

EXAMPLE.–

```
<body>
        <p><dfn>Computer network</dfn> is a collection of computers
connected to each other through wired or non-wired links with a view
to facilitating the sharing of hardware and software resources.</p>
</body>
```

NOTE.– The <dfn> tag does not accept a default style, but most browsers display this element with an italic style.

2.4.1.10. *The <abbr> tag*

The <abbr> tag defines an abbreviation or an acronym. Marking abbreviations with the <abbr> tag can provide useful information for browsers and search engines.

EXAMPLE.–

```
<body>
<abbr title="Higher Institute of Technological Studies">HITS </abbr>
is a university institution.
</body>
```

NOTE.– The "title" attribute of the <abbr> tag generally contains the text in its extended form of the abbreviation or acronym.

2.4.1.11. *The <code> tag*

The <code> tag is used to contain a portion of computer code from any programming language. In general, the <code> tag does not have a default style rule.

EXAMPLE.–

```
<body>
        <p>The following Pascal code is used to calculate the sum of
two integers</p>
        <code>
        Begin
        Readln(a,b);
        s:=a+b;
```

```
        writeln('the sumis ',s);
    end;
    </code>
</body>
```

Figure 2.16 shows the result obtained.

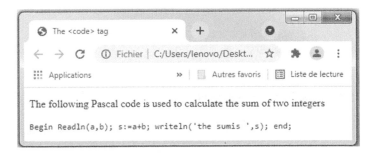

Figure 2.16. *Effect of the <code> tag*

2.4.1.12. *The <var> tag*

The <var> tag is used to wrap a piece of content that defines a variable. The text of this tag is displayed in italics.

EXAMPLE.–

```
<body>
The result of the addition of <var>x</var>+<var>y </var> is:
</body>
```

Figure 2.17 shows the result obtained.

Figure 2.17. *Effect of the <var> tag*

2.4.1.13. *The <kbd> tag*

The <kbd> tag is used to present user inputs via the keyboard.

The browser displays the content of this element in the monotype font.

EXAMPLE.–

```
<body>
      <p>Enter the following text in the Run window:
      <kbd>cmd</kbd><br/>     Then click on the OK button</p>
</body>
```

Figure 2.18 shows the result obtained.

Figure 2.18. *Effect of the <kbd> tag*

2.4.1.14. *The <samp> tag*

The <samp> tag is used to present a result from a computer program.

It is generally displayed in the monotype font.

EXAMPLE.–

```
<body>
      <p>Normal  text  -  <samp>Text  produced  by  a  program.</samp>  -
Normal text</p>
</body>
```

Figure 2.19 shows the result obtained.

Figure 2.19. *Effect of the <samp> tag*

2.4.1.15. *The <sub> tag*

The <sub> tag is used to display text that is subscript with respect to the main text block.

EXAMPLE.–

```
<body>
        <p>The water molecule is symbolized by H<sub>2</sub>O.</p>
</body>
```

Figure 2.20 shows the result obtained.

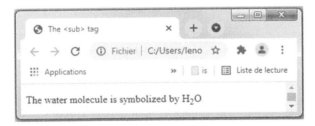

Figure 2.20. *Effect of the <sub> tag*

2.4.1.16. *The <sup> tag*

The <sup> tag is used to present a fragment of text that appears on a higher line and is often smaller than the surrounding text.

EXAMPLE.–

```
<body>
        <p>This text is set to <sup>exponent</sup></p>
</body>
```

Figure 2.21 shows the result obtained.

Figure 2.21. *Effect of the <sup> tag*

2.4.1.17. *The <time> tag*

The <time> tag is used to present a time (*using the 24-hour clock*) or a date (*using the Gregorian calendar*).

It is used to apply time-order information in a browser-readable format.

The <time> tag has the list of attributes shown in Table 2.5.

Attribute	Value	Description
datetime	Date or time or date and time	Used to assign the date and/or time element in a standardized format.
pubdate	Pubdate or "" or (empty)	Used to indicate that the given date is relative to the publication of the entire document, otherwise the nearest <article> ancestor, if one exists.

Table 2.5. *Attributes of the <time> tag*

EXAMPLE.–

```
<body>
      <p>The concert starts at <time>20:00</time>.</p>
</body>
```

Figure 2.22 shows the result obtained.

Figure 2.22. *Effect of the <time> tag*

EXAMPLE.– With datetime.

```
<body>
      <p>The concert took place on <time datetime="2019-05-15
19:00">15thMay</time>.</p>
</body>
```

Figure 2.23 shows the result obtained.

Figure 2.23. *Result of using the datetime attribute*

EXAMPLE.– With pubdate.

```
<body>
      <article>
      <p>The   book   will   be   published   on<time   pubdate>2020-12-
20</time>.</p>
      </article>
</body>
```

Figure 2.24 shows the result obtained.

Figure 2.24. *Result of using the pubdate attribute*

2.4.1.18. *The <hr /> tag*

The <hr /> tag is an empty tag that is used to define a horizontal separation between two blocks.

EXAMPLE.–

```
<body>
        <p>Paragraph 1</p>
        <hr />
        <p>Paragraph 2</p>
</body>
```

Figure 2.25 shows the result obtained.

Figure 2.25. *Effect of the <hr /> tag*

2.4.1.19. *The <br /> tag*

The <br /> tag is an empty tag that is used to produce a line break in the text. It is quite important in the context of poems and addresses, where line separation is necessary.

EXAMPLE.–

```
<body>
      <p>This is a line <br /> and this is the second line</p>
</body>
```

Figure 2.26 shows the result obtained.

Figure 2.26. *Effect of the <br /> tag*

2.4.1.20. *The <wbr> tag*

The <wbr> tag defines a text-level position where the browser can potentially add a line-break should the display window be too small, even if line-break instructions are not specified.

EXAMPLE.–

```
<body>
<p>In medicine, the longest word is
      glyco<wbr>sylpho<wbr>sphatidyletha<wbr>nolamine.</p>
</body>
```

2.4.1.21. *The <ins> tag*

The <ins> tag is used to indicate that text has been added to a document after it has been published.

This content is visually represented by underlined text.

The <ins> tag has the list of attributes shown in Table 2.6.

Attribute	Value	Description
cite	URI	Address of an external resource explaining the reasons for the change.
datetime	Date or date + time	The date and time of the change.

Table 2.6. *Attributes of the <ins> tag*

EXAMPLE.– Dated insertion of a day.

```
<body>
        <p>Google Chrome supports video formats WebM,MP4<ins
datetime="2019-12-04"> and Theora</ins></p>
</body>
```

Figure 2.27 shows the result obtained.

Figure 2.27. *Effect of the <ins> tag*

2.4.1.22. *The <del> tag*

The <del> tag is used to present a text fragment that has been deleted from a document. The deleted text is generally displayed as struck-through.

The <del> tag has the list of attributes shown in Table 2.7.

Attribute	Value	Description
cite	URL	Address of an external resource explaining the reasons for deletion.
datetime	Date or date + time	The date and time of the deletion.

Table 2.7. *Attributes of the <del> tag*

EXAMPLE.– Dated deletion of a day, with reason.

```
<body>
    <p>HTML<deldatetime="2019-01-19" cite="http://hassen.over-
    blog.com/html5"<del>5</del> is a tagging language for the Web</p>
</body>
```

Figure 2.28 shows the result obtained.

Figure 2.28. *Effect of the <del> tag. For a color version of this figure, see www.iste.co.uk/benrebah/website.zip*

2.4.1.23. *The <s> tag*

The <s> tag is used to display text that is struck-through because it is no longer important or is considered obsolete, unlike the <del> tag, which defines the deletion of an incorrect text fragment.

Text surrounded by this tag is generally displayed as struck-through.

EXAMPLE.–

```
<body>
    <p>Our computer club is made up of <s>five</s> people</p>
</body>
```

Figure 2.29 shows the result obtained.

Figure 2.29. *Effect of the <s> tag*

2.4.1.24. *The <pre> tag*

The <pre> tag represents pre-formatted text. The content of this tag is often represented with a monospaced font and is displayed as is; the spaces used on the web page will be retranscribed.

EXAMPLE.–

```
<body>
        <pre>
        _| |___|0|  |Salut |
        <_  _  _|- |_  _-|
          00  00       0  0

        </pre>
</body>
```

Figure 2.30 shows the result obtained.

```
_| |___|0|  |Salut |          — ___ _____ _||___|0| |Salut |<___ _|-|_ __ _| 00 00 0 0
<_  _  _|- |_  _-|
  00  00      0  0
```

Figure 2.30. *Preformatted text with <pre> (left) and without the <pre> tag (right)*

2.4.1.25. *The <mark> tag*

The <mark> tag is used to mark or highlight text that is generally considered relevant in its context. Text wrapped in this tag is visually displayed with a yellow background and black text.

EXAMPLE.–

```
<body>
        <p>Mahdia is a <mark>tourist</mark> area</p>
</body>
```

Figure 2.31 shows the result obtained.

Figure 2.31. *Effect of the <mark> tag*

2.4.1.26. The *<ruby> tag*

The <ruby> tag defines a ruby annotation. This kind of annotation is used to visualize the pronunciation of East Asian characters.

2.4.1.27. The *<rt> tag*

The <rt> tag is wrapped by a <ruby> parent element and is used to mark the text annotation.

2.4.1.28. The *<rp> tag*

The <rp> element is wrapped by a <ruby> parent element enabling the insertion of parentheses around the <rt> annotation for browsers that do not support this feature. These browsers will then display the parentheses.

EXAMPLE.– <ruby>, <rt> and <rp>.

```
<body>
<ruby>
        汉字<rp>(</rp><rt>Hello</rt><rp>)</rp>
</ruby>
</body>
```

2.4.1.29. The *<bdo> tag*

The <bdo> tag is used to change the direction of the text in question. It allows the user to change the direction of the text to the direction indicated by the tag.

The <bdo> tag has the attribute shown in Table 2.8.

Attribute	Value	Description
dir	ltr: text oriented from left to right. rtl: text oriented from right to left. auto: depending on the nature of the content, the browser decides the direction.	Defines the direction in which the browser reads the text.

Table 2.8. *Attributes of the <bdo> tag*

EXAMPLE.–

```
<body>
        <bdo dir="rtl">I wish you a very good day!</bdo>
</body>
```

2.4.1.30. *The <bdi> tag*

The <bdi> tag is used to isolate a text fragment that is placed in a different direction from the rest of the text surrounding it. For this tag, the "dir" attribute is set to auto.

EXAMPLE.–

```
<body>
      <bdo dir="rtl">This Arabic word <bdi>ARABIC_PLACEHOLDER</bdi>
is automatically displayed from right to left.</bdo>
</body>
```

Figure 2.32 shows the result obtained.

Figure 2.32. *Effect of the <bdi> tag*

2.4.1.31. *The <address> tag*

The <address> tag features within the parent HTML elements <article> or <body>, and can be used by authors to provide contact information, such as the names of the individuals behind a document, their web address or their email address.

EXAMPLE.–

```
<body>
      <article>
      <address>
            This book is produced by: Hassen, Hafedh& Antoine
            <a href="http://www.Lesson.com">HTML 5 and CSS3</a>
      </address>
      </article>
</body>
```

2.4.2. Bulleted lists

Lists in HTML5 are dedicated to drawing up enumerations having a semantic value. These lists are featured in the form of two structures, namely, ordered (or numbered) and unordered (bulleted) lists, which are formed by <ol> and <ul> elements, respectively, in which individual <li> elements can be added. They are generally used to create navigation menus.

2.4.2.1. The <ol> tag

The <ol> tag defines an ordered list of elements. The elements of this type of list are commonly viewed with a cardinal number in the form of a letter, a Roman numeral, a decimal number, etc.

EXAMPLE.–

```
<body>
        <p>This book consists of five chapters</p>
        <ol>
        <li>Overview and Basic Concept</li>
        <li>The Language of the Web: HTML5</li>
        <li>Style Sheets: CSS3</li>
        <li> Design and Creation of a Website</li>
        <li>Practical Exercises</li>
        </ol>
</body>
```

Figure 2.33 shows the result obtained.

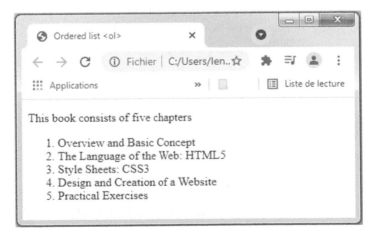

Figure 2.33. *Ordered list <ol>*

The <ol> tag has the list of attributes shown in Table 2.9.

Attribute	Value	Description
start	Integer (positive or negative)	Starting value for the list.
reversed	Reversed or "" or without value	Indicates that the list is descending.

Table 2.9. *Attributes of the <ol> tag*

EXAMPLE.–

```
<body>
      <p>This book consists of two main sections</p>
      <ol start="2" Type="A">
      <li>The Language of the Web: HTML5</li>
      <li>Style sheets: CSS3</li>
      </ol>
</body>
```

Figure 2.34 shows the result obtained.

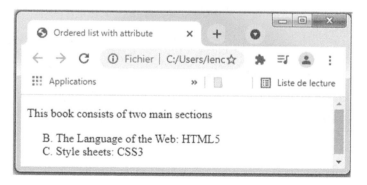

Figure 2.34. *Ordered list with attribute*

2.4.2.2. The <ul> tag

The <ul> tag defines a list of unordered elements.

It is a set of elements with the same degree of importance, and without a numerical order.

Typically, elements in a list of this type are displayed with a bullet of the type: dot, circle or square.

EXAMPLE.–

```
<body>
        <p>This book consists of five chapters</p>
        <ul>
        <li>Overview and basic concept</li>
        <li>The Language of the Web: HTML5</li>
        <li>Style sheets: CSS3</li>
        <li> Design and Creation of a Website</li>
        <li>Practical Exercises</li>
        </ul>
</body>
```

Figure 2.35 shows the result obtained.

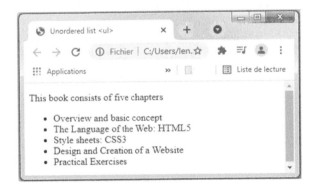

Figure 2.35. *Unordered list <ul>*

2.4.2.3. *The <li> tag*

The <li> tag is used to present an element from a list. It is generally included in an ordered <ol> or unordered <ul> list, in which it refers to a single element from that list.

2.4.2.4. *The <dl> tag*

The <dl> tag is used to present a definition list. It is formed by a list of pairs joining terms (<dt>) to their description (<dd>). The elements in this list are not in any alphabetical order and it is up to the author to sort them as they choose at source code level.

2.4.2.5. The <dd> tag

The <dd> tag is a thread of the <dl> element, used to specify the definition of a term at definition-list level. This tag can only be displayed if it is included in a definition list and should generally be placed after a <dt> element.

2.4.2.6. The <dt> tag

The <dt> tag is used to specify a term at definition-list level. This element can only be displayed as a child element of <dl>. It is commonly placed before a <dd> element.

EXAMPLE.–

```
<body>
        <dl>
        <dt>Firefox:</dt>
                <dd>is a free, open-source web browser
        developed and distributed by the Mozilla Foundation.</dd>
        <dt>Google Chrome:</dt>
                <dd>is a Google-developed web browser based on
        the Chromium open-source project running
        on Windows,Mac,Linux,Android and iOS.</dd>
        </dl>
</body>
```

Figure 2.36 shows the result obtained[2].

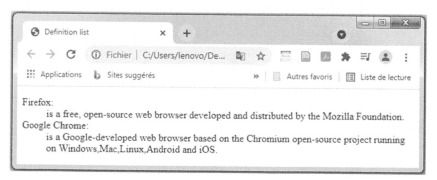

Figure 2.36. Definition list

---

2 The definitions of Google Chrome and Firefox are copied from the site: https://www.wikipedia.com.

2.4.3. *Titles*

2.4.3.1. *The <hx> tag*

<hx> tags, where *x* corresponds to a digit of the interval [1;6] representing titles of different levels. <h1> is the title of the first level, <h2> is the title of the second level, etc., up to the last level <h6>.

EXAMPLE.–

```
<body>
        <h1>Title_level 1</h1>
        <h2>Title_level 2</h2>
        <h3>Title_level 3</h3>
        <h4>Title_level 4</h4>
        <h5>Title_level 5</h5>
        <h6>Title_level 6</h6>
</body>
```

Figure 2.37 shows the result obtained.

Figure 2.37. *The six levels of the <hx> tag*

2.4.3.2. *The <hgroup> tag*

The <hgroup> tag wraps one or more titles from <h1> to <h6>. Ideally, there is no benefit to using this tag for fewer than two titles or more, because it refers to the header of a section, when the section contains more than one title or subtitle.

In general, it is advisable to use a single <h1> title on a web page and avoid omitting a title number.

EXAMPLE.–

```
<body>
      <hgroup>
               <h1>Title_level 1</h1>
               <h2>Title_level 2</h2>
               <h3>Title_level 3</h3>
      </hgroup>
</body>
```

2.5. Creating hyperlinks

A hyperlink is an HTML element that exists on a web page in graphical or textual form. Clicking on it offers users the possibility of going from one site to another or from one page to another on the same website.

2.5.1. *Inserting a hyperlink: the <a> tag*

The <a></a> tag is the base tag for creating a hyperlink. This tag accepts the list of attributes shown in Table 2.10.

NOTE.–

– By default, a hyperlink is displayed in blue and underlined.

– When the user clicks on a hyperlink using the mouse cursor, the cursor forms a hand shape.

Attribute	Value	Description
media	Mediaquery (example: screen, TV, all, print, etc.)	Specifies the media type to which a link is pointed. media="all": default value, suitable for all devices. media="tv": television-type device. media="screen": computer screen. media="projection": video projector. media="print": printer.
href	URL	Destination address of the link.
hreflang	Language code (example: ar, fr, en)	Indicates the language of the destination document if it does not match the language of the source document.
type	MIME* type	The MIME type of the link target.
download	File name after upload operation or (empty)	Specifies that the linked resource is considered for download. In case a value is assigned to the attribute, it will play the role of the file name after downloading.
rel	Alternate, author, archives, bookmark, first, external, help, last, index, nextnofollow license, prefetch, noreferrer prev, sidebar, search, tag	Indicates the type of relationship defined by the link between the source document and the target. Several values can be combined as long as they are separated by spaces. rel="author": defines a link to a page describing the author or making it possible to contact them. rel="bookmark": indicates that the hyperlink is a permanent link for the nearest <article> element. rel="first": indicates that the hyperlink points to the first resource in the sequence of the current page.
target	_blank, _parent, _self, _top	Tells the web browser how the link target will be displayed. Target="_blank": to open the hyperlink in a new window or tab. Target="_parent": to open the hyperlink in the parent frame. Target="_self": default setting, to open the hyperlink in the same window as the start page. Target="_top": to open the hyperlink in the entire body of the window.

*MIME: *Multipurpose Internet Mail Extensions.*

Table 2.10. *Attributes of the <a> tag*

2.5.2. *Types of hyperlinks*

2.5.2.1. *Absolute link*

An absolute link is a link that includes the full address to access a document (*case of a link leading to another site located on another domain name*).

> EXAMPLE.– Link to an external site.
>
> ```
> <body>
>         <p>
>         Hello, to consult the site of our institute click
>         <ahref="www.isetma.rnu.tn">here</a>
>         </p>
> </body>
> ```

2.5.2.2. *Relative link*

A relative link is a link, as its name suggests, relative to a reference path. It refers to a document located at the same level as the source file or at a different level (*subdirectory*, *parent directory* or *root directory*).

> EXAMPLE.– Link between two pages located in the same folder.
>
> ```
> <body>
>         <p>
>             Hello, see <a href="next.html">next page   </a>
>         </p>
> </body>
> ```

> EXAMPLE.– Link between two pages located in two different folders.
>
> ```
> <body>
>         <p>
>             Hello, see
>         <a href="directory_name/next.html"> the next page    </a></p>
>
>         <!-- If there are multiple directories -->
>         <p>
>             Hello, see
>         <a href="directory_name1/directory_name2/next.html">
> the     next page</a>
>         </p>
> </body>
> ```

EXAMPLE.– Link to a file placed in a parent folder.

```
<body>
      <p>
          Hello, see
      <a href="../next.html">the next page</a>
      </p>
</body>
```

2.5.2.3. *Link within the same web page*

In a web document of some importance, it is important to give the Internet user the opportunity to move to a well-defined place on the page. It is possible to use bookmarks or anchors in this case.

The creation of a link within the same page generally occurs in two stages:

– declaration of the bookmark (the anchor);

– creation of the link to the bookmark.

To create a bookmark, you simply need to add an *id* attribute to a given tag that will act as a marker.

EXAMPLE.–

```
<body>
      <h2 id="bookmark1">Text</h2>
</body>
```

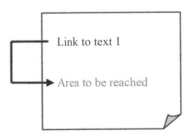

Then, you simply need to create a hyperlink in the usual way, provided that the *href* attribute contains the *hash (#)* value, followed by the bookmark name.

EXAMPLE.–

```
<body>
      <a href ="#bookmark1">Link to Text</a>
</body>
```

NOTE.– It is possible to create a hyperlink to a bookmark placed on another web page. To do so, you simply need to write the page name followed by the *hash (#)* symbol followed by the *name of the bookmark*.

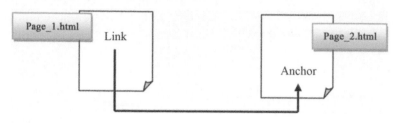

EXAMPLE.–

```
<body>
        <a href="page_2.html#bookmark">Hyperlink</a>
</body>
```

2.5.2.4. *Link to an email address*

To create a link to an email address, you simply need to use, with the *href* attribute, the *mailto* value followed by the destination email address. Clicking this link opens the email application window installed by default on the user's machine. Example: Microsoft Outlook.

EXAMPLE.–

```
<body>
        <a href="mailto:ben_rebah_h@yahoo.fr">Contact me by email
        </a>
</body>
```

NOTE.– It is possible to predefine the subject of the message in this type of link and to schedule the sending of a copy to another user.

EXAMPLE.–
```
<body>
        <a href="mailto:ben_rebah_h@yahoo.fr?
subject=book    HTML5&cc=hbr@gmail.com">
        Contact the author </a>
</body>
```

2.5.2.5. *Download link*

In order to allow a file to be downloaded, you simply need to indicate the name and extension of the file. This technique is essentially valid when both file types (*HTML and the one to be download*ed) are placed beneath the same directory.

EXAMPLE.–

```
<body>
        <a href="bookHTML5.doc">Download lesson</a>
</body>
```

2.5.2.6. *Block-type link*

Previously, it was not possible to create block-type links. With HTML5, it is possible to wrap block-level tags (*<div>*, *<p>*, etc.) in a link. This technique is considered interesting if a fragment of the web page consists of various elements (titles and images) leading to the same resource.

EXAMPLE.–

```
<body>
        <a href="page_2.html">
        <ul>
        <li>The language of the web:HTML5</li>
        <li>Style sheets:CSS3</li>
        </ul>
        </a>
</body>
```

2.5.3. *Adding a tooltip to a link*

The global *title="text"* attribute is used to provide an explanatory tooltip when hovering over the link with the mouse cursor.

EXAMPLE.–

```
<body>
        <a href="Home.html" title="Link to home page"> home</a>
</body>
```

2.6. Inserting images and multimedia objects

2.6.1. *The image*

2.6.1.1. *The <img /> tag*

The <img /> tag is used to insert an image stored in an external folder or directory within a web page.

The <img /> tag has the list of attributes shown in Table 2.11.

Attribute	Value	Description
src	URL	A mandatory attribute that defines the image file address.
width	Positive integer	The width of the image, expressed in pixels.
height	Positive integer	The height of the image, expressed in pixels.
usemap	Character string	Name of the <map> element to be used to define map-level clickable areas (client-side image map).
ismap	Ismap or "" or (empty)	Used to indicate that the image is part of a server-side clickable map.
alt	Character string	Used to define text describing the image. This text will be displayed to users if the image address is incorrect, if the image format is not supported by the browser, or until the image finishes downloading.

Table 2.11. *Attributes of the <img /> tag*

2.6.1.2. *The image formats supported by the web*

Format	Invention	Usage
GIF	1987	Small graphical elements, icons and small animated images
PNG	Open format	High-quality images
JPEG	1980–1992	Photographs

Table 2.12. *The image formats supported by the web*

EXAMPLE.– Using the <img /> tag.

```
<body>
        <h1>New Kia Rio 2020</h1>
        <imgsrc="car.jpg" alt="Kia Rio 2020" width="400" height="200"
/>
</body>
```

2.6.1.3. *Inserting a link on an image*

A link created from an image is made by simply placing the image between <a></a> tags. This type of link has the same characteristics as text links. As a result, the entire image surface is clickable.

EXAMPLE.–

```
<body>
        <h1>New Kia Rio 2020</h1>
        <a href="page2.html"><imgsrc="car.jpg" alt="Kia Rio 2020"
        width="400" height="200"/></a>
</body>
```

Figure 2.38 shows the result obtained.

Figure 2.38. *Example of use of the <img /> tag[3]. For a color version of this figure, see www.iste.co.uk/benrebah/website.zip*

3 See: https://mobile.guideautoweb.com/.

2.6.1.4. *Responsive images*

Responsive images are used to define separate hyperlinks from a portion of an image or an area specific to it. For example, on a geographical map of Tunisia, it is possible to imagine that clicking once on a city (*area*) would lead the Internet user to another web page containing all of the information about that city.

Figure 2.39. *Example of the use of the <map> tag. For a color version of this figure, see www.iste.co.uk/benrebah/website.zip*

To develop such an example, the <map> tag needs to be used in conjunction with an <img/> image as follows:

– Definition of the responsive image tag:

```
<imgsrc="file_image"usemap="#map_name"/>
```

Therefore, the principle is simple, consisting of adding the *usemap* attribute to the <img /> tag, to alert the browser that it should use a map for this and the map name in question. This will automatically add this map to the file, rather like a hyperlink bookmark. The code already uses the notation with the # character, a specific feature of bookmarks.

– Map tag definition: a map (<map>) is generally formed by one or more <area> elements, each of which refers to a clickable area characterized by a shape (*shape*) having coordinates (*coords*) and an address (*href*).

```
<mapname="map_name">
     <area shape="shape" coords="coordinates" href="destination"/>
     <!-- other area tags -->

</map>
```

No.	Meaning
1	<mapname="map_name">....</map> The <map> is assigned a name through the *name* attribute and it is this name that will be used by the *usemap* attribute of the <img /> tag.
2	<areashape="shape" coords="coordinates"href="destination"/> –<area/>: determines the responsive area of the image. – shape: attribute of the <area> tag, determines the shape of the responsive area: - shape="rect" for a rectangle; - shape="circle" for a circle; - shape="poly" for an irregular polygon; - shape="default" to manage clicks made outside of a responsive area. – coords: attribute of the <area> tag, specifies the coordinates of the geometric shape: - for a rectangle: coords="x,y,x,y"; - for a circle: coords="x,y,r"; - for a polygon: coords="x1,y1,x2,y2,x3,y3,x4,y4"; – href: attribute of the <area> tag, specifies the address of the file associated with the selected area.

Table 2.13. *Attributes of <map> and <area> tags*

EXAMPLE.–

```
<body>
<p>
     <imgsrc="cubes.gif"usemap="#cube" height="126" width="139"/>
</p>
     <mapname="cube">
     <areashape="rect"coords="38,10,73,41"href="c1.html"/>
     <areashape="rect"coords="19,47,48,80"href="c2.html"/>
     <areashape="rect"coords="62,44,94,79"href="c3.html"/>
     <areashape="rect"coords="10,85,37,120"href="c4.html"/>
     <areashape="rect"coords="49,86,78,1176"href="c5.html"/>
     <areashape="rect"coords="90,91,124,116"href="c6.html"/>
     </map>
</body>
```

Figure 2.40 shows the result obtained.

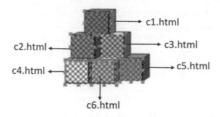

Figure 2.40. *Example of a responsive image. For a color version of this figure, see www.iste.co.uk/benrebah/website.zip*

NOTE.– If an image clarifies the text (and is not just decorative), it is preferable to place it between the <figure></figure> tags. This tag is used in conjunction with the <figcaption> tag, which provides a caption for the image.

EXAMPLE.–

```
<body>
<figure>
<imgsrc="car.jpg" alt="Kia Rio" width="400"
height="200"/>
<figcaption>Kia rio 2020</figcaption>
</figure>
</body>
```

2.6.2. Audio and video media

2.6.2.1. The <audio> tag

The embedding of an audio file into an HTML5 document occurs using the <audio></audio> tag.

2.6.2.2. Audio formats

Format	Description
MP3	This is one of the oldest, and also among the most compatible formats.
AAC	This is a good-quality format generally used by Apple on iTunes. It is readable on iPods and iPhones without any problems.
OGG	This is a widely known and widely used open-source format. It generally represents the open-source equivalent of mp3.
Wav	This is a format defined by IBM and Microsoft. Wav-type files are commonly uncompressed.

Table 2.14. *Audio formats*

NOTE.– There is no web browser that supports all of these formats at once. Table 2.15 shows the compatibility for MP3 and OGG (*the most commonly used formats*).

Browser	MP3	OGG
	✓	
	✓	✓
		✓
	✓	
		✓

Table 2.15. *Browser compatibility with audio formats. For a color version of this table, see www.iste.co.uk/benrebah/website.zip*

NOTE.– Regarding the <video> tag, when we use it, the <source> tags are used inside the video tag to deal with format support issues.

2.6.2.3. *The <video> tag*

The < video ></ video> tag is used to embed a video file in an HTML document.

2.6.2.4. *Video formats*

Format	Description
H.264	One of the most widely used and powerful formats today.
OggTheora	It is a free, open format that is less powerful than H.267. OggTheora is used on Linux, but for the Windows operating system it is necessary to install programs to read it.
WebM	This is a free, open format developed by Google.

Table 2.16. *Video formats*

2.6.2.5. *Attributes of <audio> and <video> tags*

The <audio> and <video> tags possess the list of attributes shown in Table 2.17.

Attribute	Value	Description
src	URL	A mandatory attribute that designates the source address of the audio or video file to be interpreted or downloaded. EXAMPLE.– <audio src="Mazzika.com">…</audio>
width and height	Positive integer	Only valid for the video tag and used to define the dimensions (width and height) of the display area. EXAMPLE.– <video src="Mazzika.com" width="400" height="400">…</video>
controls	"controls" or (empty)	It enables (or disables) the default presence of the player's visual control buttons on the screen (pause button, play button, etc.). EXAMPLE.– <video src="video.ogv" controls> …</video>
poster	URL	Only valid for video. It is used to indicate the URL of an image to be displayed before the video is played. EXAMPLE.– <video src="film.ogv" poster="lion.jpg" width="600" height="400">…</video>
autoplay	"autoplay" or (empty)	Specifies whether an audio or video file will play automatically as soon as it is available. EXAMPLE.– <audio src="mamusique.mp3"autoplay="autoplay">…</audio>
loop	"loop" or (empty)	Indicates that the sound or video file will be played on loop. EXAMPLE.– <audio src="mamusique.mp3" loop="loop">…</audio>
preload	"auto" or "meta" or "none"	Used to indicate to the web browser that it must download the audio or video file as soon as the page is loaded, so that it can be accessed for direct playback as soon as requested by the user. This attribute accepts the following values: – preload="none": no preloading; – preload="meta": preloading of the metadata associated with the file; – preload="auto": automatic preloading. EXAMPLE.– <video src="video.ogv" preload="auto">…</video> NOTE.–This attribute has no effect if the auto-play attribute is present.

Table 2.17. *Attributes of <audio> and <video> tags*

2.7. Tables

2.7.1. *The <table> tag*

The <table> tag is dedicated to wrapping tabular data. By doing so, the data can be stored in a structure formed by rows and columns.

Figure 2.41. *General structure of a table. For a color version of this figure, see www.iste.co.uk/benrebah/website.zip*

EXAMPLE.–

```
<body>
    <table>
    <!-- List of rows and columns -->
    </table>
</body>
```

The <table> tag accepts several child elements that can be represented in Table 2.18.

Element	Number of occurrences	Role
<caption>	0 or 1	Table caption
<colgroup>	0 or +	A group of columns with the same properties
<thead>	0 or 1	Header of columns in a table
<tfoot>	0 or 1	Footer of columns in a table
<tbody> or	0 or +	Table contents (body) (formed by tr, th and td)
<tr>	1 or +	Table rows (formed by th and td)

Table 2.18. *Child elements of <table> tag*

2.7.2. The <caption> tag

The <caption> tag is used to present the caption to a table. It should be added directly after the <table> tag, and should only be used once in this element.

2.7.3. The <thead> tag

The <thead> tag is used to define a certain number of rows as the header of the columns in a table. It is generally used in conjunction with the <tbody> and <tfoot> tags and is positioned after any <caption> and <colgroup> elements, and before <tbody> or <tfoot>.

2.7.4. The <tfoot> tag

The <tfoot> tag is used to define the footer of a table. It is used in conjunction with the <thead> and <tbody> tags and can contain zero or several <tr> tags.

NOTE.– <tfoot> must be placed in front of <tbody> in the code to give the browser the indications it holds, before loading the entire document.

2.7.5. The <tbody> tag

The <tbody> tag is used to define the body of the table, and is generally used in conjunction with the <thead> and <tfoot> tags. It wraps the <tr> rows that are used to contain the data in the table. With this tag type, no <tr> is located directly beneath <table>.

EXAMPLE.– Using the <caption>, <thread>, <tfoot> and <tbody> tags.

```
<body>
      <table>
      <!-- Table title -->
      <caption>List of students and their averages</caption>
      <!-- Headers of table columns-->
      <thead>
      <tr>
            <th>Student</th>
            <th>Average</th>
      </tr>
      </thead>
      <!-- Table footer -->
```

```
        <tfoot>
        <tr>
        <td>Class average</td>
        <td>16.76</td>
        </tr>
        </tfoot>
        <!-- Table body -->
        <tbody>
        <tr>
                <td>Hassen</td>
                <td>16.32</td>
        </tr>
        <tr>
                <td>Rayen</td>
                <td>17.20</td>
        </tr>
        </tbody>
        </table>
</body>
```

Figure 2.42 shows the result obtained.

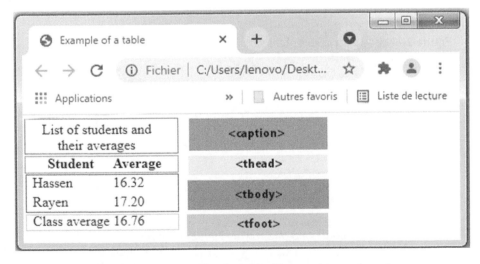

Figure 2.42. *Example of a table. For a color version of this figure, see www.iste.co.uk/benrebah/website.zip*

NOTE.– The result obtained is a borderless table. In the third chapter of the book, we will look at CSS style sheets, which allow us to add borders to tables.

2.7.6. *The <tr> tag*

The <tr> tag designates a row in the table. It wraps one or more <td> and/or <th> elements.

2.7.7. *The <td> tag*

The <td> tag is a child element of <tr>. It is generally used to contain hyperlinks, text, images, lists, etc.

EXAMPLE.– Using the <tr> and <td> tags.

```
<body>
        <table>
        <tr>
                <td>France</td><td>Canada</td><td>Tunisia</td>
        </tr>
        </table>
</body>
```

Figure 2.43 shows the result obtained.

Figure 2.43. *Example of a table*
consisting of a row and three columns

The <td> tag has the list of attributes shown in Table 2.19.

Attribute	Value	Description
headers	Identifiers	A list of character strings separated by spaces. Each element on this list refers to the <id> attribute of the <th> tag that applies to this cell.
colspan	Positive integer	Number of columns that this cell spans.
rowspan	Positive integer	Number of rows that this cell spans.

Table 2.19. *Attributes of the <td> tag*

2.7.8. *The <th> tag*

The <th> tag is a thread of the <tr> element used to specify the header of a column (or *row*) of a table.

The <th> tag has the list of attributes shown in Table 2.20.

Attribute	Value	Description
scope	Row Col Rowgroup Colgroup	Indicates whether the cell is a header cell of a column, row, row group, etc.: – row: current row; – col: current column; – rowgroup: group of rows; – colgroup: group of columns.
headers	Identifiers	A list of character strings separated by spaces. Each element on this list refers to the <id> attribute of the <th> tag that applies to this cell.
colspan	Positive integer	Number of rows to which this cell is extended.
rowspan	Positive integer	Number of rows to which this cell is extended.

Table 2.20. *Attributes of the <th> tag*

EXAMPLE.– Using the colspan and rowspan attributes.

```
<table>
      <tr>
      <th scope="col"colspan="2">Car</th>
      <th scope="col">Brand and range</th>
      </tr>
      <tr>
      <td>Golf</td>
      <td>Passat</td>
      <td rowspan="2">Volkswagen</td>
      </tr>
      <tr>
      <td>Polo</td>
      <td>Jetta</td>
      </tr>
</table>
```

Figure 2.44 shows the result obtained.

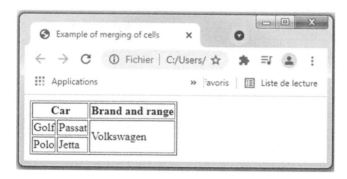

Figure 2.44. *Example of merging of cells*

2.8. Forms

2.8.1. *Benefit of a form*

Forms hold a rather important place in the majority of applications and websites.

Indeed, it is the only technique that offers the possibility for the user to send data to a web server for processing.

2.8.2. *Form construction*

2.8.2.1. *The <form> tag*

The <form></form> tag is used to indicate to the web browser that it should define a form.

Attribute	Value	Description
name	Text	Form name.
method	Get or post	Defines the method used by the browser to send data to the server.
novalidate	Novalidate or "" or (empty)	Disables automatic validation of form data by the browser.
action	URL	Indicates the address to which data are sent if the form is submitted. EXAMPLE.– action="http://www.server/processing.php" (address of a program dedicated to a given process, placed under a PHP server). action="mailto:my_email@server" (email address to easily retrieve form data). action="" (form data is processed locally).
autocomplete	On or off	On: the browser can automatically fill in values based on previous information input by the user during previous uses of the form. Off: the user must fill in the value of each field in the form themselves.
enctype	Text/plain or application/x-wwwform-urlencoded or multipart/formdata	Defines in which computer format (MIME type) data will be transferred from the form to the server. If this attribute is not defined, the default value used is *application/x-wwwform-urlencoded.* To send a file, the *multipart/form-data* value needs to be used. To send to an email address using the mailto protocol, the value will be *text/plain.*
target	_self or _parent or _top or _blank	A name or keyword that indicates where the response will be displayed after submitting the form. _self (default value): used to display the response in the same current navigation frame. _parent: displays the response in the frame that wraps the current page (parent window). _top: displays the answer in the entire uppermost window. _blank: displays the response in another window of the browser.

Table 2.21. *Attributes of the <form> tag*

It can contain various items, including check boxes, drop-down lists and buttons.

EXAMPLE.–

```
<body>
        <form><!-- Form elements --></form>
</body>
```

The < form> tag has the list of attributes shown in Table 2.21.

NOTE.– If the form data is processed locally, the *method* and *enctype* attributes are of no interest since there is no exchange with the server.

2.8.2.2. *The <fieldset> tag*

The <fieldset> tag is used to group input fields according to their theme. The purpose of this grouping is to make controls simpler and more understandable.

2.8.2.3. *The <legend> tag*

The <legend> tag is used to define a title (*illustrative legend*) for the content of the <fieldset> parent element.

2.8.2.4. *The <label> tag*

A <label> allows a label to be associated with a form element. The content of this label makes it easier to understand the form, especially from an accessibility point of view, i.e. activating this element through the clicking action, for example, makes it possible to give focus to the form field with which it is associated. This link is provided between the *id* attribute of the form element and the *for* attribute of <label>.

EXAMPLE.– Form with <fieldset>, <legend> and <label>.

```
<body>
        <form method="post" action="">
        <fieldset>
                <legend>Personal information</legend>
                <label for="secondname">Enter your second name</label>
                <input id="secondname" name="secondname" type="text"/>
                <label for="firstname">Enter your first name</label>
                <input id="firstname" name="firstname" type="text"/>
        </fieldset>
        </form>
</body>
```

Figure 2.45 shows the result obtained.

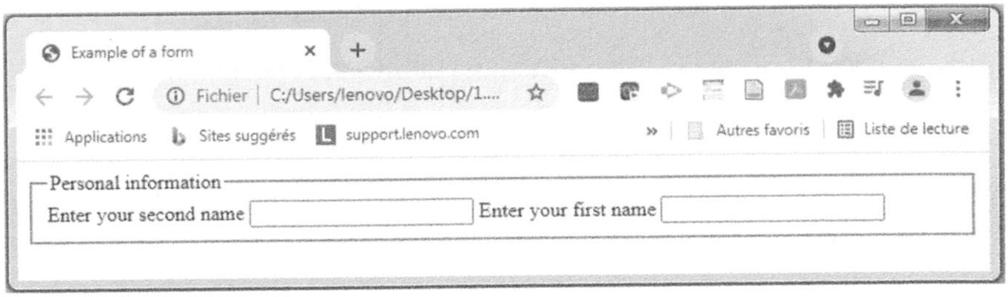

Figure 2.45. *Example of a form with <fieldset>, <legend> and <label>*

2.8.3. *The form <input /> tag and its variants*

In HTML, <input /> is a specific element that makes use of its *type* attribute to enable various appearances and features. Its interest lies in retrieving all types of information input by the user by providing them with all of the necessary means, in order to clearly define their inputs and choices.

2.8.3.1. *Text type*

This is the most standard <input> type; it is used to input text.

```
<input type="text" name="firstname"/>
```

Text input field

<input type="text"/> has the list of attributes shown in Table 2.22.

Attribute	Value	Description
name	Text	The name of the field associated with the piece of data issued by the form.
value	Text	The value of the field when the form is sent.

Table 2.22. *Attributes of the <input type="text" /> tag*

2.8.3.2. *Password type*

Closely related to text type, this is a password input field whose characters are generally visually obscured by asterisks or dots.

```
Password: <input type="password" name="psw"/>
```

Password: ┊········┊

> Password field

`<input type="password"/>` has the list of attributes shown in Table 2.23.

Attribute	Value	Description
name	Text	The name of the field associated with the data issued by the form.
value	Text	The value of the field when the form is sent.

Table 2.23. *Attributes of the <input type="password" /> tag*

2.8.3.3. *Tel type*

This is a text field intended to receive a telephone number.

```
Telephone:<input type="tel" name="telephone"/>
```

`<input type="tel"/>` has the list of attributes shown in Table 2.24.

Attribute	Value	Description
name	Text	The name of the field associated with the data issued by the form.
value	Text	The value of the field when the form is sent.

Table 2.24. *Attributes of the <input type="tel" /> tag*

2.8.3.4. *URL type*

This is a text field intended to receive a URL.

```
URL:<input type="url" name="webaddress"/>
```
`<input type="url"/>` has the list of attributes shown in Table 2.25.

Attribute	Value	Description
name	Text	The name of the field associated with the data issued by the form.
value	Text	The value of the field when the form is sent.

Table 2.25. *Attributes of the <input type="url" /> tag*

2.8.3.5. *Email type*

This is a text field intended to receive an email address.

```
Email: <input type="email" name="emailaddress"/>
```

`<input type="email"/>` has the list of attributes shown in Table 2.26.

Attribute	Value	Description
multiple	Multiple or "" or (empty)	Indicates that a list of email addresses can be input.
name	Text	The name of the field associated with the data issued by the form.
value	Text	The value of the field when the form is sent.

Table 2.26. *Attributes of the <input type="email" /> tag*

2.8.3.6. *Search type*

This is a text field that is used to input keywords or terms for a search.

```
Search: <input type="search" name="word"/>
```

`<input type="search"/>` has the list of attributes shown in Table 2.27.

Attribute	Value	Description
name	Text	The name of the field associated with the data issued by the form.
value	Text	The value of the field when the form is sent.

Table 2.27. *Attributes of the <input type="search" /> tag*

2.8.3.7. *Hidden type*

This is a hidden field that offers programmers the ability to enter data that cannot be seen by users when the form is validated.

```
Search: <input type="hidden" name="action" value="registration"/>
```

`<input type="hidden"/>` has the list of attributes shown in Table 2.28.

Attribute	Value	Description
name	Text	The name of the field associated with the data issued by the form.
value	Text	The value of the field when the form is sent.

Table 2.28. *Attributes of the <input type="hidden" /> tag*

2.8.3.8. *Radio type*

A radio button is a form element that generally belongs to a group of other buttons, from which the user can choose only one option. A list of radio buttons generally has the same name (*name*).

```
<input type="radio" name="type" value="male" id="ma"/>
<label for="ma">man</label>
<input type="radio" name="type" value="female" id="fm"/>
<label for="fm">woman</label>
```

Radio buttons   ● man   ● woman

`<input type="radio"/>` has the list of attributes shown in Table 2.29.

Attribute	Value	Description
checked	Checked or "" or (empty)	Default state (checked).
name	Text	The name of the field associated with the data issued by the form.
value	Text	The value of the field when the form is sent.

Table 2.29. *Attributes of the <input type="radio" /> tag*

2.8.3.9. *Checkbox type*

These are buttons that are quite similar to radio buttons (single-choice button), but in this case it is possible to choose several options at the same time.

```
<h5>Choose your favorite subject</h5>
<input type="checkbox" name="subject1" value="algo" id="algo"/>
<label for="algo">Algorithmics</label>
<input type="checkbox" name="subject2" value="HTML5" id="html"/>
<label for="html">HTML5</label>
```

Choose your favorite subject

Checkbox   ☐ Algorithmics ☐ HTML 5

`<input type="checkbox"/>` has the list of attributes shown in Table 2.30.

Attribute	Value	Description
checked	Checked or "" or (empty)	Default state (checked).
name	Text	The name of the field associated with the data issued by the form.
value	Text	The value of the field when the form is sent.

Table 2.30. *Attributes of the <input type="checkbox" /> tag*

2.8.3.10. *Button type*

The *button* <input /> element enables a push button to be created, which is generally used to control functionalities on the form thanks to a script.

```
<input type="button" value="Cancel"/>
```

Any button   **Cancel**

`<input type="button"/>` has the list of attributes shown in Table 2.31.

Attribute	Value	Description
name	Text	The name of the field associated with the data issued by the form.
value	Text	The value of the field when the form is sent.

Table 2.31. *Attributes of the <input type="button" /> tag*

2.8.3.11. *Reset type*

This is a control button that enables all fields in the form to be reset to their initial values.

```
<label for="first name">First name:</label>
<input type="text" name="firstname" id="firstname"/>
<input type="reset" value="Reset"/>
```

First name: Hassen   Reset

Reset button:

First name: Reset

`<input type="reset"/>` has the list of attributes shown in Table 2.32.

Attribute	Value	Description
name	Text	The name of the field associated with the data issued by the form.
value	Text	The value of the field when the form is sent.

Table 2.32. *Attributes of the <input type="reset" /> tag*

2.8.3.12. *Submit type*

The *submit*-type <input /> element is used to create a button used to validate the form data. Clicking a button of this type will trigger the submission of the form data to the server.

```
<form method="post" action="test.php">
        <label for="user">Identifier:</label>
        <input type="email" id="user" name="login"/>
        <input type="submit" value="submit"/>
</form>
```

Submit button   **Submit**

`<input type="submit"/>` has the list of attributes shown in Table 2.33.

Attribute	Value	Description
name	Text	The name of the field associated with the data issued by the form.
value	Text	The value of the field when the form is sent.

Table 2.33. *Attributes of the <input type="submit" /> tag*

2.8.3.13. *Image type*

This is a graphical button used to send a form.

```
<input type="image"src="image.png" name="button"/>
```

`<input type="image"/>` has the list of attributes shown in Table 2.34.

Attribute	Value	Description
name	Text	The name of the field associated with the data issued by the form.
height	Non-negative integer	Height of the image, in pixels.
width	Non-negative integer	Widths of the image, in pixel.
ALT	Text	Text alternative.
src	URL	Image source (URL).

Table 2.34. *Attributes of the <input type="image" /> tag*

2.8.3.14. *File type*

The *file* type makes it possible for the user to transfer one or more files from their personal computer to a remote server. A *file* type is generally represented by a *text* field with a *Browse ...* or *Select a file* button.

```
<input type="file" name="myfile"/>
```

Browse button   Select a file   No file selected

`<input type="file"/>` has the list of attributes shown in Table 2.35.

Attribute	Value	Description
multiple	Multiple or "" or (empty)	Indicates that the file element can acquire multiple files.
accept	MIME-type list	Specifies to the web browser the list of file types accepted by the server (the elements in this list are generally separated by commas).
name	Text	The name of the field associated with the data issued by the form.

Table 2.35. *Attributes of the <input type="file" /> tag*

2.8.3.15. *Date type*

The *date* type is used to input a date (day, month and year).

```
<input type="date" name="dateofbirth"/>
```

Date type

`<input type="date"/>` has the list of attributes shown in Table 2.36.

Attribute	Value	Description
min	Date	Minimum value allowed.
max	Date	Maximum value allowed.
step	Any or positive integer	Selection step size.
name	Text	The name of the field associated with the data issued by the form.
value	Date	The value of the field when the form is sent.

Table 2.36. *Attributes of the <input type="date" /> tag*

EXAMPLE.– *min* and *max* attributes.

```
<input type="date" name="booking" min="2019-05-06" max="2020-05-08"/>
```

2.8.3.16. *Time type*

The *time* type is used to input a time without a time zone.

```
<input type="time" name="contacttime"/>
```

Time type   01 : 45 ✕ ⬍

`<input type="time"/>` has the list of attributes shown in Table 2.37.

Attribute	Value	Description
min	Time	Minimum value allowed.
max	Time	Maximum value allowed.
step	Any or positive floating-point number	Selection step size.
name	Text	The name of the field associated with the data issued by the form.
value	Time	The value of the field when the form is sent.

Table 2.37. *Attributes of the <input type="time" /> tag*

2.8.3.17. Datetime type

The *datetime* type is used to input a date and time, based on UTC time (hour, minute, second and fraction of a second).

```
<input type="datetime" name="event"/>
```

Daytime type in opera   2011-03-13   ▼ 13:37 📅 UTC

`<input type="datetime"/>` has the list of attributes shown in Table 2.38.

Attribute	Value	Description
min	Date and time	Minimum value allowed.
max	Date and time	Maximum value allowed.
step	Any or positive floating-point number	Selection step size.
name	Text	The name of the field associated with the data issued by the form.
value	Date and time	The value of the field when the form is sent.

Table 2.38. *Attributes of the <input type="datetime" /> tag*

2.8.3.18. *Datetime-local type*

The *datetime-local* type is used to input a date (a year, a month and a day) and a time (*an hour and a minute*) without a time zone.

```
<input type="datetime-local" name="appointment"/>
```

`<input type="datetime-local"/>` has the list of attributes shown in Table 2.39.

Attribute	Value	Description
min	Date and time (local)	Minimum value allowed.
max	Date and time (local)	Maximum value allowed.
step	Any or positive floating-point number	Selection step size.
name	Text	The name of the field associated with the data issued by the form.
value	Date and time	The value of the field when the form is sent.

Table 2.39. *Attributes of the <input type="datetime-local" /> tag*

2.8.3.19. *Month type*

The *month* type is used to input a month and year in the form "YYYY-MM", without a time zone.

```
<input type="month" name="month"/>
```

Month type   October 2014   × ↕ ▼

`<input type="month"/>` has the list of attributes shown in Table 2.40.

Attribute	Value	Description
min	Month	Minimum value allowed.
max	Month	Maximum value allowed.
step	Positive integer	Selection step size.
name	Text	The name of the field associated with the data issued by the form.
value	Month	The value of the field when the form is sent.

Table 2.40. *Attributes of the <input type="month" /> tag*

2.8.3.20. *The week type*

The *week* type is very similar to *month*; it is used to define a field that allows the input of a year and a number of the week during that year.

```
<input type="week" name="month"/>
```

Week type   Week 01, 2015

`<input type="week"/>` has the list of attributes shown in Table 2.41.

Attribute	Value	Description
min	Week	Minimum value allowed.
max	Week	Maximum value allowed.
step	Any or positive integer	Selection step size.
name	Text	The name of the field associated with the data issued by the form.
value	Month	The value of the field when the form is sent.

Table 2.41. *Attributes of the <input type="week" /> tag*

2.8.3.21. *Number type*

A *number*-type field is used to input numbers generally belonging to an interval whose lower and upper limits are fixed by the *min* and *max* attributes.

```
<input type="number" name="age"/>
```

`<input type="number"/>` has the list of attributes shown in Table 2.42.

Attribute	Value	Description
min	Floating-point number	Minimum value allowed.
max	Floating-point number	Maximum value allowed.
step	Any or positive floating-point number	Selection step size.
name	Text	The name of the field associated with the data issued by the form.
value	Floating-point number	The value of the field when the form is sent.

Table 2.42. *Attributes of the <input type="number" /> tag*

2.8.3.22. Range type

The *range* type is used to input a numerical value between two limits. For this type, the precise value is assumed to be unimportant.

```
<input type="range" name="volume"/>
```

Range-type variation field

`<input type="range"/>` has the list of attributes shown in Table 2.43.

Attribute	Value	Description
min	Floating-point number	Minimum value allowed.
max	Floating-point number	Maximum value allowed.
step	Any or positive floating-point number	Selection step size.
name	Text	The name of the field associated with the data issued by the form.
value	Floating-point number	The value of the field when the form is sent.

Table 2.43. *Attributes of the <input type="range" /> tag*

2.8.3.23. Color type

The *color* type is used to define a *color*. It provides a color selection interface that does not require features other than accepting colors as text.

```
<input type="color" name="colors" value="#FF8810"/>
```

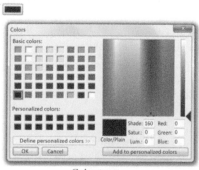

Color type

`<input type="color"/>` has the list of attributes shown in Table 2.44.

Attribute	Value	Description
value	Hexadecimal color code	Color value. Example: #FF0000 for red.
name	Floating-point number	Maximum value allowed.

Table 2.44. *Attributes of the <input type="color" /> tag*

2.8.3.24. *The <datalist> tag*

The <datalist> tag added to a text-type *input* tag opens a list of encoding suggestions with the focus on the latter. The user can retain a suggestion or code a value of their choice. This is similar to what Google Suggestion presents when a keyword is input into its search bar.

EXAMPLE.–

```
<form action="">
        Choose a book:
        <input type="text" list="books"/>
        <datalist id="books">
        <option value="Math"></option>
        <option value="Physics"></option>
        <option value="Information Technology"></option>
        </datalist>
</form>
```

Figure 2.46 shows the result obtained.

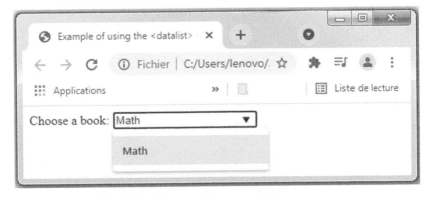

Figure 2.46. *Example of using the <datalist> tag*

2.8.4. *Other form tags*

2.8.4.1. *The <textarea> tag*

The <textarea> tag represents a multi-line input field, allowing simple text to be edited.

The <textarea> tag has the list of attributes shown in Table 2.45.

Attribute	Value	Description
rows	Positive integer	Specifies the visible height of the text box in terms of the number of lines.
cols	Positive integer	Specifies the visible width of the text box in terms of the number of columns.
wrap	Hard or soft	Specifies the addition of line breaks by the web browser when the form is sent. Hard: add line breaks to the returned value, i.e. each line contains no more characters than the value indicated by the cols attribute. Soft: do not add line breaks.

Table 2.45. *Attributes of the <textarea> tag*

EXAMPLE.–

```
<body>
        <form action="">
        <p>Comments:</p>
        <textarea rows="6" cols="32"></textarea>
        </form>
</body>
```

Figure 2.47 shows the result obtained.

Figure 2.47. *Example of using the <textarea> tag*

2.8.4.2. *the <select> tag*

This is a pick list generally consisting of one or more <option> elements and the value of which is specified through the *value* attribute.

The <select> tag has the list of attributes shown in Table 2.46.

Attribute	Value	Description
size	Positive integer	List of options visible to the user.
name	Text	The name of the field associated with the data issued by the form.
multiple	Multiple or "" or (empty)	If present, the user has the possibility of selecting several options at the same time. If absent, the user has the possibility of choosing only one option.

Table 2.46. *Attributes of the <select> tag*

EXAMPLE.−

```
<form action="">
      <p>your favorite car:
      <select>
            <option value="1">Golf 7</option>
            <option value="2">Audi A4</option>
            <option value="3">Peugot 2008</option>
            <option value="4">Kinbo S2</option>
            <option value="5">Audi Q3</option>
      </select>
      </p>
</form>
```

Figure 2.48 shows the result obtained.

Figure 2.48. *Example of using the <select> tag*

2.8.4.3. *The <option> tag*

The <option> tag is used to define a single option in a <select> pick list.

The <option> tag has the list of attributes shown in Table 2.47.

Attribute	Value	Description
selected	Selected or "" or (empty)	If existing, the option is selected by default.
label	Text	Specifies a short description of the option.
name	Text	The name of the field associated with the data issued by the form.
value	Text	The value of the field when the form is sent.

Table 2.47. *Attributes of the <option> tag*

EXAMPLE.–

```
<form action="">
        <select size="4" multiple>
                <option label="yellow">Yellow color</option>
                <option label="green">Green color</option>
                <option label="blue">Blue color</option>
                <option label="red">Red color</option>
        </select>
</form>
```

Figure 2.49 shows the result obtained.

Figure 2.49. *Example of use of the <option> multiple*

2.8.4.4. *The <optgroup> tag*

The <optgroup> tag is used to group options from a web form within a <select> element.

The <optgroup> tag has the attribute shown in Table 2.48.

Attribute	Value	Description
label	Text	A legend for a group of options, generally visible to the user.

Table 2.48. *Attribute of the <optgroup> tag*

EXAMPLE.–

```
<form action="">
<select>
        <optgroup label="1st year">
                <option>LI 1.1</option>
        </optgroup>
        <optgroup label="2nd year">
                <option>DMW 2.1</option>
                <option>DSI 2.1</option>
        </optgroup>
                <optgroup label="3rd year">
                <option><DMW3.1</option>
                <option>DSI 3.1</option>
                <option>RSI 3.1</option>
        </optgroup>
</select>
</form>
```

Figure 2.50 shows the result obtained.

NOTE.– In the <optgroup> tag, the group caption cannot be selected at pick-list level. It has no exploitable value.

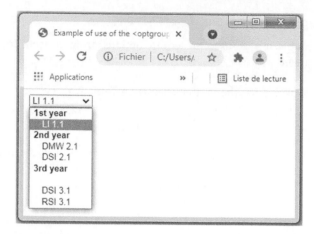

Figure 2.50. *Example of use of the <optgroup> tag*

2.8.4.5. *The <button> tag*

The <button> tag is used to create a clickable button. It has the list of attributes shown in Table 2.49.

Attribute	Value	Description
name	Text	The name of the field associated with the data issued by the form.
value	Text	The value of the field when the form is sent.
type	Button or submit or reset	Standard button. Button for sending data from a form. Form initialization button.

Table 2.49. *Attributes of the <button> tag*

EXAMPLE.–

```
<button type="button">OK</button>
<button type="submit">Submit</button>
```

2.8.4.6. *The <output> tag*

The < output > tag is used to define the result of a calculation in a web form. In particular, it is used to display such a result as a result of a script, without submitting the form.

The <output> tag has the list of attributes shown in Table 2.50.

Attribute	Value	Description
for	A list of identifiers separated by spaces	A list of the identifiers of a set of form elements having participated in a calculation operation, generally as a data input source.
name	Text	The name of the field associated with the data issued by the form.

Table 2.50. *Attributes of the <output> tag*

2.8.4.7. *The <progress> tag*

The <progress> tag is used to view the progress of a task. The specifics of the display are managed by the browser. In most cases, the browser displays a progress bar.

EXAMPLE.–

```
<p>
Progress bar:
<progress value="40" max="100">40%</progress>
</p>
```

Figure 2.51 shows the result obtained.

Figure 2.51. *Example of use of the <progress> tag*

The <progress> tag has the list of attributes shown in Table 2.51.

Attribute	Value	Description
name	Text	The name of the field associated with the data issued by the form.
value	Positive floating-point number	The value of the field when the form is sent.
max	Positive floating-point number	Maximum value to be reached (to be specified, default max="1").

Table 2.51. *Attributes of the <progress> tag*

2.8.4.8. *The <meter> tag*

The <meter> element is used to define a gage similar to <progress>, but which instead represents a scalar measurement within a well-defined range and not a percentage of progress.

The <meter> tag has the list of attributes shown in Table 2.52.

Attribute	Value	Description
name	Text	The name of the field associated with the data issued by the form.
value	Floating-point number	Value of the measurement, one gage level.
max	Floating-point number	Maximum value of the interval.
min	Floating-point number	Minimum value of the interval.
low	Floating-point number	The maximum value of the interval as of which the measurement is classified as low.
high	Floating-point number	The minimum value of the interval as of which the measurement is classified as high.
optimum	Floating-point number	Ideal value of position in the interval.

Table 2.52. *Attributes of the <meter> tag*

EXAMPLE.–

```
<p>
   Climate temperature during summer:
<meter min="35" max="49" value="39">39°C</meter>
</p>
<p>
Occupancy of a memory card:
<meter low="0" high="800" max="1000" value="950"
optimum="500">950MB</meter>
</p>
<p>
   Energy consumption rate in liters:
<meter low="6" high="12" max="20" value="4">4/20</meter>
</p>
```

Figure 2.52 shows the result obtained.

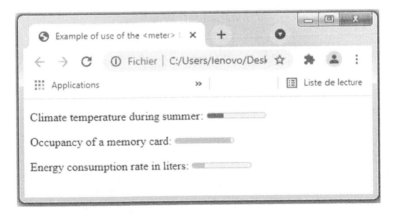

Figure 2.52. *Example of use of the <meter>*
tag. For a color version of this figure, see
www.iste.co.uk/benrebah/website.zip

2.8.5. *Common attributes for form elements*

Table 2.53 shows the list of common attributes for form elements.

Attribute	Role	<input/> types and other form tags	HTML5
accept	Accepted file types	File	
alt	Text as an alternative to the image	Image	
autocomplete	Semi-automatic input	Text, search, password, URL, tel, email, date, datetime, datetime-local, month, week, time, number, range, color, <textarea>, <form>	Yes
autofocus	Automatically focuses on an element	Text, search, password, URL, tel, email, date, datetime, datetime-local, month, week, time, number, range, color, <textarea>, <button>, <select>	Yes
checked	Button checked by default	Radio, checkbox	
dirname	Direction of input text	All	Yes
disabled	Deactivates an element	All	Yes
height	Height of an image	Image	Yes
high	High value of an interval	<meter>	Yes
list	List of proposals	Text, search, URL, tel, email, date, datetime, datetime-local, month, week, time, number, range, color	Yes
low	Low value of an interval	<meter>	Yes
max	Maximum measurement value	Date, datetime, datetime-local, month, week, time, number, range, <meter>, <progress>	Yes
maxlength	Maximum number of characters	Text, search, password, URL, tel, email, <textarea>	
min	Minimum measurement value	Date, datetime, datetime-local, month, week, time, number, range, <meter>, <progress>	Yes
multiple	Multi-selection	Email, file, <select>	Yes
name	Field name	All	Yes
optimum	Ideal value	<meter>	Yes
readonly	Read-only	All	Yes
placeholder	Indication on the expected value	Text, search, password, URL, tel, email, <textarea>	Yes

Attribute	Role	\<input/\> types and other form tags	HTML5
pattern	Model against which the syntax of an element is verified	Text, search, password, URL, tel, email	Yes
required	Required field	Text, search, password, URL, tel, email, date, datetime, datetime-local, month, week, time, number, checkbox, radio, file, \<textarea\>	Yes
size	Default size of an element	Text, search, password, URL, tel, email	
src	Image source	Image	
step	Step size	Date, datetime, datetime-local, month, week, time, number, range, \<meter\>, \<progress\>	Yes
type	Field type	\<input/\> in general	
value	Default value	For standard buttons: button label For buttons with images: the value of the validated field For radio buttons and check boxes: the value of the chosen field For text fields, variations of \<input/\>, and hidden fields: the default value of the element Attribute not used with the type="file"	
width	Width of the image	Image	Yes

Table 2.53. *Common attributes for form elements*

2.8.6. *Several new attributes added with HTML5*

2.8.6.1. *The placeholder attribute*

The *placeholder* attribute is used to provide a hint as to the value expected to be input in a form field. In general, this index is automatically cleared as soon as the field obtains the *focus*.

EXAMPLE.–

```
<form action="">
      <label for="np">Firstname&lastname:</label>
      <input type="text" id="np" placeholder="Enter your first name
and last name..."/>
      <input type="submit" value="Submit"/>
</form>
```

Figure 2.53 shows the result obtained.

Figure 2.53. *Example of use of the placeholder attribute*

2.8.6.2. *The autofocus attribute*

The *autofocus* attribute is used to directly focus on a field in the form as soon as the web page is loaded.

This attribute should only be used with one element of a given web page.

EXAMPLE.–

```
<input type="search" name="search" autofocus/>
```

Figure 2.54 shows the result obtained.

Figure 2.54. *Example of use of the autofocus attribute*

2.8.6.3. *The autocomplete attribute*

The *autocomplete* attribute is used to define how the browser predicts to the user the type of data expected in a form field.

It accepts two values: *on* and *off*.

EXAMPLE.–

```
<input type="search" name="search"autocomplete="off"/>
```

2.8.6.4. *The required attribute*

The *required* attribute is used to indicate that the completion of a field is mandatory. With this attribute, the browser only allows the form to be submitted if the field is completed by the user.

EXAMPLE.–

```
<form action="">
        <input type="tel" name="telephone" required/>
        <input type="submit" value="Submit"/>
</form>
```

Figure 2.55 shows the result obtained.

Figure 2.55. *Example of use of the required attribute*

2.8.6.5. *The multiple attribute*

The *multiple* attribute is a Boolean that gives the user the ability to input multiple values simultaneously. For a *file*-type field, it is possible to select multiple files at the same time for the same HTML element.

EXAMPLE.–

```
<input type="email" name="addresses" multiple/>
```

2.8.6.6. *The dirname attribute*

The *dirname* attribute is used to determine the direction in which the text has been input, after submitting the form. This technique seems to be useful mainly with Middle Eastern or Asian scripts. The web browser assigns to the variable (*name of the field concerned at the form level*) the value of the *dirname* attribute with rtl (*right to left*) or ltr (*left to right*).

EXAMPLE.–

```
<form action="" method="get">
    Name:<input type="text" name="name" required/>
    Comment:
    <input type="text" name="comment"    dirname="comment.dir"/>
    <input type="submit" value="Validate"/>
</form>
```

Figure 2.56 shows the result obtained.

Figure 2.56. *Example of use of the dirname attribute*

2.8.6.7. *The pattern attribute*

The *pattern* attribute is generally used with text fields to check, using a regular expression, whether their value meets certain constraints. If a value is incorrect, the form cannot be submitted.

EXAMPLE.–

```
<form action="">
<!-- Alphanumeric characters are allowed to be input -->
    <input type="text" name="login" pattern="[a-z0-9]"/>
    <input type="submit" value="Submit"/>
</form>
```

Figure 2.57 shows the result obtained.

Figure 2.57. *Example of use of the pattern attribute*

3

Style Sheets: CSS3

CSS – Cascading Style Sheets – is commonly used to format HTML-type web pages using display properties (colors, fonts, borders, etc.) and positioning properties (height, width, top-down, side-by-side, etc.). The display result of a web page can be completely changed without adding additional code to the web page. Indeed, the main purpose of style sheets is to separate the content of the page from its visual appearance. This approach makes it possible to:

– avoid repeating the same formatting code in each web page;

– employ common styles, using clear names (e.g. employing the same shaded style for images or text);

– modify the appearance of an entire website by changing only one single file (the style sheet);

– understand the code of the web page.

It should be noted that CSS is part of the standards published by W3C (World Wide Web Consortium).

3.1. Overview

3.1.1. *Origins of CSS3*

3.1.1.1. *CSS1: arduous adaptations in the battle of the browsers*

The final specification of CSS1 was revealed on December 17, 1996, presenting 50 properties. The W3C definition of CSS1 is a "simple style sheet mechanism that allows authors and readers to attach styles to the HTML document"[1]. In order to

---

1 https://www.w3.org/TR/REC-CSS1/.

facilitate the task for web developers, CSS1 is a language that can be easily read and written immediately by its human users, and it features a lexicon consistent with common uses in computer publishing.

3.1.1.2. *CSS2: hasty ambitions*

CSS was assigned in 1997 to a new working team within the W3C, led by Chris Lilley, in order to meet the requirements not covered by the first CSS1 specification. In May 1998, this team released the second level of CSS as a recommendation that offered more theoretical opportunities for cascading style sheets, adding almost 70 additional properties.

In 2007, this team was made up of additional representatives from Google, Apple, Microsoft, Adobe, IBM, Mozilla and Opera.

3.1.1.3. *CSS2.1: a return to implementations*

CSS2 implementations were back, leading the W3C CSS working group to draw up a revised version, CSS2.1 (CSS Level 2, Revision 1), as of 2001, based on what was actually chosen by the different browsers. CSS2.1 corrected CSS2 on several details, with this version either completely or partially removing certain sections (sound styles to define the media type, downloadable fonts, print styles, etc.). CSS2.1 was announced in July 2007 after eight successive versions, as a candidate recommendation, rather like a standard that implementations should follow.

3.1.1.4. *CSS3*

The development of the third level of cascading style sheets began in 1999, alongside CSS2.1.

To assist with updates, CSS3 has evolved to become "modular", with this modularity facilitating its implementation by users with a continuous variety of capabilities and requirements (*mobile browsers*, *graphical browsers* and *voice browsers*). Browsers are thus able to implement CSS3 modules.

With CSS3, new modules are added, the most important of which are as follows:

– selectors;

– box model;

– backgrounds and boundaries;

– the values of the image and the replaced content;

– text effects;

– 2D/3D transformation;

– animations;

– multi-column layout;

– user interface.

3.1.1.5. CSS4

As of 2010, the level-four edition of CSS began simultaneously with CSS modules. This fourth generation is still being researched.

3.1.2. Syntax and structure of the CSS3 language

3.1.2.1. Basic syntax rules

3.1.2.1.1. Case

CSS does not take uppercase and lowercase into account; they are therefore case insensitive. Exceptions are the values of the id and class attributes (which are named by the developer), the names of the character font families (e.g. "Times New Roman") and URLs, which are case sensitive.

3.1.2.1.2. Source code formatting

Spaces and line breaks have no influence in CSS code.

3.1.2.1.3. Identifiers

Identifiers (name, id and class) cannot start with a number, they can only contain alphanumeric characters: A-Z, a-z, 0-9, as well as the hyphen (-) and underscore (_).

3.1.2.1.4. Character strings

Detectable character strings (as in the case of the *quote* property or pseudo-elements *:after* and *:before*) are delimited by single quotation marks: ' (apostrophes) or double quotation marks: ".

– The character is preceded by a backslash: \' and \", respectively, to introduce a single or double quotation mark in the detectable string.

– We add the character "\000a" or "\a" to introduce a line break; we put a single backslash at the end of the line if we wish to continue the line in the code.

– If the character set declaration (*charset*) is missing, character strings can only contain ASCII characters. Unicode characters are obtained by placing the hexadecimal code preceded by a backslash, such as "\0040" for "@", "\0024" for

"$" (leading zeros can be ignored). If the sheet is included in the HTML file (delimited by the <style></style> tags), it uses the same character set as the HTML page. A style sheet put in a separate file must define the code by the *@charset* rule (such as: *@charset "UTF-8";*).

3.1.2.1.5. Comments

Comments begin with a backslash followed by an asterisk: "/*" and end with the character set inverted: "*/". They are optional for small display changes but mandatory for important layouts and formats.

3.1.2.2. *General structure*

3.1.2.2.1. Style rules

The operating principle of a CSS is based on *declarations*.

```
selector {property: value;}
```

A declaration is composed of at least two elements:

– the *selector*: the element of the web page to which one wishes to apply a style;

– the *property* and *value*: the group of rules that define the style.

EXAMPLE.–

```
p  {
color: green;
}
```

In this example, the formatted element is p (*paragraph*) and the rule group, between two braces, comprises the rule "color this element in green". A rule comprises a property (here, *color*), then a colon (:), and finally the value of the property (here, *green*).

It is certainly possible to define several rules, corresponding to the same element, and separate them with semicolons (;) in this way:

```
p    {
color: green;
font-family: "Arial"
}
```

It is also possible to define a common rule set for different identifiers separated by commas (,):

```
p ,span {
color: green;
font-family: "Arial";
}
```

3.1.2.2.2. Modular styles

Styles included in different style files can be imported for modular classification. There are several possible practices, such as:

– dividing styles corresponding to the layout, such as positioning of page elements, and styles corresponding to typography (*borders, fonts, colors,* etc.);

– cascading a general sheet for a set of pages and a specific sheet for the page in question (*possibility of having a more complicated cascade with styles by page families*).

For this, it is possible to use the syntax:

```
@import "style.css";
```

where *style.css* is the name of the file containing the styles we wish to import.

3.1.2.3. *Embedding CSS styles into a web page*

3.1.2.3.1. Style declaration

In the <head> header of the HTML file

This method involves embedding CSS styles within the header of the HTML file, <head>, delimited by the <style> and </style> tags. In this way, CSS styles are only definitely valid for the current page, so this method will generally be kept for learning or for styles specific to a single page.

EXAMPLE.–

```
<html>
<head>
<style type="text/css">
h1 {
color: blue;
}
</style>
</head>
        <body>
        <p>HTML page with embedded CSS style</p>
```

```
        </body>
</html >
```

In a .css file

This method consists of defining CSS styles in a different file with the *.css* extension.

This file will be referenced in the header of the HTML page using a *link* tag (*this file can be referenced in multiple HTML pages. This is therefore the most recommended method*).

EXAMPLE.– the HTML file.

```
<html>
<head>
        <link rel="stylesheet" type="text/css" href="styles.css">
</head>
<body>
        <p>HTML web page with external CSS style</p>
</body>
</html>
```

page.html

EXAMPLE.– The style.css file.

```
P {
        color: blue;
}
```

style.css

NOTE.–

– The *CSS* file path is either absolute or relative (for the previous example, both files, *page.html* and *style.css*, are placed in the same directory).

– There is another way to import external CSS styles. This is to use the CSS *@import* rule to import a style sheet between two tags, <style> and </style>.

EXAMPLE.–

```
<html>
<head>
        <style type="text/css">
 @import"style.css"
        </style>
</head>
<body>
<p>HTML web page with external CSS styles</p>
</body>
</html>
```

Directly in the tag

This method allows the *style* attribute to be added to any tag. It is the least recommended method.

EXAMPLE.–

```
<body>
        <p style="color: red"; > Welcome to ISET Mahdia</p>
</body>
```

3.1.2.3.2. Adapting styles to the display device

The web page display device is not always the computer screen. It can also be the printer for printing papers, a video projector for a large-format presentation or a mobile web browser. The styles used for the screen are often not adaptable to other media.

Style sheets can be adapted to the display device using the output *media* indication, directly in the style sheet or during importation of an external sheet.

EXAMPLE.– The *media* indication is shown directly in the style sheet.

```
@media screen {
        /* style rule*/;
}
```

EXAMPLE.– The *media* indication is shown when importing an external style sheet.

```
<html>
<head>
```

```
        <link rel="stylesheet" type="text/css" href="styles.css"
        media="screen"/>
        <link rel="stylesheet" type="text/css" href="printing.css"
        media="print"/>
</head>
<body>
        <p>HTML page with adaptive CSS styles</p>
</body>
</html>
```

3.1.2.4. *Cascade and interpretation order of styles*

3.1.2.4.1. A cascade of styles

If numerous style sheets are used in the same web page, CSS rules are created simultaneously with the reading of each rule, in the invoked order of the style sheets. As a result, if opposing rules appear in the styles, it is the rule that is read last that takes precedence.

EXAMPLE.– styles.css and colors.css scripts.

```
/* styles.css*/
p {color: green; }
 /* colors.css*/
p {color: blue;}
```

In the case where the styles are imported as follows, the text of the paragraphs will be colored green.

```
@import "styles.css"
@import "colors.css"
```

3.1.2.4.2. Rule priority

To prevent the style of a well-defined part of the page (*such as the menu*) from being changed by a fairly general rule like the one in the previous paragraph, the concept of rule priority applies. Therefore, in the cascade, a rule that appears previously can only change a style if its priority is greater or equal.

EXAMPLE.– Take the following HTML code:

```
<body>
<div id="nav">
<h1>Navigation Section</h1>
<ul>
```

```
<li><h1>Navigation input 1</h1></li>
</ul>
</div>
</body>
```

In order for the navigation menu titles not to have a similar color to the text titles, the following style needs to be applied:

```
h1, h2, h3 {
color: red;
}
div#nav h1 {color:red;}
```

3.1.2.4.3. Order of rule specificities

It is clear from the last example that the navigation menu titles should not be treated in the same way as other titles. In addition, if the element selector is *precise* in its target, its priority will be important. The precision of the selector is known as *specificity* in the CSS lexicon. The order of the specificities is as follows, in increasing order of priority:

– HTML element, such as *h2 {color: blue;}*: obtains one priority point;

– succession of elements, such as *div h2 {color: blue}*: obtains two priority points, one per selector element;

– using a class (*class attribute*), such as *h2.blue {color: blue}*: obtains 11 priority points: 1 point for the element and 10 for the class;

– using an identifier (*id attribute*), such as *h2#site-title {color: blue}*: obtains 101 priority points: 1 point for the element and 100 for the identifier;

– a style inside an HTML tag, such as *<h2 style="color: blue">...* *</h1>*: obtains 1,000 priority points.

NOTE.– A low-priority style can never change a high-priority style. However, there is a way to override this rule: the *! important* notation. This notation is introduced just after a CSS property value and signals to the browser that opposite styles should not be retained thereafter.

EXAMPLE.–

```
p {color: blue! important }
```

3.1.2.4.4. Calculating specificity

The specificity of a rule is calculated starting from the most typical to the least typical elements. At all steps, the count of the number of selectors matching the specificity shows the priority level.

EXAMPLE.–

`div#page p em` is more specific than `div#page em` but less than `div#page p em.blue`.

Therefore, if we run through the specificities in descending order, we have:

– `div#page`: gives all rules equal priority;

– `em.blue`: shows that the last rule takes priority;

– `p em`: gives the first rule the highest priority;

– `em`: gives the second rule top priority.

NOTE.– It is always advisable to use selectors sparingly in order to simplify the addition of more specific rules.

EXAMPLE.–

```
<div id="page">
<p>
        <ul>
        <li><a> Hello and welcome to our web page.</a></li>
        </ul>
</p>
</div>
```

To change the style of the <a> link in the list, a simple rule such as "div#page a" rather than "div#page p ul li a" needs to be used. If there are other <a> links outside the <ul> list, then it is recommended to use the "div#page li a" rule.

3.1.3. *Selectors*

The term CSS *selector* refers to a class of page elements apparently of a different type or a relationship between two elements. It is possible, for example, to select all paragraphs on the page, or alternatively all elements that have been marked in blue. To do this, CSS selectors distinguish the elements of the page according to their type, their attributes, their succession in the web page code or according to the interaction with the user such as links.

The user may apply as many selectors as possible to specify the element whose style they wish to change. It is possible, therefore, to combine as desired the different types of selectors described below. This specific feature grants ample versatility to CSS rules.

3.1.3.1. *General selectors*

3.1.3.1.1. Universal selector

The asterisk (*) selector selects all tags on the web page.

EXAMPLE.– Changing the font of all text on the web page.

```
*  {
Font-family: Arial;
}
```

The general selector can discover other applications in the succession of elements. It is then optional when pasted to a different selector, often rendering it of little use.

EXAMPLE.–

```
*.class   {
font-family: Arial;
}
```

is similar to:

```
. class   {
font-family: Arial;
}
```

3.1.3.1.2. Type selectors

This is a selector corresponding to the name of a tag in an HTML page.

EXAMPLE.– Setting the font size of an H1 title to 16 px.

```
h1   {
font-size: 16px;
}
```

3.1.3.2. *Attribute selectors*

This is a selector referring to an attribute of an element of an HTML page. The two most commonly used attributes are generally *class* and *id*, but it is possible to refer to any other attribute.

3.1.3.2.1. Class selectors (the class attribute)

This is a selector that applies specifically to elements that repeat in the web page. It is defined in CSS by a period (.) and it can concern all or only one of the elements of the HTML page using this class.

EXAMPLE.–

```
<!DOCTYPE html>
<html>
<head>
      <meta http-equiv="content-type" content="text/html;charset=UTF-
      8"/>
      <link rel="stylesheet" href="style.css"/>
      <title>Class selector</title>
</head>
<body>
<h1>WebprogrammingHTML 5 & CSS 3</h1>
      <p class="introduction">I wish you pleasant reading</p>
</body>
</html>
```

To color the text of the paragraph <p> in blue and italicize it, you simply need to define the following style:

```
.introduction{
color = blue;
font-style : italic; }
```

NOTE.– The CSS syntax of the class selector can be defined in two ways:

.class_name {/* declaration of CSS properties */ }

or:

element.class_name{ /* declaration of CSS properties */ }

EXAMPLE.– If in an HTML5 document we have:

```
<p class="c1">…..</p>
<ul class="c1">
<li>……</li>
</ul>
```

where applicable, in the style sheet we find:

```
.c1 { color:gray;}
p.c1{font-style: italic;}
```

This style allows c1 classes to be displayed in gray, and paragraphs are also in italics.

3.1.3.2.2. Identifier selectors (the id attribute)

It is only possible to apply this selector to a single element in the code of an HTML page. It then concerns unique elements for structuring the web page, such as the essential blocks (*logo, header, column(s), footer,* etc.). This selector is defined in CSS by a hash character (*#*).

EXAMPLE.–

```
<img src="images/logo.png" alt="website logo" id="logo"/>
```

To define a style property for this logo, you simply need to:

```
# logo { /* CSS style here */ }
```

NOTE.– The CSS syntax of the identifier selector can be defined in two ways:

id_name{/* declaration (s) */ }

or:

element#id_name { /* declaration (s) */ }

3.1.3.2.3. Attribute selectors

The various other attributes are referenced by adding to a type selector [attribute_name].

EXAMPLE.– The <a> tag and the [title] attribute.

```
<a   href="  http:   //site.com"  title="Choose  this  link">Visit  our
site</a>
```

The possible style rules for this link are:

– CSS1 rule: select the set of links that have a [title] attribute:

```
a [title] {/* style properties*/ }
```

– CSS2 rule: selecting the set of links that have a [title] attribute is equivalent to the value "Choose this link":

```
a [title=" Choose this link "] {/* style properties*/ }
```

– CSS3 rule: select the set of links that have a [title] attribute that includes the word "to" in its value:

```
a [title *="to"] {/* style properties*/ }
```

NOTE.– General syntax of the attribute selector:

   – a tag that has an attribute: [attribute] tag;

   – a tag with an attribute having an exact value: tag [attribute= "value"];

   – a tag with an attribute having a precise word in its value: tag [attribute*="value"].

3.1.3.3. *Hierarchical selectors*

In CSS, it is possible to specify rules for elements included in other elements by not adding a class or identifier. In practice it is possible, for example, to change the style of a strong text according to whether it is in a list or paragraph. This can be done using the concept of web-page element hierarchy, according to the tag nesting noted in the web page code.

3.1.3.3.1. Descendant selector

Using the *descendant selector*, which is noted in the form of one or more space(s), it is possible to designate the descendant elements of another element (*or of several other elements*), or connected to each other by any relationship.

EXAMPLE.– Select all <strong> tags located in an <h2> tag.

```
H2 strong { }
```

EXAMPLE.– Matching HTML code.

```
<h2>Title with <strong>important text</ strong ></h2>
```

NOTE.– *selector1 selector2{style properties}*: used to select all elements of type *selector2* included in *selector1*, regardless of their level.

EXAMPLE.–

```
<div id="Par1">
<h1>Title of the Site</h1>
        <div id="Par2">
        <h2>First Title</h2>
        <p> ............................</p>
        </div>
</div>
```

To select all <h2> titles and change their styles, you simply need to note:
```
#Par1 h2 {/*style properties*/}
```

To select the grandchild <h2> (the second title), you simply need to note:
```
#Par1 * h2 {/*style properties*/}
```

3.1.3.3.2. Child selector

It is possible to designate an element by direct filiation with another element using the *child selector*, written >. The relationship then only looks at children and not grandchildren. We note the parent element followed by > and then the child element.

EXAMPLE.– Selection of the <h2> title of the second <div> of the previous example.

```
#Par2>h2 {                }
```

3.1.3.3.3. Adjacent sibling selector

It is possible to define a style for a child element *promptly* followed by a different child element from the same parent element using the *adjacent sibling selector*, which is noted +.

EXAMPLE.– Selection of an <h2> title located after the <p> tag.

```
p+h2  {                    }
```

EXAMPLE.– Corresponding HTML code.

```
<p> paragraph </p>
<h2> Title </h2>
```

3.1.3.4. *Pseudo-classes and pseudo-elements*

The selectors studied previously are satisfactory for styling an HTML web page that is not complex. However, more precise selectors exist that are used to change the styles of elements in a typical state, such as links that are or are not consulted, states that correspond to the user's reaction or elements meeting specific conditions.

3.1.3.4.1. Pseudo-classes of links

The pseudo-classes `:visited` and `:link` are intended for hypertext links only (*<a href=""></a> in the HTML page code*). The pseudo-class *:link* is used to select previously unvisited links and the pseudo-class *:visited* is used to select previously visited links.

EXAMPLE.–

```
a:link { color: blue;}
a:visited { color: gray;}
```

/* This style is used to put the links of an HTML page in blue when it has not yet been visited, and in gray after it has been visited */.

3.1.3.4.2. Interactive pseudo-classes

It is possible to select elements according to their interaction with the user using pseudo-classes `:active,` `:hover` and `:focus`. The W3C gives the following definitions:

– the pseudo-class *:hover* matches when the user shows an element (*with any tool*) but does not activate it. For example, this pseudo-class is applied by the browser if the (*mouse*) cursor is hovering over the box bounding the element;

– the pseudo-class *:active* matches when an element is being activated by the user. For example, during the time between the user pressing the mouse button and releasing it;

– the pseudo-class *:focus* matches when an element has focus (*this includes events from all input forms such as the keyboard, for example*).

EXAMPLE.– Pseudo-class *:hover*.

```
img {border: none;}
img:hover {border: underline;}
```

/* This style makes it possible to remove the default underlining of links and have it appear only when hovered over with the mouse */.

EXAMPLE.– Pseudo-class *:focus*.

```
input {color: #222; background-color: #bababa;}
input:focus {color: #333; background-color: #ddd;}
```

/* This style changes the color of the text and background of a text field when it switches from inactive state to return-to-focus state */.

3.1.3.4.3. Pseudo-elements

The pseudo-elements *:first-letter* and *:first-line* indicate in order the first character and first line of a text, specifically a paragraph.

EXAMPLE.–

```
div#P1 p:first-line {font-size: 150%}
```

/* This style allows the first line in the paragraph to be displayed larger than the rest */.

The *:after* and *:before* pseudo-elements refer to the content of the element. They allow text to be added after or before the text inside the element using the *content* property (note the \00BB and \00AB codifications designating French closing and opening double quotation marks, in that order).

NOTE.– To differentiate pseudo-classes from pseudo-elements, CSS3 adds ":" to pseudo-elements.

EXAMPLE.– the pseudo *:before* will be notated in CSS3 by *::before*.

EXAMPLE.–

```
q:before {
content: " « \00AB»"
color :blue;
}
q:after {
```

```
content: " « \00BB»"
color: red;
}
```

/* This style allows the quotation to be framed by two quotation marks colored blue and red */.

Table 3.1 shows a list of pseudo-elements and pseudo-classes.

Pseudo-classes/pseudo-elements	Role
:link	Link
:visited	Link visited
:hover	Element hovered over
:active	Active element
Pseudo-classes/pseudo-elements	Role
:focus	Element with the focus
:first-child	First child
:last-child	Last child
:nth-child(n)	nth child
:nth-last-of-child(n)	nth last child
:nth-of-type(n)	nth type of element
:nth-last-of-type(n)	nth last type of element
:first-of-type	First type of element
:last-of-type	Last type of element
:only-of-type	Element of unique type
:checked	Status checked
:enabled	Activated state
::first-letter	First letter
::first-line	First line

Table 3.1. *List of pseudo-classes and pseudo-elements*[2]

---

2 http://archive.org/stream/GoFreebooks.comHTMLFr3/go-freebooks.com-HTML-fr%20(3)_djvu.txt.

3.1.4. *Values and units used*

3.1.4.1. *Distances and dimensions*

In a style sheet, it is possible to use several measurement units, such as inch, centimeter, millimeter, point, pica, pixel and percentage. Absolute values, which remain constant for any hardware or software used, are distinguished from relative values, which vary depending on the computer used.

Absolute values are shown in Table 3.2.

Unit	Name	Description	Value	Example
pt	Point	72 pt = 1 in	Integer	32 pt
pc	Pica	1 pc = 12 pt	Actual	3.78 pc
mm	Millimeter	1 mm = 24 pc	Integer	45 mm
cm	Centimeter	1 cm = 10 mm	Integer	7 cm
in	Inch	1 in = 2.45 cm	Actual	1.5 in

Table 3.2. *The absolute values of the dimensions*[3]

Relative values are shown in Table 3.3.

Unit	Description	Value	Example
em	A relative unit that is based on the default font size of the web document	Actual	1.8 em
rem	Relative unit (rem = "root em") represents the size of the font in the root element of the web page	Actual	1.5 rem
ex	Unit relative to the height of the lowercase letter of the element chosen	Actual	1.3 ex
px	The pixel is the smallest particle in an image. It depends on the screen resolution	Integer	220 px
%	Percentage	Integer	80%

Table 3.3. *The relative values of the dimensions*

---

3 *Idem.*

NOTE.–

– Measurement units are always noted by an abbreviation composed of two letters.

– It is often recommended to use the em unit to define the size of fonts for more stability between separate operating systems and browsers.

3.1.4.2. Colors

Colors can be declared using multiple notations in CSS, such as:

– *standard hexadecimal notation*, e.g. *#aabb55*. This notation represents the color, or preferably its three components, red (r), green (g) and blue (b), through a hexadecimal notation of the form *#rrggbb*;

– *simplified hexadecimal notation*, e.g. *#cb4*. In this way it is possible to gain several characters. Each digit is thus tacitly duplicated, such that *#cb4* coincides with the notation *#ccbb44* (the color #fb4a5c has no abbreviation);

– *decimal notation*, e.g. *color :rgb(255,0,0)*. A hexadecimal value is not used to encode the color in RGB, but an integer between 0 and 255 is used;

– *percentage notation*, e.g. *color :rgb(50%,0%,75%)*. A value of 100% means that the component is at its maximum and 0% means that it is absent;

– *keywords* such as *color :red*. There are 17 colors indicated, representing the basic colors.

The CSS3 specificity has added to these notations:

– the *RGBa notation*, which follows the same rules as standard RGB notation, aside from one component added to the value *:rgb(10,10,10)*. This thus becomes *rgba(10,10,10,1)*. The final value designating the degree of transparency or opacity between 0 and 1;

– the *HSL* (*Hue Saturation Luminance*) *notation*. This notation comprises three values. The first value is defined in degrees between 0° and 359° (the ° symbol, however, does not appear in the notation). It coincides with a color on the color wheel: magenta (300°), blue (240°), cyan (180°), green (120°), yellow (60°) and red (0°). The second and third values are defined as a percentage and mark the saturation and luminosity, in that order. Such as: *color :hsl(60,50%,100%)* for yellow;

– the *HSLa notation*, enabling the addition of a value between 0 and 1 for opacity or transparency. Such as: *color :hsl(60,50%,100%,0.5)* for a semi-transparent yellow.

Name	Notation	Result
Maroon	#800000	
Red	#ff0000	
Orange	#ffA500	
Yellow	#ffff00	
Olive	#808000	
Purple	#800080	
Fuchsia	#ff00ff	
White	#ffffff	
Lime	#00ff00	
Green	#008000	
Navy	#000080	
Blue	#0000ff	
Aqua	#00ffff	
Teal	#008080	
Black	#000000	
Silver	#c0c0c0	
Gray	#808080	

Table 3.4. *The 17 colors of the web[4]. For a color version of this table, see www.iste.co.uk/benrebah/website.zip*

3.2. Text formatting

3.2.1. *Character size*

The CSS *font-size* property needs to be used to exchange the size of the text. There are many techniques, such as:

– specifying an absolute size: in centimeters, millimeters or pixels. This way is very precise but it is not advised unless necessary as there is a risk of specifying a size that is excessively small for some readers;

– specifying a relative size: in (em) or (ex) or as a percentage; this approach has the advantage of being flexible. It provides a size that is more easily adaptable to the needs of visitors.

---

4 https://fr.m.wikibooks.org/wiki/Le_langage_CSS/Version_imprimable.

SYNTAX.– *Font-size*:

- – value in em;

- – or value in px;

- – or value in pt;

- – or small, x-small, xx-small, medium, xx-large, x-wide, wide;

- – or larger or `smaller` than the parent element.

EXAMPLE.– Absolute size.

```
p {
font-size: 14px; /* Paragraphs of 14 pixels */
}
```

NOTE.–

– The size can be indicated in pixels (px) or points (pt). Point notation is used more for pages intended for printing and the pixel is used more for display on a screen.

– It is possible to indicate the values in cm, mm, in, ex or pica, but these are not widely used for character display.

– Spaces must not be placed between the value and the unit, such that 14px is correct and 14 px is incorrect.

– It is possible to indicate the value relative to the height of a font: em. The value 1 em coincides with 100% of the current font size, 1.5 em to 150% and 0.75 em to 75%. The use of the em unit is limited to the size of the character fonts.

– The values small, x-small, xx-small, medium, xx-large, x-wide and wide present a flaw in that they define only seven sizes.

– The *larger* and *smaller* values are also referred to as relative values since they depend on the font size of the parent element.

3.2.2. *Font type*

The presentation of a document depends very much on the character font, an important element both on-screen and during printing. It is possible to define the font used with the *font-family* property.

Syntax.– *Font-family*.

Specifying the font or font family.

EXAMPLE.–

```
p {
font-family: Verdana;
}
```

NOTE.– To prevent problems when the user does not have exactly the same font as yours, certain font names are generally cited with commas separating them. Here, the first font indicated will be used by the browser, but it must be present on the user's operating system. Otherwise, it will access the next one. In the event that none of the indicated fonts are to be found on the system, the default font will be used by the browser.

EXAMPLE.–

```
p { font-family: Verdana,Arial,Times;}
```

– Where the font name contains spaces, the entire name must be delimited by quotation marks (single or double).

EXAMPLE.–

```
h1 {font-family:'Times New Roman';}
```

– The font name is case insensitive.

– Instead of the font name, you can indicate font families or general font names (such as serif – Bodoni, Garamond, Georgia, Times New Roman, etc.).

3.2.3. *Italic text*

The style property that allows text to be italicized is *font-style*.

Syntax.– *Font-style*:

– italic; /* italicizes the text */;

– or oblique; /* slants the text (a slightly different result from italics, precisely speaking */;

– or normal; /* the text will be normal (default value). This cancels the italic formatting */.

EXAMPLE.–

```
h1 {
font-style: italic;
}
```

3.2.4. *Bold text*

With this *font-weight* property, text can be put in bold.

SYNTAX.– *Font-weight*:

– bold; /* the font is put in bold */;

– or bolder; /* increases the boldness relative to the parent element */;

– or lighter; /* reduces the boldness relative to the parent element */;

– or normal; /* the text will be normal */;

– or a value between 100 and 900; /* possible values: 100, 200, 300, 400, 500, 600, 700, 800 and 900 (500 coincides with normal, 700 coincides with bold and 900 coincides with bolder) */.

EXAMPLE.–

```
h2 {
font-weight: bolder;
}
```

3.2.5. *Text decoration and underlining*

Using the *text-decoration* property, it is possible to change the decoration of a text.

SYNTAX.– *Text-decoration*:

– underline; /* a line will be drawn immediately under the text */;

– or overline; /* a line will be drawn immediately above the text */;

– or line-through; /* the text will be struck-through */;

– or blink; /* the text will be flashing; this works on some browsers, not all */;

– or none; /* the text will be normal (default value) */.

EXAMPLE.–

```
h1 {
text-decoration: overline;
}
```

NOTE.– By applying the *text-decoration: none*; style declaration to the <a> hyperlink tag, the underline will be removed from the links.

3.2.6. *Small capitals*

Using the *font-variant* property, text can be placed in small capitals.

SYNTAX.– *Font-variant*:

– small-caps; /* the text will be placed in capital letters that are smaller in size than normal capitals */;

– or normal; /* the text is normal (default value)*/.

EXAMPLE.–

```
h1 {
font-variant: small-caps;
}
```

3.2.7. *Text coloring*

With the *color* property, the color of a text can be changed.

SYNTAX.– *Color*:

– color designation;

– or hexadecimal notation with the form #rrggbb;

– or abbreviated hexadecimal notation with the form #rgb;

– or RGB notation using integers from 0 to 255;

– or RGB notation using percentages between 0 and 100;

– or RGBa notation with a between 0 and 1;

– or HSL notation;

– or HSLa notation with a between 0 and 1;

– or transparent.

EXAMPLE.–

```
h1, h2 {
color: blue;
}
```

NOTE.– The *color* property can be applied to different elements such as backgrounds, form elements or horizontal lines.

3.2.8. *Transforming text to lowercase or uppercase*

Using the *text-transform* property, text can be placed in lowercase or uppercase.

SYNTAX.– *Text-transform*:

– capitalize /* the first letter of any word is capitalized */;

– or uppercase /* all letters are uppercase */;

– or lowercase /* all letters are lowercase */;

– or none /* the letters remain unchanged */.

EXAMPLE.–

```
h2 {
text-transform: capitalize;
}
```

3.2.9. *Indenting the first line of a paragraph*

With the *text-indent* property, it is possible to indent the first line of a paragraph.

SYNTAX.– *Text-indent*:

– an exact value (such as 15 px);

– or a relative value noted as a percentage relative to the width of the paragraph.

EXAMPLE.–

```
p {
text-indent: 25px;
}
```

3.2.10. *Letter spacing*

With the *letter-spacing* property, it is possible to change the value of the space between characters.

SYNTAX.– *Letter-spacing*:

– a length value (such as 5 px);

– or normal (default value).

EXAMPLE.–

```
p {
Letter-spacing: 8px;
}
H3 {
Letter-spacing: -2px;
}
```

3.2.11. *Word spacing*

Using the *word-spacing* property, it is possible to change the value of the space between words.

SYNTAX.– *Word-spacing*:

– a length value (such as 5px);

– or normal (default value).

EXAMPLE.–

```
p {
word-spacing: 5px;
}
```

3.2.12. *Paragraph spacing*

With the *line-height* property, the line spacing can be changed.

SYNTAX.– *Line-height*:

– a numerical value;

– or length value (such as 15 px);

– or percentage;

– or normal (default value).

3.2.13. *Horizontal text alignment*

With the *text-align* property, it is possible to align text horizontally (*right, left, centered or justified*).

SYNTAX.– *Text-align*:

– right /* align text to the right */;

– or left /* align text to the left (by default) */;

– or center /* center the text */;

– or justify /* justify the text */;

– or auto /* default alignment value */.

EXAMPLE.–

```
p {
text-align: right;
}
```

NOTE.– It is not possible to change the text alignment for an inline tag (such as <strong>, <a>, <em>, etc.); it only works on block tags (<div>, <p>, <h2>, <h1>, etc.).

3.2.14. *Vertical text alignment*

Using the vertical-align property, it is possible to align text vertically with another element. It is possible to apply this property only to cells in a table or to inline-type elements.

SYNTAX.– *Vertical-align*:

– top;

– or middle;

– or bottom;

– baseline;

– or sub;

– or super;

– none (no indication);

– or length value (such as 5 px);

– or percentage.

EXAMPLE.–

```
.alignmiddle {
vertical-align: middle;
}
```

NOTE.–

– The *sup*, *super* and *baseline* values are used relative to a line of text:

- *baseline* aligns the bottom of the element to the text baseline;

- *super* puts the text in superscript.

– The alignments *none*, *length value* or *percentage* leave it to the browser to display the aligned text.

– The *bottom*, *middle* and *top* values make it possible to align proportionally to the parent element such as text or one or more cells in a table:

- *top* aligns to the highest level of the parent element;

- *middle* aligns to the middle of the parent element;

- *bottom* aligns to the lowest level of the parent element.

– If the length value is positive, the alignment is on the baseline.

– If the value is negative, the alignment is below the baseline.

– If the percentage is positive, the alignment is on the baseline.

– If the percentage is negative, the alignment is below the baseline.

3.2.15. *Text direction*

Using the *direction* property, it is possible to change the direction of text (from right to left or vice versa).

SYNTAX.– *Direction*:

  – lrt; /* left-to-right direction */;

  – or rtl; /* right-to-left direction */.

EXAMPLE.–

```
.arabicdir {
direction: ltr;
}
```

3.2.16. *Text length and height*

With the *width* and *height* style properties, several text tags can be associated with the width and height of a strip enclosing the contained text. These properties are very useful because they avoid using the trick of unreal tables to display text inside an area in the form of a rectangle.

SYNTAX.–

  Width: a width value or a percentage.

  Height: a height value or a percentage.

3.2.17. *Floating*

With the *float* property, it is possible to float an element all around the text.

SYNTAX.– *Float*:

  – left /* float the element to the left */;

  – or right /* float the element to the right */.

EXAMPLE.– An image will float to the left of a text.

```
<!-- Here is the HTML code for the example-->

<p><img src="flash.png" class="imagefloat" alt="image float"/> This
is normal paragraph text, written after the image, which will wrap it
as the image is floating.</p>

/* The CSS style to be applied to the HTML*/ code.
.imagefloat
```

```
{
float: left;
}
```

Figure 3.1 shows the result obtained.

 Lorem ipsum dolor sit amet, consectetuer adipiscing elit. Donec vitae lorem imperdiet lacus molestie molestie. Cum sociis natoque penatibus

Figure 3.1. *Effect of* float *style*

NOTE.– When applying wrapping to an object, the element that floats needs to be placed beforehand in the HTML code, otherwise the effect will not work.

3.3. List formatting

A list is defined as an organized paragraph consisting of a series of sections. In HTML, there are three types of lists:

– ordered lists;

– unordered lists;

– lists of definitions.

There are several properties offered by CSS that make it possible to change the appearance of the lists mentioned above.

3.3.1. Different bullet numbering styles

With the *list-style-type* property, it is possible to determine the appearance of the numbering style or the bullet of a list.

SYNTAX.– *List-style-type*.

Ordered lists:

– decimal /* such as 1, 2, 3, etc. */;

– decimal-leading-zero /* such as 01, 02, etc. */;

– upper-roman /* such as I, II, III, etc. */;

– lower-roman /* such as i, ii, iii, etc. */;

– upper-alpha /* such as A, B, C, etc. */;

– lower-alpha /* such as a, b, c, etc. */.

Unordered lists:

– disc /* a full disc */;

– circle /* an empty circle */;

– square /* a square */.

EXAMPLE.–

```
.style1 {
List-style-type: square;
}
```

3.3.2. *Graphic style of bullets*

Using the *list-style-image* property, it is possible to change the bullets to an image.

SYNTAX.– List-style-image:

– url /* location of the image */ ;

– none/* no indication */.

EXAMPLE.–

```
ul {
List-style-image: url(image.png);
}
```

3.3.3. *Removing lines from a bullet list*

The *list-style-position* property can be used to specify the position of the second line (and subsequent lines) of a list element in proportion to the bullet or numbering.

SYNTAX. *List-style-position*:

– outside /* outside (default value) */;

– inside /* inside */.

EXAMPLE.–

```
.positionin {
list-style-position: inside;
}

.positionext {
list-style-position: outside;
}
```

Figure 3.2 shows the result obtained.

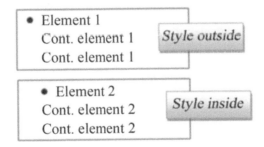

Figure 3.2. *Effect of the* list-style-position *property*

3.4. Backgrounds, borders and shadows

3.4.1. *Backgrounds*

3.4.1.1. *Background color*

Using the *background-color* property, it is possible to change the background color.

SYNTAX.– *Background-color*:

– color designation;

– hexadecimal notation or abbreviated hexadecimal notation;

– notation in RGB mode with integers between 0 and 25;

– RGB notation with percentages between 0 and 100;

– RGBa notation;

– HSL or HSLa notation;

– transparent.

EXAMPLE.–

```
div {
background-color: red; /* the page background is red */
color: yellow; /* the page text is yellow */
}
```

3.4.1.2. *Inserting a background image*

With the *background-image* property, the positioning of a background image can be standard or tiled.

SYNTAX.– *Background-image*:

– url (location of the image);

– none /* no background image */.

EXAMPLE.–

```
div {
background-image: url(background.png);
}
```

NOTE.–

– The *background-image* property can be complemented by several options in order to change the attitude of the background image:

- first option, *background-attachment*: used to fix the background. With this option, you can see the text scroll relative to the background. This option can have one of the following values: *fixed*: fix the background image; *scroll*: scroll the background image at the same time as the text.

EXAMPLE.–

```
body { background-image: url(bubbles.jpg);
background-attachment: scroll;

}
```

- Second option, *background-repeat*: used to tile the image by default. This option can have one of the following four values: *no-repeat*: do not repeat the background; *repeat-x*: repeat the background on the first row only; *repeat-y*: repeat the background on the first column only; *repeat*: tile the background (default value).

EXAMPLE.–

```
body { background-image: url(bubbles.jpg);
background-repeat: repeat-x;}
```

- Third option, *background-position*: used to precisely position the background image of an element. This option is only important if it is used in conjunction with *background-repeat: no-repeat*. This option can have one of the following three values: 1st pixel value 2nd pixel value; 1st percentage 2nd percentage; *right* or *center* or *left bottom* or *center* or *top*.

EXAMPLE.–

```
background-position: 75px 225px;
/* the background is placed at 75 pixels from the left and 225 pixels
from the top */.

background-position: 75%  25%;

background-position: bottom left;
```

FULL EXAMPLE.–

```
body {
Background-image :url(background.jpg;
background-attachment: scroll; /* the background scrolls with the
text */
background-repeat: repeat; /* the background will be repeated */
background-position: bottom left; /* the background will be placed in
the bottom-left corner */
}
```

– Where numerous background properties are used, this syntax can be used:

```
body {background: url(background.jpg) scroll repeat-x bottom left;
}
```

– Many background images can be given for an element by separating the declarations with a comma.

```
body {background: url(background.jpg) scroll repeat-y bottom left,
url (image.gif) scroll;
}
```

/* Given its importance, the image declaration order requires the first image in the list to be placed above the others */.

3.4.1.3. *Opacity or transparency*

It is possible with CSS3s, and using the *opacity* property, to change the transparency or opacity of an element.

SYNTAX.– *Opacity*.

A value between 1 and 0 (if the value = 1, opacity will be total and transparency will be zero. If the value = 0, the opacity will be zero and the transparency will be total).

EXAMPLE.–

```
div {
background-color: blue; color: yellow; opacity: 0.5;
}
```

NOTE.– The RGBa notation can be used to change the transparency of an element.

EXAMPLE.–

```
div{ background-color: rgba(0,255,0,0.7); }
```

3.4.2. *Borders and shadows*

With CSS, we have a wide choice of borders to decorate the boundaries of an element on an HTML page.

There are several CSS properties that make it possible to change the appearance of these borders.

3.4.2.1. *Border color*

With CSS3, the *border-color* property makes it possible to change the color of a border.

SYNTAX.– *Border-color*:

– color designation;

– hexadecimal notation with the form #xxxxxx;

– brief hexadecimal notation with the form #xxx;

– RGB notation with integers between 0 and 255;

– RGBa notation, a is a real number between 0 and 1;

– HSL notation;

– HSLa notation, a is a real number between 0 and 1.

NOTE.–

– With the *border-color* property, it is possible to define the color (*alone*) of all four sides of an element on an HTML page.

– The color can only be applied where the border type (*border-style*) and its thickness (*border-width*) are defined.

– It is also possible to define the colors on each side of the element separately with the properties:

- *border-top-color* (color of the top border);

- *border-right-color* (color of the right border);

- *border-bottom-color* (color of the bottom border);

- *border-left-color* (color of the left border).

EXAMPLE.–

```
p{ border-style: dashed;
Border-width: 10px;
border-bottom-color: rgb(121,145,212);
text-align: justify;
}
```

3.4.2.2. *Border thickness*

With the *border-width* property, it is possible to specify the thickness of the four borders simultaneously.

SYNTAX.– *Border-width*:

– a value of length /* such as 5 px */;

– thin /* value to indicate a thin border */;

– medium /* value to indicate a medium border */;

– thick /* value to indicate a thick border */.

NOTE.–

– The thickness is only displayed if the border type (*border-style*) has been defined.

– The thickness of each side can also be defined separately with the following properties:

- *border-right-width*;

- *border-top-width*;

- *border-left-width*;

- *border-bottom-width*.

– It is possible to surpass the long notation of the properties *border-bottom-width*, *border-top-width*, *border-left-width* and *border-right-width* by specifying 1, 2, 3 or 4 thicknesses for the *border-width* property.

– Where only one thickness is indicated, it will apply to all four sides.

– Where two thicknesses are indicated, the first will apply to the top side and the second will apply to the lateral sides (*left and right*).

– Where three thicknesses are indicated, the first will apply to the top side, the second will apply to the lateral sides and the third will apply to the bottom side.

– Where four thicknesses are indicated, they will be assigned in a clockwise direction.

– This same writing difficulty applies with *border-color*.

EXAMPLE.–

```
p {  border-style: dashed;
border-width: 5px;
border-top-color: rgb(221,211,125);
border-width: thick thin;
}
```

3.4.2.3. *Border style*

With CSS3, using the *border-style* property, it is possible to designate the style of the borders of an element on the web page.

SYNTAX.– *Border-style*:

– solid;

– dotted;

– dashed;

– double;

– ridge;

– groove;

– outset;

– inset;

– hidden /* without any border */;

– none /* identical to border-width: 0 px*/.

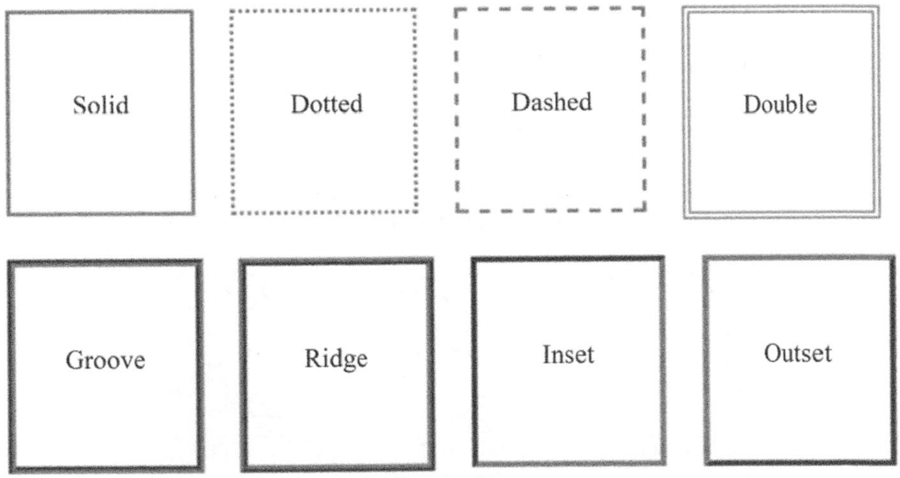

Solid	Dotted	Dashed	Double
Groove	Ridge	Inset	Outset

Figure 3.3. *The different border types. For a color version of this figure, see www.iste.co.uk/benrebah/website.zip*

NOTE.–

– The border style can only be displayed when the width of the border (*border-width*) has already been defined.

– The style can also be defined separately on either side with the following properties:

- *border-bottom-style*;

- *border-top-style*;

- *border-left-style*;

- *border-right-style*.

– It is possible to surpass the long notation of the properties *border-bottom-style*, *border-top-style*, *border-left-style* and *border-right-style*, by specifying 1, 2, 3 or 4 style types for the *border-style* property (this is the same principle used for *border-width* and *border-color*).

3.4.2.4. *Rounded border*

With CSS3, using the *border-radius* property, it is possible to easily round the corners of any element on a web page. To do so, the size of the rounding (*its importance*) needs to be indicated in pixels.

SYNTAX.– *Border-radius*.

x y; /* *x* and *y* are in px or as a percentage */.

The horizontal and vertical radii of the quarter ellipse are determined by the *x* and *y* values, which will cause the angle to bend. Examples are given in Figure 3.4.

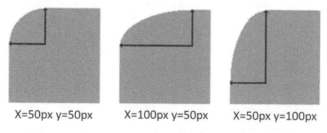

X=50px y=50px   X=100px y=50px   X=50px y=100px

Figure 3.4. *Example of using* border-radius*: round radius*

NOTE.–

– A single value can be given to *border-radius* (*border-radius*: 20 px). Here, the value of x is the same as the value of y.

– It is possible to specify an angle for any end separately, as usual in CSS, using the following properties:

- *border-top-left-radius*;

- *border-bottom-right-radius*;

- *border-top-right-radius*;

- *border-bottom-left-radius*.

EXAMPLE.–

```
#rounded {
width: 185px; height: 75px;
Background-color: rgb (205, 185, 215);
border: 2px solid black;
border-radius: 1.2em;
}
```

Figure 3.5 shows the result obtained.

Figure 3.5. *Complete example using* border-radius

3.4.2.5. *Image border*

With CSS3, using the *border-image* property, it is possible to indicate the style of the borders of any element on the web page. To do this we take a rectangular-shaped image, which will be divided into nine sections (see Figure 3.6). The eight border sections are therefore used for the sides and angles. The center will be hidden in order to allow the content to be displayed.

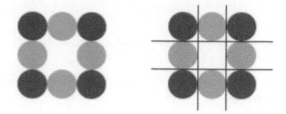

Figure 3.6. *Image decomposition process using the* border-image *property. For a color version of this figure, see www.iste.co.uk/benrebah/website.zip*

SYNTAX.– *Border-image.*

url(image location*) a b c d* value1 value2; where:

– url(image location) indicates the relative address of the image file that will be used to produce the outlines;

– *a*, *b*, *c* and *d* indicate the measurement of a section of the grid on the sides of the outline;

– values such as: repeat, stretch or round.

EXAMPLE.–

```
Border-image: url(border.jpg) 15 15 15 15 stretch stretch;
```

NOTE.–

– It is possible to indicate a single parameter. Here, this parameter applies to all four sides. If two parameters are used, they designate the dimension of the top/bottom and right/left sides. If three parameters are cited, it is the top, right/left and bottom side, in that order. Finally, if four parameters are cited, it is the top, right, bottom and left, respectively.

– The term *round* reproduces the images and changes their dimensions so that they precisely fit the height and width of the element.

– The term *repeat* (not functional for some browsers) performs the same action as *round*, only without adjustment.

– The term *stretch* (the default value) stretches the image to the element's measurements.

3.4.2.6. *Shadows*

With CSS3, using shadowing properties, it is now possible to add a shadow effect for text or for all elements on an HTML page.

3.4.2.6.1. Shadows on text

SYNTAX.– *Text-shadow.*

> *x y z* color; where:
>
> – *x* is the distance from the beginning of the shadow to the right;
>
> – *y* is the distance from the beginning of the shadow downward;
>
> – *z* is the gradient or blur enhancement (optional, default = 0);
>
> – color is that of the shadow.

EXAMPLE.–

```
.shadows {text-shadow: 3px 3px 5px #bbb;}
```

3.4.2.6.2. Shadows on box elements

SYNTAX.– *Box-shadow.*

> *x y z* color; where:
>
> – *x* is the distance from the beginning of the shadow to the right;
>
> – *y* is the distance from the beginning of the shadow downward;
>
> – *z* is the gradient or blur enhancement (optional, default = 0);
>
> – color is that of the shadow.

EXAMPLE.–

```
div{box-shadow: 5px 5px 0px #000 ; }
```

Figure 3.7 presents the result obtained.

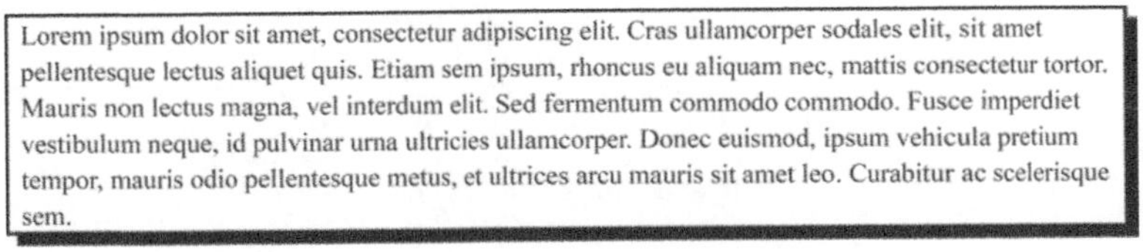

> Lorem ipsum dolor sit amet, consectetur adipiscing elit. Cras ullamcorper sodales elit, sit amet pellentesque lectus aliquet quis. Etiam sem ipsum, rhoncus eu aliquam nec, mattis consectetur tortor. Mauris non lectus magna, vel interdum elit. Sed fermentum commodo commodo. Fusce imperdiet vestibulum neque, id pulvinar urna ultricies ullamcorper. Donec euismod, ipsum vehicula pretium tempor, mauris odio pellentesque metus, et ultrices arcu mauris sit amet leo. Curabitur ac scelerisque sem.

Figure 3.7. *Example of using* box-shadow *on a div block*

3.5. Table formatting

3.5.1. *Space between cells*

The style property to specify the spacing between each cell in a table is *border-spacing*. This is the equivalent of the HTML 4.0 *cellspacing* attribute.

SYNTAX.– *Border-spacing*:

– a numerical value expressed in px;

– a numeric value expressed in pt;

– a percentage.

EXAMPLE.–

```
table {
      width: 185px;
      text-align: center;
      border: 2px solid #bbb;
      border-spacing: 15px;
      }
td {
      border: 2px solid #bbb;
      background-color: rgb(185,225,215);
}
```

Figure 3.8 presents the result obtained.

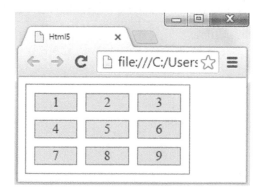

Figure 3.8. *Effect of the* border-spacing *style*

NOTE.–

– If the *border-spacing* property is missing, the table is thus displayed by default:

1	2	3
4	5	6
7	8	9

– It is possible to have a single table border if *border-spacing*: 0 px:

1	2	3
4	5	6
7	8	9

3.5.2. *Borders*

By default, the browser displays two borders in tables as in Figure 3.8: here, the outline and the borders that enclose the cells.

This case can be managed with the CSS *border-collapse* property.

SYNTAX.– *Border-collapse*:

– collapse /* with this value adjacent borders can be merged, giving the appearance of a single border */;

– separate /* with this value it is possible to present separate borders, which is the default case */.

EXAMPLE.–

```
table {
        width: 185px;
        text-align: center;
        border: 2px solid #bbb;
        border-collapse: collapse;
}
td {
        border: 2px solid #bbb;
}
```

Figure 3.9 presents the result obtained.

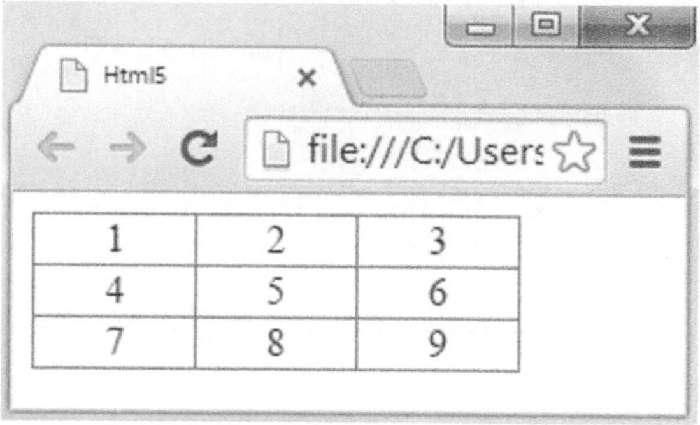

Figure 3.9. *Effect of the*
border-collapse *style*

3.5.3. *Empty cells*

With the *empty-cells* property, it is possible to guide the browser's behavior when it finds empty cells in tables.

SYNTAX.– *Empty-cells*:

– show /* this value is used to show the empty cell. This displays the borders and background */;

– hide /* this value is used to hide the empty cell. This hides the borders and background */.

EXAMPLE.–

```
table {
      width: 185px;
      text-align: center;
}
td {
      border: 2px solid #bbb;
      background-color: rgb(195,225,235);
}
.show{empty-cells:show;}
.hide {empty-cells:hide;}
```

Figure 3.10 displays the result obtained.

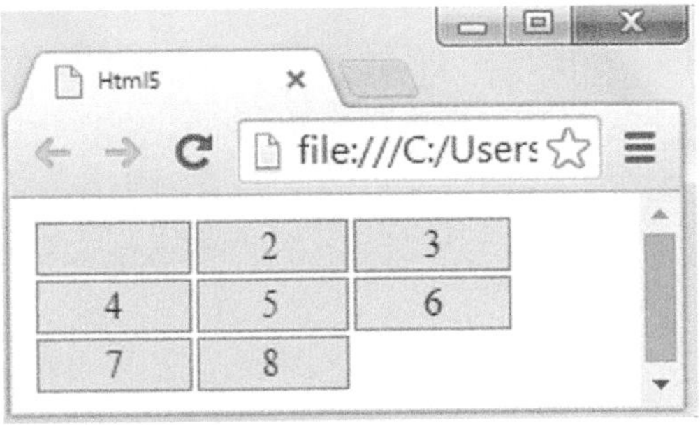

Figure 3.10. *Effect of the* empty-cells *style*

3.5.4. *Caption position*

With CSS3, and the *caption-side* property, the position of the legend of a table can be designated.

SYNTAX.– *Caption-side*:

– top /* this value is used to position the caption before the table (this is the default case) */;

– bottom /* this value is used to position the caption after the table */.

EXAMPLE.–

```
table {
      width: 185px;
      text-align: center;
      border: 2px solid #bbb;
      border-collapse: collapse;
}
td {
      border: 2px solid #bbb;
}
caption{
      Caption-side: bottom;
}
```

Figure 3.11 displays the result obtained.

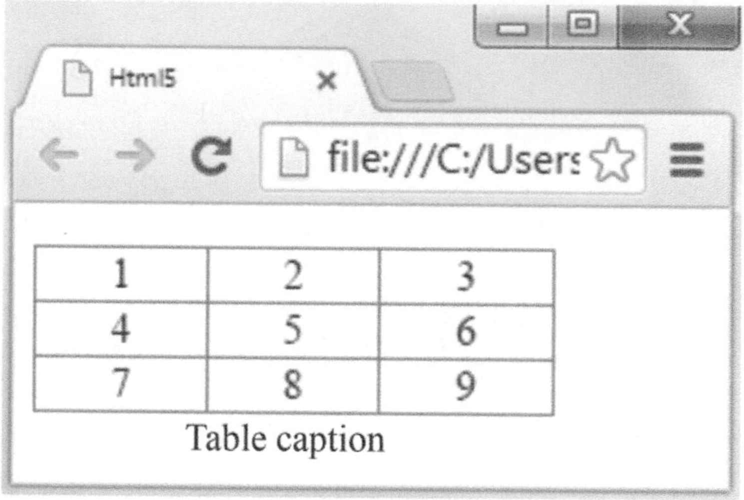

Figure 3.11. *Effect of the caption-side style*

3.6. Layout of the site

3.6.1. *Concept of the box model*

In CSS, the box element is an important concept. This element is also referred to as a container or block.

A box element is defined by the W3C as a rectangular area composed of:

– border (*border*);

– outer margin (*margin*);

– content;

– inner margin (*padding*).

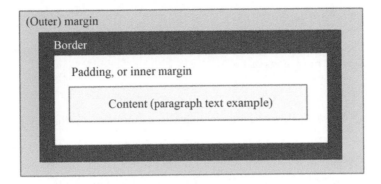

Figure 3.12. *Box model. For a color version of this figure, see www.iste.co.uk/benrebah/website.zip*

NOTE.–

– CSS makes it possible to adjust separately:

- four outer margins in all directions;

- four borders (fix: dimension, style and color);

- four inner margins in all directions;

- measurements: width and height of the content.

– The overall dimension of the box element, which can be calculated as follows: content measurement (*height* + *width*) + borders + outer margins + inner margins.

EXAMPLE.–

```
p {  width: 185px;
border: 15px solid rgb(110,150,210);
padding: 15px;
margin: 15px;
background-color: rgb(205,225,235);
}
```

Box concept in CSS

3.6.2. *Block or inline element*

With CSS, the very powerful *display* property is able to change an inline element to a block element or vice versa.

SYNTAX.– *Display*:

– inline /* an inline element, placing one next to another, horizontally */;

– block /* block element, placing one below the other, vertically, with it being possible to resize them */;

– inline-block /* elements placed next to each other (horizontally), yet they can be resized like blocks */;

– none /* elements not visible */.

NOTE.– In HTML language, there are two types of tags:

– *block* tag: this involuntarily creates a line break in front and behind (like the <p></p> tag);

– *inline* tag: this will always be nested in a *block* tag. This tag does not create a line break (like <header>, <nav>, <a>, etc.).

EXAMPLE.– Apply the *display: inline* property for a list (which represents a *block* tag).

```
<!DOCTYPE html>
<html>
<head>
<title>Block tag</title>
        <meta charset="UTF-8"/>
        <style type="text/css">
                ul { padding: 5px;
                list-style: none;}
                li { border: 2px solid #bbb;
                display: inline;
                background-color: rgb(220,224,235);
                margin-right: 5px;
                text-align: center;
                padding-left: 10px; padding-right: 10px;}
        </style>
        </head>
<body>
```

```
        <ul>
                <li> Link 1</li>
                <li> Link 2</li>
                <li> Link 3</li>
                <li> Link 4</li>
        </ul>
</body>
</html>
```

Figure 3.13 displays the result obtained.

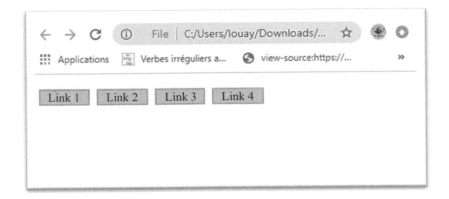

Figure 3.13. *Example of how to use the* display *property. For a color version of this figure, see www.iste.co.uk/benrebah/website.zip*

3.6.3. *Width and height of a box element*

With the *width* and *height* style properties, it is possible to set the width and height of a block (box) element, in that order.

SYNTAX.–

Width:

– auto;

– or a width value such as 20 px;

– or percentage.

Height:

– auto;

– or a height value such as 20 px;

– or percentage.

NOTE.–

– The width and height of the content are specified by the *width* and *height* values (no borders, no outer margins and no inner margins).

– The content dimension is automatically adjusted by the auto value.

– A fixed value is specified by the length value.

– A relative value is specified by the percentage.

– With CSS2, the maximum and minimum size of a box-type element can be determined by the following properties:

- *min-height*: sets the minimum height;

- *max-height*: sets the maximum height;

- *min-width*: sets the minimum width;

- *max-width*: sets the maximum width.

EXAMPLE.–

```
<!DOCTYPE html>
<html>
<head>
<title>HTML5 example</title>
<meta charset="utf-8"/>
</head>
<body>
<p>width</p>
<div style= "border: 2px solid #000; width: 250px;">
xxxxxxxxxxxxxxxxxxxxxxxxx
</div>
<p>min-width</p>
<div style="border: 1px solid #000; min-width: 245px;">
xxxxxxxxxxxxxxxxxxxxxxxxxxxxx
</div>
<p>max-width</p>
```

```
<div style="border: 1px solid #000; width: 250px; max-width: 150px;">
xxxxxxxxxxxxxxxxxxxxxxxxx
</div>
</body>
</html>
```

```
┌──────────────────────────────────────────────────────────────┐
│ width                                                          │
│  ┌──────────────────────────────────────────┐                 │
│  │ xxx xxx xxx xxx xxx xxx xxx xxx           │                 │
│  └──────────────────────────────────────────┘                 │
│ min-width                                                      │
│  ┌───────────────────────────────────────────────────────────┐│
│  │ xxx xxx xxx xxx xxx xxx xxx xxx                            ││
│  └───────────────────────────────────────────────────────────┘│
│ max-width                                                      │
│  ┌────────────────────────────────┐                           │
│  │ xxx xxx xxx xxx xxx xxx         │                           │
│  │ xxx xxx                         │                           │
│  └────────────────────────────────┘                           │
└──────────────────────────────────────────────────────────────┘
```

3.6.4. *Outer margins*

With the *margin* property, it is possible to define the *outer margin* of the block-type element.

SYNTAX.– *Margin*:

– auto /* leaves it to the browser to display outer margins */;

– or length value /* a value that precisely defines the outer margins */;

– or percentage /* a percentage that defines the length with respect to a parent element */.

NOTE.–

– The outer margin of each side of the box element can also be defined separately with the properties: *margin-right* (right border), *margin-top* (top border), *margin-left* (left border) and *margin-bottom* (bottom border).

– The outer margin properties (*margin-right, margin-top, margin-left* and *margin-bottom*) can be shortened in writing, by indicating 2, 3 or 4 values for the *margin* property:

- with two margins: the first is applied to the top and bottom sides and the second to the lateral sides (right and left);

- with three margins: the first is applied to the top side, the second to the lateral sides and the last to the bottom side;

- with four margins: the four values are assigned clockwise (top, right, bottom and left).

EXAMPLE.–

```
<!DOCTYPE html>
<html>
<head>
<Title>outer margins</title>
<meta charset="UTF-8"/>
<style type="text/css">
    body {margin: 5px;
    }
    .box {border: 2px solid #000;
    margin: 15px 15px 15px 15px;
    text-align: center;
    }
</style>
</head>
<body>
<div class="box">
    outer margin
</div>
</body>
</html>
```

Figure 3.14 displays the result obtained.

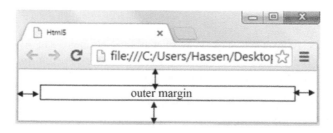

Figure 3.14. *Example of using the CSS* margin *property*

3.6.5. *Inner margins*

With the *padding* property, the inner margin of the block-type element (box) can be designated.

SYNTAX.– *Padding*:

– auto /* the browser is responsible for displaying the inner margins */;

– or a length value /* to exactly define the inner margins */;

– or a percentage /* to define the length relative to a parent element */.

NOTE.–

– The inner margin on each side of the element can be defined individually with the properties: *padding-right, padding-top, padding-left* and *padding-bottom*.

– It is possible to shorten the declaration of inner margin properties (*padding-right, padding-top, padding-left* and *padding-bottom*) by specifying 2, 3 or 4 values for the padding property:

- with two margins: the first is applied to the top and bottom sides and the second to the lateral sides (right and left);

- with three margins: the first is applied to the top side, the second to the lateral sides and the last to the bottom side;

- with four margins: the four values are assigned clockwise (top, right, bottom and left).

EXAMPLE.–

```
<!DOCTYPE html>
<html>
<head>
<title>HTML5 example</title>
<meta charset="UTF-8"/>
<style type="text/css">
.margeleft {width: 250px;
padding-left: 40px;
border:solid 2px #bbb;
}
</style>
</head>
<body>
```

```
        <div class=" margeleft">
        Lorem ipsum dolorsitamet, consectetueradipiscingelit. Sed non
        risus. Suspendisse lectustortor, dignissimsitamet, adipiscing
        nec, ultriciessed, dolor. Cras elementumultrices diam.
</div>
</body>
</html>
```

Figure 3.15 displays the result obtained.

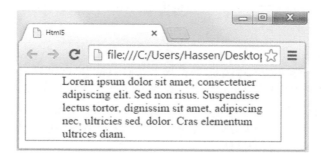

Figure 3.15. *Effect of the CSS* padding-left *property*

NOTE.– Center alignment of blocks.

To center a block in an HTML page using margins, the following rule needs to be applied:

– assign a width to the box (using the *width* property);

– signal that the outer margins will be automatic (*margin:auto;*).

EXAMPLE.–

```
P {
width: 400px; /* A width ( required ) has been designated */
margin: auto; /* It is thus possible to request the centering of the
block with auto */
border: 2px solid #000;
text-align: left;
padding: 15px;
margin-bottom: 25px;
}
```

3.6.6. *Element positioning*

An element can be positioned in four distinct ways.

3.6.6.1. *Static positioning*

As per standard browser behavior, this is the element's default positioning.

It is defined by:

SYNTAX.– *Position: static;*.

/* In this case, the designer is not able to control the visibility and position of the element */.

3.6.6.2. *Relative positioning*

This is the position of an element relative to its *static* position. This element will be *off-center* relative to its *normal* position.

The position is determined by the (x,y) coordinates with:

– x representing the relative distance to the left end of the parent element or the browser window (the horizontal axis). Therefore, *left* is the distance from the left of the page to the left of the element and *right* represents the distance from the right of the page to the right of the element.

– y representing the relative distance to the top end of the parent element or the browser window (the vertical axis). Therefore, *top* is the distance from the top edge of the page to the top edge of the element, and *bottom* represents the distance from the bottom edge of the page to the bottom edge of the element.

Thus, relative positioning is defined by:

SYNTAX.– *Position: relative;*:

  – right: value or %;

  – bottom: value or %;

  – left: value or %;

  – top: value or %.

EXAMPLE.–

```
< !DOCTYPE HTML>
<html>
<head>
<title>HTML5 example</title>
<meta charset="UTF-8"/>
<style type="text/css">
      .posrelative {position: relative;
      top: 75px;
      left: 125px;
      width: 200px;
      border: 1px solid #bbb;
      text-align: center;
      }
</style>
</head>
<body>
<div class="posrelative">
      The relative position
</div>
</body>
</html>
```

Figure 3.16 shows the result obtained.

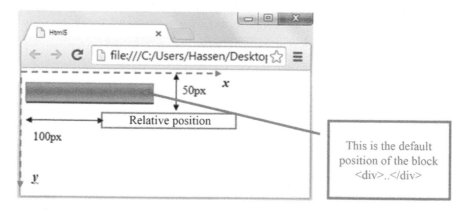

Figure 3.16. *Example of relative positioning. For a color version of this figure, see www.iste.co.uk/benrebah/website.zip*

3.6.6.3. *Absolute positioning*

Independent of the rest of the web page, absolute positioning creates an element. The elements put in absolute position are moved away from the regular flow and are placed at the exact location determined by the designer.

The position is determined by the (x,y) coordinates with:

$- x$ representing the relative distance to the left end of the parent element or the browser window (the horizontal axis). Therefore, *left* is the distance from the left of the page to the left of the element and *right* represents the distance from the right of the page to the right of the element;

$- y$ representing the relative distance to the top end of the parent element or the browser window (the vertical axis). Therefore, *top* is the distance from the top edge of the page to the top edge of the element, and *bottom* represents the distance from the bottom edge of the page to the bottom edge of the element.

Thus, absolute positioning is defined by:

SYNTAX.– *Position: absolute;*:

   – right: valuc or %;

   – bottom: value or %;

   – left: value or %;

   – top: value or %.

EXAMPLE.–

```
<!DOCTYPE HTML>
<html>
<head>
<title>HTML5 example</title>
<meta charset="UTF-8"/>
<style type="text/css">
       .division1{
               width:220;
               border:1px solid #bbb;
               background-color:#f00;
       }
       .division3{position:relative;
               top:50px;
               width:190px;
```

```
                    border:1px solid #bbb;
                    background-color: #0f0;
           }
        .division2 {position:absolute;
                left:180px;
                top: 75px;
                width: 210px;
                border: 1px solid #bbb;
                background-color:#00f;
           }
</style>
<div class="division1">
      block 1 block 1 block 1
</div>
<div class="division2">
      block2 block 2 block 2
</div>
<div class="division3">
      block3 block 3 block 3
</div>
</body>
</html>
```

Figure 3.17 displays the result obtained.

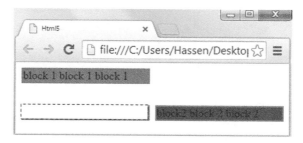

Figure 3.17. *Absolute positioning. For a color version of this figure, see www.iste.co.uk/benrebah/website.zip*

3.6.6.4. *Fixed positioning*

The position of an element can be defined independently, using *fixed* positioning. In our case, the element remains stationary even when the web page scrolls.

Thus, fixed positioning is defined by:

SYNTAX.– *Position: fixed;*:

  – right: value or %;

  – bottom: value or %;

  – left: value or %;

  – top: value or %.

EXAMPLE.–

```
<!DOCTYPE HTML>
<html>
<head>
<title>HTML5 example</title>
<meta charset="UTF-8"/>
      <style type="text/css">
             .fixedPosition {position:fixed;
             top: 45%.
             left: 45;
             width: 180px;
             border: 1px solid #000;
             text-align: center;
             }
      </style>
</head>
<body>
      <div class="fixedPosition"> The fixed position
      </div>
      <div>
             Paragraph1 <br/>
             Paragraph2 <br/>
             Paragraph3 <br/>
             Paragraph4 <br/>
             Paragraph5 <br/>
      </div>
</body>
</html>
```

Figure 3.18 displays the result obtained.

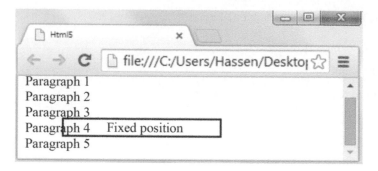

Figure 3.18. *Fixed positioning*

3.6.7. *Element floating*

With the *float* property, a block-type element can be removed from the normal flow of the page and placed *as far left* or *as far right* as possible within its *parent element*, or more precisely, its *container*.

SYNTAX.– *Float*:

– right;

– or left;

– or none.

NOTE.–

– Right: in order to align the requested element to the right, so the *right* value will push the separate elements to align right.

– Left: in order to align the requested element to the left, so the *left* value will push the separate elements to align left.

– Whereas the *none* value does nothing and leaves control to the browser.

Float cannot be applied in the case of an absolute position.

EXAMPLE.–

```
<!DOCTYPE HTML>
<html>
<head>
<title>HTML5 example</title>
<meta charset="UTF-8"/>
```

```
<style type="text/CSS">
      img{float: right;}
</style>
</head>
<body>
<div>
      <img width="150" height="150"/>
      <p>Yuri Alekseyevich Gagarin, born March 9, 1934 and died March
27, 1968, was the first person to fly into space during the Vostok 1
mission on April 12, 1961, as part of the Soviet space program.</p>
</div>
</body>
</html>
```

Figure 3.19 displays the result obtained.

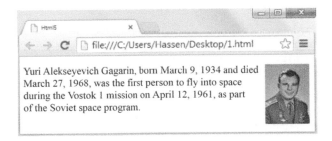

Figure 3.19. *Example of floating. For a color version of this figure, see www.iste.co.uk/benrebah/website.zip*

3.6.8. *Element stacking*

With the *z-index* property, it is possible to add a depth axis to position elements on or under another element.

SYNTAX.– *Z-index*.

Positive integer.

NOTE.–

– Absolute positioning is needed for this property to work.

– If an element has the property *z-index: 4;* it will appear before or on the element with the property *z-index: 1;*.

EXAMPLE.—

```
<!DOCTYPE html>
<html>
<head>
<title>HTML5 example</title>
<meta charset="UTF-8"/>
<style type="text/css">
      .bloc1 {
              position: absolute;
              left: 35px; top: 35px;
              width: 120px; height: 50px;
              padding: 5px;
              border: 1px solid #bbb;
              background-color: rgb(135,155,215);
              z-index: 1;
      }
      . bloc2 {
              position: absolute;
              left: 45px; top: 55px;
              width: 120px; height: 50px;
              padding: 5px;
              border: 1px solid #bbb;
              background-color: rgb(220,240,250);
              z-index: 2;
      }
</style>
</head>
<body>
<div class=" bloc1">
      z-index 1
</div>
<div class=" bloc2">
      z-index 2
</div>
</body>
</html>
```

Figure 3.20 displays the result obtained.

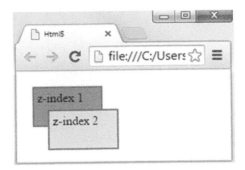

Figure 3.20. *The* z-index *property*

4

Design and Creation of a Website

An Internet site, or website, remains first and foremost an information medium or a showcase. It is a good means of identification and communication. As a result, it can be beneficial for web designers to study in detail how this kind of application is implemented and not to approach it like a conventional project, since it involves providing various users with different tastes and preferences, access to a mass of structured and coherent information. This condition requires particular interest to be placed in this medium, with regard to both content and presentation.

4.1. Process of creating a website

The process of creating a website is not only limited to the technical phase (*development of web pages*). It also needs to be planned using a structured and creative approach: the definition of a certain number of steps, ideas and solutions to problems.

The steps for creating a website can be summarized as follows:

– development;

– hosting;

– referencing;

– updating.

4.1.1. *Development*

The development phase essentially covers the following steps.

_____

For a color version of all the figures in this chapter, see: www.iste.co.uk/benrebah/website.zip.

4.1.1.1. *Preliminary study*

A website generally needs to satisfy a need and not simply a desire, to the point that in this phase the designer is required to set the list of objectives, select the orientations and estimate the feasibility of the site.

The preliminary study leads to a global reflection about the website realized: it focuses first on the objectives of the site (*company site, sources of information, portal, online commerce*, etc.) and the target audience (*group of friends, clients*, etc.). Second, on the logistical means offered (*development tools, performance and duration of connections*, etc.) and the implementation budget.

It is during this step that the idea of creating the website will be taken up or canceled.

4.1.1.2. *Specifications*

The specifications document presents a set of information regarding the characteristics of the website to be created (theme of the site, objectives, the supervisor, the creator(s), the hardware and software requirements, the time frame for design and implementation, the requirements regarding work quality and quantity, the form of the end product and the evaluation rules).

The specifications will play the role of a reference document for the steps that follow the website development phase.

4.1.1.3. *Design of the structure of the site and content of web pages (preparation of a storyboard)*

As soon as the specifications have been put in place, it is worth specifying the structure of the site, i.e. how to organize the information to be presented. An overview of the possible techniques for moving around within the website structure also needs to be specified. Therefore, for each link, it is important to define all the possible effects that could be perceived by the user as well as the direction of navigation (*back, forward*) and the type to be put in place (*menu, standard button, image*, etc.).

In this phase, it is possible to simply use paper and a pencil to draw frames to represent the web pages of the site and arrows to designate the links while defining the content of each of these pages (*information, buttons, links* and *images*). Throughout this exercise, the designer must keep in mind the purpose of the site and the target audience.

Several templates exist for organizing the pages of a website.

Figure 4.1. *Example of a storyboard. "Accueil" is French for "home page"*

4.1.1.3.1. Linear architecture or sequential architecture

This is the term used for a site formed by a set of pages structured sequentially, i.e. the first page (home page) refers to the second, and the second refers to the third and so on. This structure is essentially a characteristic of older websites. It is not very interactive and favors narrativity and browsing.

Application types: learning sites or tutorials, slide show, comic strip.

Figure 4.2. *Linear architecture*

4.1.1.3.2. Hierarchical architecture

This is the term for a site that generally consists of a home page leading the user to other pages. Each of these pages will direct the user to a set of pages formed by links that refer to that page. Sequential architecture represents a special case of hierarchical architecture.

This way of organizing information into independent, hierarchical blocks requires fairly substantial work in terms of prior analysis of the site content, as this kind of architecture will only be effective if the available information is carefully organized.

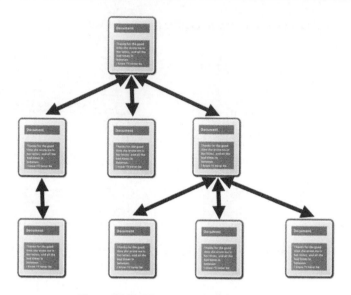

Figure 4.3. *Hierarchical architecture*

4.1.1.3.3. Composite architecture (non-hierarchical)

This is the structure most commonly used for current websites. The user can reach the different levels of the site starting from the home page, and vice versa.

Type of application: the permanent menu bar.

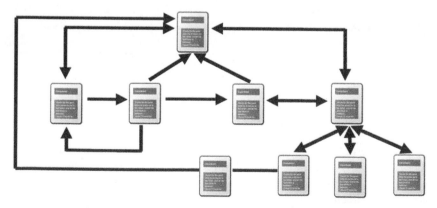

Figure 4.4. *Composite architecture*

NOTE.– Drawing a structure for your website and preparing the storyboard saves time during the development phase.

4.1.1.4. *Technical development*

This step consists of:

– data collection: this involves preparing the objects necessary for integration into the site (*text*, *images*, *sounds* and *videos*). This operation consists of collecting these objects from various sources or creating them using the appropriate hardware and software tools. Of course, it can be beneficial to organize these objects in different directories in order to facilitate the following step:

– integration: this involves collecting the objects prepared during the collection phase, whilst adhering to the storyboard of the site already planned. This step also covers the web page development, testing and remediation phases. Therefore, it is important to have a local browser to test the display of all components of the site.

Figure 4.5. *Example of implementing a storyboard*

4.1.2. *Hosting*

4.1.2.1. *Definition*

This step consists of making an Internet site accessible from the Web. It therefore involves copying all the files from the site to the disk of a server (powerful computer) that is, in general, permanently connected to the Internet network.

To implement this process, first of all it is necessary to obtain a domain name. This is an internationally unique site identifier. It is the name that the user will enter into the browser address bar.

EXAMPLE.–

– http://hassen.over-blog.com/: for the personal blog of Hassen Ben Rebah.

– http://www.mes.tn: for the website of the Ministry of Higher Education of Tunisia.

After the domain name is reserved, the site must be stored on the hosting server disk and then the home page will be associated with the domain name already chosen: the home page files are named index.htm, index.html, default.htm or default.html. These files must be named in this way so that the server knows which file to automatically direct individuals wishing to access a website address (URL).

EXAMPLE.–

If the user types the following address: http://www.mes.tn, the server will automatically direct the user to the home page as follows: http://mes.tn/index.html.

1. Creation of the website on your local disk
2. Site publication
3. Once published, the site is available online

Figure 4.6. *Website hosting process*

4.1.2.2. *Hosting types*

On the Web, various hosting formulas exist. Below are some examples:

– Multi-tenant hosting: this is one of the cheapest hosting formulas, consisting of sharing a server's storage space between several websites, hence the name "multi-tenant hosting". Choosing this option means that the hosting service is responsible for ensuring and verifying the smooth operation of the site at all times. For this type of choice, the customer is invited only to register with the Web hosting service, who will handle all ensuing tasks.

– Dedicated web hosting: this is a type of hosting that consists of reserving an entire web server for exclusive use. It offers customers who have chosen this option the ability to exploit all available server resources and host multiple sites at the same time.

– Free web hosting (category 1): the web hosting provider offers you a free space to host your website by inserting advertising into your site or simply by minimizing the services to encourage you to opt for a premium option at a later date.

– Free web hosting (category 2): this is a type of hosting that offers users the opportunity to enjoy a free hosting space in order to put their websites online, provided that they distribute some advertising articles at the site level. For this type of hosting, the services offered to clients are very limited.

There are several ways to host a website:

– making direct contact with the host in order to offer the website to them on a storage medium;

– sending the site to a storage medium via the workstation to the host, which will take care of the hosting task;

– emailing the site to the host;

– using file transfer software to copy website files from a local computer to a remote hosting server. This is the most widely used technique.

4.1.3. *Referencing*

Referencing is the set of methods and techniques that aim to ensure a website's recognition on the Internet, i.e. to improve its visibility to search engines so that the pages of the site are displayed in the first results found by the search engine. This step essentially includes:

– Indexing (submission): this involves ensuring the site is recognized by search engines by using the forms that they propose.

EXAMPLE.–

– Sitemap creation at the Google search engine level: https://search.google.com/search-console/welcome;

– or by making use of the services offered by utilities such as dedicated software or a "multi-referencing" site. The operation in this direction simply consists of completing a form whose data will be sent to search engines and directories for use.

A form from a free referencing site is shown in Figure 4.7.

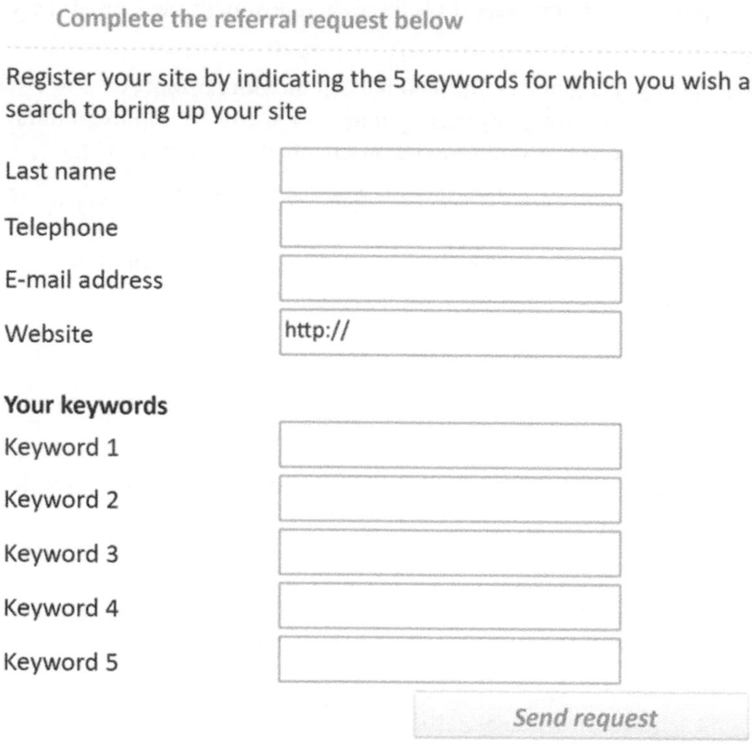

Complete the referral request below

Register your site by indicating the 5 keywords for which you wish a Google search to bring up your site

Last name

Telephone

E-mail address

Website   http://

Your keywords

Keyword 1

Keyword 2

Keyword 3

Keyword 4

Keyword 5

Send request

Figure 4.7. *Form from a free referencing site*[1]

– Positioning: this consists of optimizing the web pages of a site using certain keywords, with the aim of improving the site's position among the results found by the search engine (*appearing on the first page of search-engine results*).

EXAMPLE.– Using the *meta* and *title* HTML tags to optimize the referencing of a site.

```
<title>personal site of Hassen Ben Rebah</title>
<metaname="Content-Type" content="UTF-8"/>
<metaname="Content-Language" content="en"/>
<metaname="Description" content="this is a personal site that
contains my information technology lesson material, tutorials and
practical work, my CV and my projects."/>
```

---

1 http://www.referencementseogratuit.com/offre-referencement-gratuite.php.

```
<metaname="Keywords" content="Hassen Ben Rebah IT technologist
lessons CSS HTML XML Algorithmics ISET"/>
<metaname="Subject" content="personal site"/>
```

– Ranking: this is among the most significant natural referencing metrics; its purpose is generally comparable to positioning, but concerns more elaborate expressions.

4.1.4. *Updating*

In order for a website to remain accessible and continue to be appreciated by its target audience, it is beneficial to update its content periodically. This step is similar to hosting and generally consists of replacing the previous version of the site with a new version. This operation can affect only a few pages.

4.1.5. *Evaluation*

In order to evaluate a website, it is possible to use the conventional rules for reviewing and evaluating a document. In general, these rules relate essentially to the context, i.e. the quality of the information and its presentation.

These evaluation criteria commonly exist in the form of several grids, each covering a clearly defined aspect of the site, namely: navigation architecture, ergonomics, information distribution and interactivity.

4.2. Ergonomics of the website

4.2.1. *Concept of ergonomics*

Ergonomics is the study of the activities of human beings and the relationships they maintain with their work environment. This already identified knowledge will be used in the design and improvement of these systems. Ergonomics is generally characterized by two components:

– efficiency is used to adopt adequate solutions for the use of a product, beyond the common sense of the designer;

– usability is used to identify the degree to which a solution matches the user's capabilities. It is composed essentially of:

- user-friendliness, which consists of reducing nervous and physical fatigue,

- security, which consists of defining the most appropriate solutions to provide better protection for users.

The application of the concept of ergonomics in the field of website design consists of giving users access to an application that effectively meets their expectations in terms of security and browsing comfort.

The main difficulty that web designers may encounter is the variety in the profiles of site visitors. The following criteria are to be taken into consideration when defining the ergonomics of a website:

– user expectations: not all Internet users necessarily seek the same type of information and they do not have the same taste in terms of graphic design;

– user habits: refer to behaviors generally acquired by users;

– age of the user: corresponds to the adaptability of the user and their browsing speed;

– equipment: corresponds to the way in which the site is displayed, which may vary from one piece of equipment to another. The website ergonomics must take into account the equipment used by visitors;

– level of knowledge: not all users have the same IT skills. The website ergonomics must take into account the least experienced users.

4.2.2. *Ergonomics criterion*

The main ergonomics criteria are shown in Table 4.1.

Criterion	Sub-criterion	Description
Soberness	Simplicity	A very neat website will enhance the appearance of its owner organization.
	Streamlined	It is preferable not to use animated images. Animations are usually recommended in order to display important messages because they attract users' attention.
Readability	Clarity	It needs to be taken into account that text on the screen is less easy to read than on paper. As a result, the text needs to be sufficiently clear.
	Structure	The text should be organized through the use of paragraphs and titles of different levels in order to facilitate reading.
	Organization	Information elements should be organized in a hierarchical manner so that the most relevant elements are placed at the start of the page.
Usability	Ease of navigation	Typically, access to information should not exceed three clicks (three-click rule).

Criterion	Sub-criterion	Description
Usability (cont'd)	Position identification	At any time, the user must be able to identify their position within the site. As a result, the same graphic charter should be used on all pages to give the visitor the impression that they are still navigating the same site. The site map is a good way of allowing the visitor to know their location.
	Freedom to navigate	The site should provide the user with the possibility of consulting the home page as well as the main topics, regardless of their location. Wherever possible, the user will need to navigate between the pages of the site through transverse paths. Avoiding introductory and interstitial pages is necessary, as these can often be a source of annoyance for many users.
	Address visibility	The URL of the page in which the user is located must be sufficiently explicit and constantly visible so that the user can easily identify their position in order to be able to return to the previous page.
	Tangibility of information	It is necessary for the information presented on the site to be qualified, i.e. there should be clues to identify, for example, the web page's updated date or the site author. Similarly, it is disappointing for a user when a site has an attractive interface but they later find that other sections are still under construction.
	Homogeneity of the structure	Navigation elements should be presented on a uniform manner throughout the website and should also be positioned in the same location from one page to the next.
Rapidity	Loading time	The time it takes to display a web page should be as short as possible, as generally speaking the majority of users do not wish to wait more than 15 seconds. This time factor is, on the whole, dependent on page size, connection quality, image types used and server capacity.
	Optimized images	It is necessary to minimize the size of the images when creating a website (they should generally not exceed 40 KB). Please note that PNG (Portable Network Graphics) is the format most recommended for use on the Net, but generally it is also possible to use other formats according to your needs.
	Unresized images	For quality reasons, it is best to keep the images in their actual size, without modification.

Criterion	Sub-criterion	Description
Interactivity	Hyperlinks	Interactivity refers to all types of interactions between the Internet user and the website. Hyperlinks favor a variety of possibilities in this domain and allow users to take several different paths according to their wishes. It is necessary to define enough links between the pages of a site in order to facilitate navigation and reading.
	Breaking down of information	In order to facilitate the assimilation of information by users, and in some cases to arouse their curiosity, it is advisable to break information down. This breakdown can be translated in particular by hyperlinks to the different parts of the article.
	Facilitation of exchanges	It is preferable to put everything in place in order to make it easier to exchange with users, in particular to gather their opinions and requests, with the aim of improving the site. As a result, the user must have the means to easily contact the site administrator (an email address, a contact form, etc.).
Adaptability	Adaptability	Adaptability refers to the possibility of customizing the website with the intervention of the Internet user.
	Font repositioning	It is preferable to define site-level text fonts in absolute values, to give users the possibility of resizing them according to their preference.
Adaptivity	Adaptivity	Adaptivity means that the display of the website needs to adapt to different screen types, namely, a personal computer, tablet and smartphone.
Accessibility	Universality of access	Accessibility refers to the fact that the site needs to be accessed on a universal scale, that is, by anyone able to connect to the Internet. This objective can be achieved by applying a number of accessibility rules, independently of users' hardware or software configuration.
	Interoperability	When developing a website, it is advisable to respect accessibility rules such as those of the W3C (World Wide Wed Consortium), in order to ensure good interoperability, i.e. the site can be accessed by different browsers.
	Transparency of formats	It is preferable for the formats to be transparent, i.e. the user should be able to view them in text mode. It is also advisable for images or animations to be used as a complement only and not as a replacement for text information.

Criterion	Sub-criterion	Description
Accessibility (cont'd)	Caption	It is preferable to accompany images and illustrate them with a caption, which should appear in the event of an image display problem (using the *alt* attribute). The purpose of this action is to allow users with visual impairments to identify the meaning of the image.
	Choice of colors	It is advisable to closely examine the choice of colors to be used in order to prevent readability problems for users and especially for individuals who are color blind.
	Sound use of style sheets	Text content at site level needs to be accessible even without a style sheet.
	Adapted contrast	A good level of contrast is needed between the text and the background color of the page in order to avoid readability problems.
	Modifiable font size	It is preferable for the font size to be in adaptable mode so that the text can be enlarged if needed. Fonts that are too small are not recommended because they can cause legibility and fatigue issues when reading.

Table 4.1. *Main criteria for the ergonomics of a website*

4.2.3. *Graphic charter*

The graphic charter or "graphic specification" is a summary document that contains the set of fundamental rules describing the graphic elements of a website, thus constituting its visual identity.

The graphic charter refers to everything related to the framing and graphic design of the web page, namely, the size of the fonts, the location of the images and objects within the document, and the appearance of the text and buttons.

4.2.4. *Mockup*

A mockup is a summary prototype of a website showing the graphics of its different pages and its navigation. It is generally used to define and then validate the formal design of the site before starting the technical implementation phase. The mockup involves a static presentation of the main pages of the site, regardless of the content, and can also simulate some dynamic elements, such as search engines.

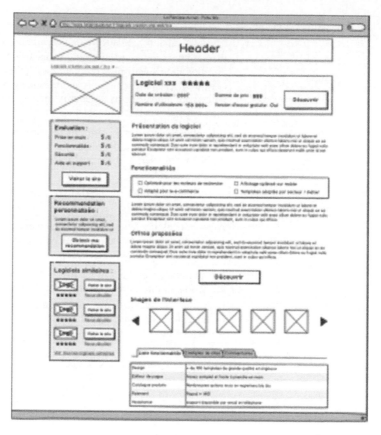

Figure 4.8. *Example of a mockup of a web page[2]*

4.2.5. *Dimensions of web pages*

A web page's dimensions generally depend on users' display definition. In the case of width, the best solution is to choose a value lower than the horizontal definition of most users, so as not to require them to scroll down the screen by using the horizontal scroll bar. A short page makes it easy for visitors to quickly browse its content in order to retrieve the information they are interested in. In terms of length, it is preferable to not exceed three to five screen heights. As a result, long pages risk being ignored or not being read in full. In order to guarantee a good display for all visitors, it is advisable to use the *adaptive design* principle, which automatically adjusts the display of a site to the screen size of the equipment used.

2 https://www.lafabriquedunet.fr/blog/logiciel-mockup-maquettage-site/.

4.3. Different website types

4.3.1. *Search engine/metasearch engine*

A search engine is a database formed of sites accessible via keyword search. The best-known free search engines are: Google, Ask.com and Yahoo.

A metasearch engine, or a search aggregator, is a software that retrieves its information from multiple search engines. More specifically, the metasearch engine sends its requests to a set of search engines, retrieves the results from each of them and then discards similar results. Finally, it plans a classification of these results.

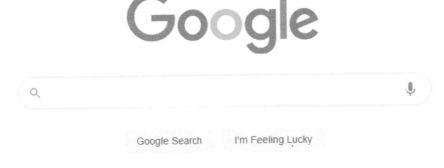

Figure 4.9. *Google search engine*

4.3.2. *Web directory*

A web directory, or Internet directory, is a website that offers a list of sites classified into categories and addressing the interests of users.

Each category comprises:

– sub-categories relating to more specific contexts of a given topic;

– hyperlinks to sites accompanied by a description.

There are three types of directories:

– general directories, which broadly cover the majority of interests;

– specialized directories, which refer to websites and web pages covering a certain number of topics;

– geographical directories, which can be both general and specialized. They generally correspond to a country, region or locality.

Figure 4.10. *French general directory*[3]

4.3.3. *Merchant site (e-commerce)*

This is a dynamic website through which a company presents its products and services 24 hours a day, 7 days a week. With this type of site, the user has the possibility of placing orders, and payment is generally made online by credit card, transfer or check.

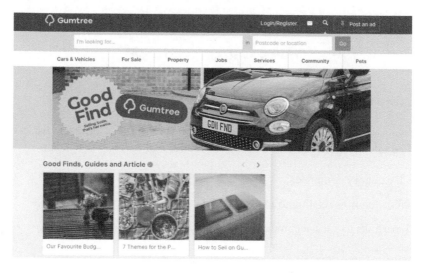

Figure 4.11. *E-commerce site*[4]

---

3 www.france-annuaire.net.
4 www.affariyet.com.

4.3.4. *Educational site (e-learning)*

An educational site is a site designed to present users with lessons, tutorials or training modules accessible from the Net. The use of this type of site in the field of education requires one to adopt new pedagogical approaches different from those used in the classroom.

Figure 4.12. *Educational site for children[5]*

4.3.5. *Advertising site*

This is a site that may present information relating to a company, product, promotion, etc. The webmaster of a site of this kind must attract the greatest number of people, through:

– implementation of high-quality content;

– application of updates on a regular basis;

– better referencing of the site with search engines;

5 www.brainpop.fr.

– definition within the site of a simple and easy-to-use navigation structure;

– taking into account visitor tastes and preferences.

The webmaster of an information site can take advantage of advertisements to earn money. The principle is to partner with sellers who can take advantage of the site in order to distribute advertising messages to their customers.

Practical Exercises

In this chapter, we present practical cases to explain theoretical concepts previously discussed in this book.

5.1. PE1: structure of an HTML5 web page

5.1.1. *Purpose*

In this workshop, we present the design of a web page by referring to the HTML5 semantic tags and using some CSS3 style properties.

5.1.2. *Presentation*

1) This workshop presents a simple structure of a web page with its associated style sheet. It covers the following concepts:

– structuring an HTML page (head/body/header/nav/main/article/aside/footer);

– importing elements (font/icons/style sheet/conditional import);

– organizing the elements of an HTML page (container/header/menu/sidebar/footer);

– adding style properties to these elements.

For a color version of all the figures in this chapter, see: www.iste.co.uk/benrebah/website.zip.

2) Referring to the following screenshot (see Figure 5.1), you are asked to create an HTML web page, as well as its CSS, while respecting the following indications:

– create the elements of your HTML page: <header>, <nav>, <main>, <footer>;

– in the <main> add an <article> element and an <aside> element;

– create a CSS: "style.css";

– import the following Google fonts, icons and CSS: https://fonts. googleapis.com/css?family=Roboto (Roboto font); https://cdnjs. cloudflare.com/ ajax/libs/font-awesome/5.13.0/css/all.min.css (icons);

– import a JavaScript code snippet to verify that HTML5 works with older versions of the IE browser: https://cdnjs.cloudflare.com/ajax/libs/html5shiv/ 3.7.3/html5shiv.js (JS script);

– add style properties to the HTML elements of your web page as already defined according to Table 5.1.

Selector	Style
body	Font: Roboto Font size: 16 px Background image: /images/background-image.jpg
container (class)	Width: 1,024 px Outer margin: automatic Rounded border radius: 5 px Border: width: 1 px; type: solid; color: #bbbbbb Background color: #dddddd Inner margin: 10 px
nav (element)	Width: 100% Text alignment: right
menu class of the ul element	Inner margin: 0 Outer margin: 0 List style: none
li element of the menu class of the ul element	Left outer margin: 2 px Text alignment: centered

Selector	Style
a element in li of the menu class of the ul element	Display: block /* by default an *a* link is inline */ Float: left /* float left positioning */ Width: 100 px Inner margin: 5 px Rounded border radius: 5 px Border: width: 1 px; type: solid; color: white Background color: #597aed /* a color can be designated by its hexadecimal code */ Text color: white /* a color can be designated by its shortcut */ Text decoration: none /* to prevent the *a* tag from displaying an underline under the text */
a element hovered over in li of the menu class of the ul element	Background color: #1226ed /* a color can be designated by its hexadecimal code */ Text color: white /* a color can be designated by its shortcut */
input of type=search in the form	Width: 220 px
aside	Float: right Width: 25% Right outer margin: 0 Left outer margin: 1% Inner margin: 10 px Background color: white Rounded border radius: 5 px Border: width: 1 px; type: solid; color: #bbbbbb
article	Text alignment: justified
footer	Background color: white Rounded border radius: 5 px Border: width: 1 px; type: solid; color: #bbbbbb Inner margin: 10 px Font size: 0.8 em
title class in div of the footer	Font size: 14 in bold
p of the footer	Text alignment: centered Outer margin: 0 px

Table 5.1. *Style properties of the page Mysite.html*

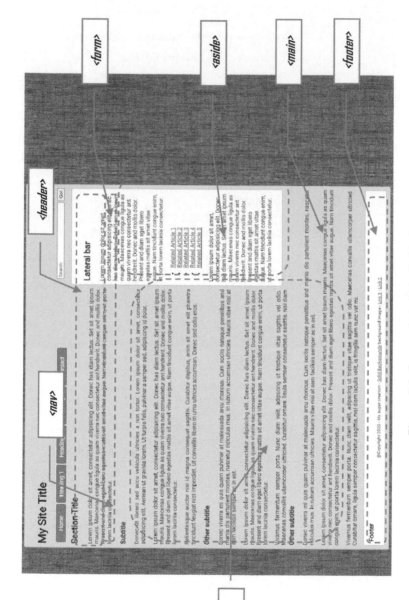

Figure 5.1. *Screenshot of Mysite.html*

5.1.3. *Solution*

Mysite.html

```
<!DOCTYPE html>
<html>
<head>
<meta charset="utf-8">
<title>Title of my Page</title>
<!-- Import of a Google font -->
<link href="https://fonts.googleapis.com/css?family=Roboto"
rel="stylesheet" type="text/css">
<!-- Link to CSS stylesheet of HTML page -->
<link rel="stylesheet" href="sets/css/style.css">
<!-- Import of an icon library -->
<link href="https://cdnjs.cloudflare.com/ajax/libs/font-
awesome/5.13.0/css/all.min.css" rel="stylesheet" type="text/css">
<!-- Conditional structure to verify that HTML5 works with older
versions of IE browser -->
<!--[if lt IE 9]>
<script
src="https://cdnjs.cloudflare.com/ajax/libs/html5shiv/3.7.3/html5shiv.
js"></script>
<![endif]-->
</head>
<body>
<div class="container">
<!-- Title -->
<header>
<h1>Title of my Site</h1>
</header>
<!-- Horizontal menu -->
<nav>
<ul class="menu">
<li><a href="#">Home</a></li>
```

```
<li><a href="#">Section 1</a></li>
<li><a href="#">Section 2</a></li>
<li><a href="#">Section 3</a></li>
<li><a href="#">Contact</a></li>
</ul>
<form>
<input type="search" name="q" placeholder="Search">
<input type="submit" value="Go !">
</form>
</nav>
<!--Content of the page -->
<main>
<!-- Sidebar -->
<aside>
<h2>Sidebar</h2>
<p>Lorem ipsum dolorsitamet, consecteturadipisicingelit. Donec a
diamlectus. Set sitamet ipsum mauris. Maecenascongueligula as
quamviverranecconsecteturanthendrerit. Donec et mollisdolor. Praesent
et diameget libero egestasmattissitamet vitae augue. Nam
tinciduntcongueenim, ut porta loremlaciniaconsectetur.</p>
<ul>
<li><a href="#">Related article 1</a></li>
<li><a href="#">Related article 2</a></li>
<li><a href="#">Related article 3</a></li>
<li><a href="#">Related article 4</a></li>
<li><a href="#">Related article 5</a></li>
</ul>
<p>Lorem ipsum dolorsitamet, consecteturadipisicingelit. Donec a
diamlectus. Set sitamet ipsum mauris. Maecenascongueligula as
quamviverranecconsecteturanthendrerit. Donec et mollisdolor. Praesent
et diameget libero egestasmattissitamet vitae augue. Nam
tinciduntcongueenim, ut porta loremlaciniaconsectetur.</p>
</aside>
<!-- Article -->
```

```
<article>
<h2>Title of the Section</h2>
<p>Lorem ipsum dolorsitamet, consecteturadipisicingelit. Donec a diam
lectus. Set sitamet ipsum mauris. Maecenascongueligula as quamviverra
nec consecteturanthendrerit. Donecet mollis dolor. Praesent et
diameget libero egestasmattissitamet vitae augue. Nam
tinciduntcongueenim, ut porta loremlaciniaconsectetur. </p>
<h3>Sub-title</h3>
<p>Donecutlibrerosedaccuvehiculaultricies a non tortor. Lorem ipsum
dolorsitamet, consecteturadipisicingelit. Aeneanutgravidalorem. Ut
turpisfelis, pulvinar a semper sed, adipiscing id dolor. </p>
<p>Lorem ipsum dolorsitamet, consecteturadipisicingelit. Donec a
diamlectus. Set sitamet ipsum mauris. Maecenascongueligula as
quamviverranecconsecteturanthendrerit. Donec et mollisdolor. Praesent
et diameget libero egestasmattissitamet vitae augue. Nam
tinciduntcongueenim, ut porta loremlaciniaconsectetur. </p>
Pelientesqueauctornisi id magna consequatsagittis. Curabiturdapibus,
enimsitametelitpharetratinciduntfeugiatnistimperdiet. Ut convallis
libero in urnaultricesaccumsan. Donecsedodioeros. </p>
<h3>Other sub-title</h3>
<p>Donecvivivra mi quisquam pulvinar at malesuadaarcu rhoncus. Cum
soclisnatoquepenatibus and manisextiturient montes, nasceturrimus mus.
In rutrumaccumsanultricies. Mauris vitae nisi at semfacilisis sememper
ac in est. </p>
<p>Vivamusfermentum semper porta. Nunc diamvelit, adipscinguttristic
vitae sagittisvelodio. Maecenasconvallisullamcorperultricid.
Curabiturornare, ligula semper consectetursagittis, nisi
diamiaculisvelit, isfringillesemnuncvetmi. </p>
<h3>Other sub-title</h3>
<p>Donecvivivra mi quisquam pulvinar at malesuadaarcu rhoncus. Cum
soclisnatoquepenatibus and manisextiturient montes, nasceturrimus mus.
In rutrumaccumsanultricies. Mauris vitae nisi at semfacilisis sememper
ac in est. </p>
<p>Lorem ipsum dolorsitamet, consecteturadipisicingelit. Donec a
```

diamlectus. Set sitamet ipsum mauris. Maecenascongueligula as
quamviverranecconsecteturanthendrerit. Donec et mollisdolor. Praesent
et diameget libero egestasmattissitamet vitae augue. Nam
tinciduntcongueenim, ut porta loremlaciniaconsectetur. </p>
Vivamofermentum semper porta. Nunc diamvelit, adipscinguttristic vitae
sagittisvelodio. Maecenasconvallisullamcorperultricid.
Curabiturornare, ligula semper consectetursagittis, nisi
diamiaculisvelit, isfringillesemnuncvetmi. </p>
<h3>Other sub-title</h3>
<p>Donecvivivra mi quisquam pulvinar at malesuadaarcu rhoncus. Cum
soclisnatoquepenatibus and manisextiturient montes, nasceturrimus mus.
In rutrumaccumsanultricies. Mauris vitae nisi at semfacilisis sememper
ac in est. </p>
<p>Lorem ipsum dolorsitamet, consecteturadipisicingelit. Donec a
diamlectus. Set sitamet ipsum mauris. Maecenascongueligula as
quamviverranecconsecteturanthendrerit. Donec et mollisdolor. Praesent
et diameget libero egestasmattissitamet vitae augue. Nam
tinciduntcongueenim, ut porta loremlaciniaconsectetur. </p>
Vivamofermentum semper porta. Nunc diamvelit, adipscinguttristic vitae
sagittisvelodio. Maecenasconvallisullamcorperultricid.
Curabiturornare, ligula semper consectetursagittis, nisi
diamiaculisvelit, isfringillesemnuncvetmi. </p>
</article>
</main>
<!-- Footer -->
<footer>
<div class="title">Footer</div>
<p>@Copyright 2021 - My super creation - Background image <a
href="https://www.solidbackgrounds.com/">Solid Backgrounds</a> - <a
href="#">Link 1</a> - <a href="#">Link 2</a></p>
</footer>
</div>
</body>
</html>

Style.css

```css
/* Style applied directly to the body of the HTML page */
body {
font-family: 'Roboto'; /* All texts will use Google font */
font-size: 16px;
background:url("../images/background-image.jpg");
}
.container {
width:1024px;
margin: auto;
border-radius: 5px;
border:1px solid#bbbbbb;
background-color: #dddddd;
padding:10px;
}
nav {
width:100%;
text-align: right;
}
/*CSS used for the menu*/
ul.menu {
padding:0;
margin:0;
list-style-type: none; /* To remove the bullet in front of the LI text
*/
}
ul.menuli {
margin-left: 2px;
text-align: center;
}
ul.menulia {
display: block; /* By default an a link is displayed inline */

float:left; /* Float left positioning */
```

```
width:100px;

padding:5px;

border-radius: 5px;

border:1px solid white;

background-color: #597aed; /* A color can be designated by its

hexadecimal code */

color: white; /* A color can be designated by its shortcut */

text-decoration: none; /* to avoid the a tag displaying an underline

under the text */

}

ul.menulia:hover {

background-color: 1226ed;

color:white;

}

forminput[type=search] {

width:220px;

}

/*CSS used for the sidebar */

aside{

float:right;

width:25%;

margin-right: 0;

margin-left: 1%.

padding:10px;

background-color: white;

border-radius: 5px;

border:1px solid#bbbbbb;

}

/*CSS used for the article */

article {

text-align: justify;

}

/*CSS used for the footer*/

footer{
```

```
background-color: white;
border-radius: 5px;
border:1px solid#bbbbbb;
padding:10px;
font-size: 0.8em;
}
footerdiv.title {
font-size: 1.4em;
font-weight: bold;
}
footerp {
text-align: center;
margin:0;
}
```

5.2. PE2: simple forms

5.2.1. *Purpose*

In this workshop, we focus on presenting examples of the usual forms used in the creation of websites, namely, the login, registration and contact forms.

5.2.2. *Presentation*

1) This workshop presents the development of several sample forms and their style sheets. It covers the following concepts:

– field types (input, select, textarea, button, etc.);

– input field types (checkbox, radio, date, email, password, etc.);

– form encryption types;

– validation attributes (required, minlength, maxlength, etc.);

– image sending;

– retrieving sent values.

2) Based on the following list of screenshots (see Figures 5.2–5.4), you are asked to create an HTML web page, as well as its CSS, while respecting the following indications:

– create the <header> element containing a table icon, an <h1> title;

– create a <div> element as the container;

– create a first <section> element containing the following elements: right sidebar <aside>, containing an <h2> title and an unordered list; <article> containing an <h2> title and a paragraph and a login form;

– create a second <section> element containing the following elements: right sidebar <aside>, containing an <h2> title and an unordered list; <article> containing an <h2> title and a paragraph and a registration form;

– create a third <section> element containing the following elements: right sidebar <aside>, containing an <h2> title and an unordered list; <article> containing an <h2> title and a paragraph and a contact form;

– create a CSS: "style.css";

– import Google fonts, icons and the CSS: https://fonts.googleapis. com/css?family=Roboto (Robot font); https://cdnjs.cloudflare.com/ajax/libs/font-awesome/5.13.0/css/all.min.css (icons);

– add styles properties to the HTML elements of your web page already defined according to Table 5.2.

Selector	Style
<body>	Font: Roboto, Helvetica, Arial, Sans-serif Font size: 16 px Outer margin: 0
header-fix	Height: 85 px Width: 100% Sets the positioning to fixed Sets the screen positioning for the Y-axis Sets the screen positioning for the X-axis Background color: #eee Bottom border: 1 px solid #ddd Box shadow: 0 px 3 px 5 px 0 px rgba(0,0,0,0.75)

Selector	Style
(header class)	Width: 1,024 px Outer margin: 0
header-container (class of the div element of the header)	Width: 1,024 px Outer margin: 84 px auto 10 px Rounded border radius: 5 px Border: 1 px solid #bbbbbb Background color: #eeeeee Inner margin: 10 px
container	Float: right Width: 25% Left outer margin: 1% Right outer margin: 0 Inner margin: 10 px Rounded border radius: 5 px Border: 1 px solid #bbbbbb Background color: white
(first div class)	Bottom outer margin: 0 px
aside (class of the aside element)	Top outer margin: 10 px
H3 in the aside element	Text alignment: justified
ul in the aside element	Display: table
article	Display: table row
form.form-element: class of form elements	Display: table cell Bottom outer margin: 10 px
form.form-element div: div in the form element class	Right inner margin: 10 px
form.form-elementspan, label, input, select, textarea: in the form element class	Text alignment: right

Table 5.2. *Style properties of the page Form.html*

NOTE.– To simplify the presentation of the content of the page *Form.html*, we have tried to break the page down into several sections, detailed in Figures 5.2–5.4.

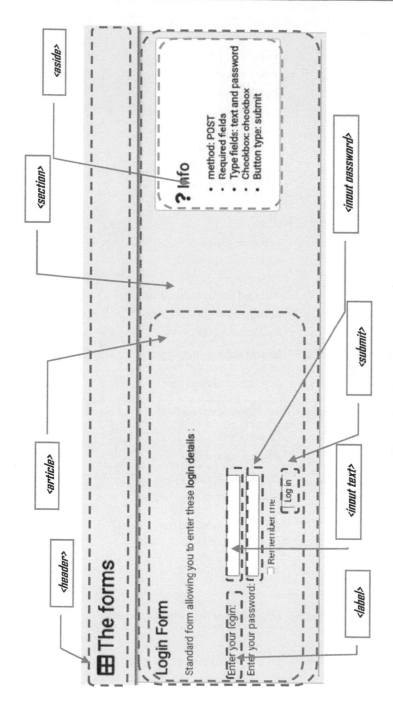

Figure 5.2. *Screenshot of login form*

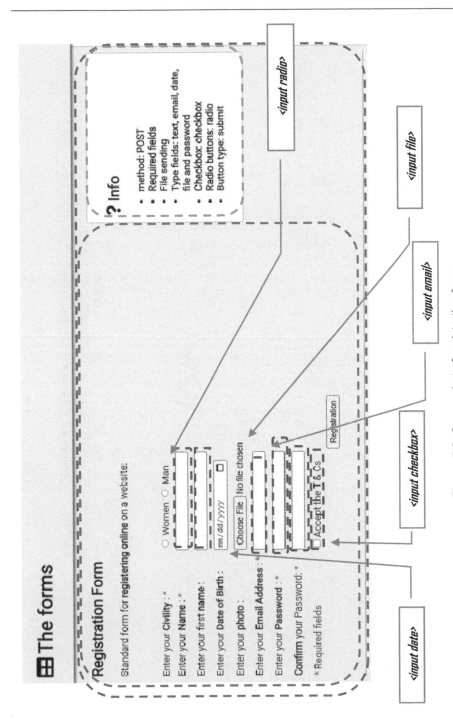

Figure 5.3. *Screenshot of registration form*

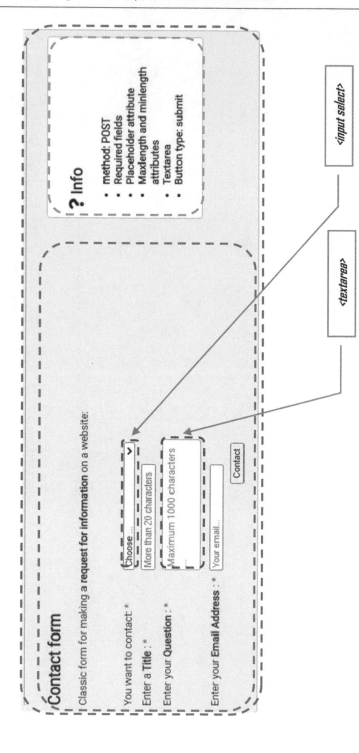

Figure 5.4. *Screenshot of contact form*

5.2.3. *Solution*

Form.html

```html
<!DOCTYPE html>
<html>
<head>
<meta charset="utf-8">
<title>Example 4: Forms</title>
<!-- Import of a Google font -->
<link href="https://fonts.googleapis.com/css?family=Roboto"
rel="stylesheet" type="text/css">
<!-- Link to CSS style sheet of HTML page -->
<link rel="stylesheet" href="sets/css/style.css">
<!-- Import of an icon library -->
<link href="https://cdnjs.cloudflare.com/ajax/libs/font-
awesome/5.13.0/css/all.min.css" rel="stylesheet" type="text/css">
<!-- Conditional structure to verify that HTML5 works with older
versions of IE browser -->
<!--[if lt IE 9]>
<script
src="https://cdnjs.cloudflare.com/ajax/libs/html5shiv/3.7.3/html5shiv.
js"></script>
<![endif]-->
</head>
<body>
<!-- Fixed Position Block -->
<header class="header-fix">
<div class="header-container">
<h1><a href=""><i class="fas fa-table"></i> Forms</h1></a>
</div>
</header>
<!--Content of the page -->
<div class="container">
<section id="login-article">
```

```
<!-- Sidebar -->
<aside>
<h2><i class="fas fa-question"></i>Info</h2>
<ul>
<li><b>method: POST</b></li>
<li><b>Mandatory fields</b></li>
<li><b>Standard field: text and password</b></li>
<li><b>Checkbox: checkbox</b></li>
<li><b>Standard button: submit</b></li>
</ul>
</aside>
<!-- Article -->
<article>
<h2>Login Form</h2>
<p class="marginBot50">Standard form to enter these <b>login
credentials</b>: </p>
<form action=" name="login-form" method="post" class="form-element">
<div>
<label for="login">Enter your login: </label>
<input type="text" name="login" id="login" required>
</div>
<div>
<label for="password">Enter your password: </label>
<input type="password" name="password" id="password" required>
</div>
<div>
<span></span>
<input type="checkbox" name="remember_me" id="remember_me"
value="ok"><label for="remember_me" style="display: inline;">Remember
me</label>
</div>
<div class="align-right">
<span></span>
<input type="submit" name="form" value="Login">
```

```
</div>
</form>
<?php if(!empty($_POST) &&$_POST['form']==="Login") { ?>
<div class="result">
<b>Values returned by the form:</b><br>
<ul>
<?php foreach($_Postas$key =>$value) {
echo'<li>'.$key.' =>'.$value.'</li>';
                           } ?>
</ul>
</div>
<?php }?>
</article>
</section>
<hr style="margin-top:30px;">
<style section="margin-top:30px;">
<!-- Sidebar -->
<aside>
<h2><i class="fas fa-question"></i>Info</h2>
<ul>
<li><b>method: POST</b></li>
<li><b>Mandatory fields</b></li>
<Li><b>File sending</b></li>
<li><b>Standard field: text, email, date, file and password</b></li>
<li><b>Checkbox: checkbox</b></li>
<li><b>Radio button: submit</b></li>
<li><b>Standard button: submit</b></li>
</ul>
</aside>
<!-- Article -->
<article id="registration-article">
<h2>RegistrationForm</h2>
<p class="marginBot50">Standard form for <b>online registration</b> on
a website: </p>
```

```
<form action="#registration-article" name="login-form" method="post"
class="form-element" enctype="multipart/form-data">
<div>
<label for="gender">Enteryour<b>Gender</b>:<span class="mandatory"
style="display: inline;">*</span></label>
<input type="radio" name="gender" id="genderF" value="F" required>
Female <standard input="radio" name="gender" id="genderM" value="M"
required> Male
</div>
<div>
<label for="last-name">Enteryour<b>Lastname</b>:<span
class="mandatory" style="display: inline;">*</span></label>
<input type="text" name="last-name" id="last-name" required>
</div>
<div>
<label for="first-name">Enter your <b>First name</b>: </label>
<input type="text" name="first-name" id="first-name">
</div>
<div>
<label for="date-of-birth">Enter your <b>Date of Birth</b>: </label>
<input type="date" name="date-of-birthday" id="date-of-birth">
</div>
<div>
<label for="photo">Enteryour<b>photo</b>:</label>
<input type="file" name="photo" id="photo" accept="image/*">
</div>
<div>
<label for="email">Enteryour<b>Email address</b>:<span
class="mandatory" style="display: inline;">*</span></label>
<input type="email" name="email" id="email" required>
</div>
<div>
<label for="password">Enter your <b>Password</b>: <span
class="mandatory" style="display: inline;">*</span></label>
```

```
<input type="password" name="password" id="password" required>
</div>
<div>
<label for="password-confirmation"><b>Confirm</b> your Password: <span
class="mandatory" style="display: inline;">*</span></label>
<input type="password" name="password-confirmation" id="password-
confirmation" required>
</div>
<div>
<labelclass="mandatory">* mandatory fields</label>
<input type="checkbox" name="tos" id="tos" value="ok" required><label
for="tos" style="display: inline;">Accept TOS</label>
</div>
<div class="align-right">
<span></span>
<input type="submit" name="form" value="Registration">
</div>
</form>
<?php if(!empty($_POST) &&$_POST['form']==="Registration") { ?>
<div class="result">
<b>Values returned by the form:</b><br>
<ul>
<?php foreach($_POSTas$key =>$value) {
echo'<li>'.$key.' =>'.$value.'</li>';
                                        } ?>
</ul>
<?php
if(!empty($_FILES) && !empty($_FILES['photo'])) {
$target_dir = "uploads/";
$target_file = $target_dir .basename($_FILES["photo"]["name"]);
if (move_uploaded_file($_FILES["photo"]["tmp_name"], $target_file)) {
echo'<br><b>Image preview:</b><br>';
echo'<imgsrc="'. $target_file.'" class="thumbnail">';
                                        }
```

```
                                    }
?>
</div>
<?php }?>
</article>
</section>
<hr style="margin-top:30px;">
<style section="margin-top:30px;">
<!-- Sidebar -->
<aside>
<h2><i class="fas fa-question"></i>Info</h2>
<ul>
<li><b>method: POST</b></li>
<li><b>Mandatory fields</b></li>
<li><b>Placeholder attribute</b></li>
<Li><b>Maxlength and minlength attributes</b></li>
<li><b>Textarea</b></li>
<li><b>Standard button: submit</b></li>
</ul>
</aside>
<article id="contact-article">
<h2>Contact Form</h2>
<p class="marginBot50">Standard form for making an <b>information
request</b> on a website: </p>
<form action="#contact-article" name="contact-form" method="post"
class="form-element">
<div>
<label for="request-type">Youwishtocontact:<span class="mandatory"
style="display: inline;">*</span></label>
<select id="request-type" required>
<option value="">Select...</option>
<option value="sales"> Sales Department</option>
<option value="communication"> Communication Department</option>
<option value="technical"> Technical Department</option>
```

```
</select>
</div>
<div>
<label for="title">Enter a <b>Title</b>:<span class="mandatory"
style="display: inline;">*</span></label>
<input type="text" name="title" id="title" placeholder="More than 20
characters" minlength="20" required>
</div>
<div>
<label for="question" class="vertical-
top">Enteryour<b>Question</b>:<span class="mandatory" style="display:
inline;">*</span></label>
<textarea name="question" id="question" placeholder="Maximum 1000
characters..." maxlength="1000" required></textarea>
</div>
<div>
<label for="email">Enteryour<b>Email address</b>:<span
class="mandatory" style="display: inline;">*</span></label>
<input type="email" name="email" id="email" placeholder="Your
Email..." required>
</div>
<div class="align-right">
<span></span>
<input type="submit" name="form" value="Contact">
</div>
</form>
<?php if(!empty($_POST) &&$_POST['form']==="Contact") { ?>
<div class="result">
<b>Values returned by the form:</b><br>
<ul>
<?php foreach($_POSTas$key =>$value) {
echo'<li>'.$key.' =>'.$value.'</li>';
                                 } ?>
</ul>
```

```
</div>
<?php }?>
</article>
</section>
</div>
</body>
</html>
```

Style.css

```css
/* Style applied directly to the body of the HTML page */
body {
font-family: 'Roboto', helvetica, arial, sans-serif; /* All texts will
use Google Font */
font-size: 16px;
margin:0;
}
header.header-fix {
height:85px;
width:100%;
position:fixed; /* Sets the positioning to fixed */
top:0; /* Sets the screen positioning for the Y-axis */
Left:0; /* Sets the screen positioning for the X-axis */
background-color: #eee;
border-bottom: 1px solid#ddd;
box-shadow: 03px 5px 0rgba(0,0,0,0.75);
}
div.header-container {
width:1024px;
margin: auto;
}
div.header-containerh1a{
color:inherit;
text-decoration: none;
}
```

```
.container {
width:1024px;
margin:84px auto 10px;
border-radius: 5px;
border:1px solid#bbbbbb;
background-color: #eeeeee;
padding:10px;
}
/*CSS used for the sidebar*/
aside{
float:right;
width:25%;
margin-right: 0;
margin-left: 1%.
padding:10px;
background-color: white;
border-radius: 5px;
border:1px solid#bbbbbb;
}
asideh3 {
margin-bottom: 0;
}
asideul {
margin-top: 10px;
}
/*CSS used for the article*/
article {
text-align: justify;
}
.marginBot50 {
margin-bottom: 50px;
}
/* Form formatting*/
form.form-element {
```

```css
display: table;
}
form.form-elementdiv {
display: table-row;
}
form.form-elementspan, label, input, select, textarea {
display: table-cell;
margin-bottom: 10px;
}
form.form-elementlabel {
padding-right: 10px;
}
form.form-element .align-right{
text-align: right;
}
form.form-elementselect, textarea{
width:100%;
}
form.form-elementtextarea{
font-family: 'Roboto', helvetica, arial, sans-serif;;
font-size: 0.95em;
padding: 4px;
resize:none;
width:calc(100% -5px);
border-radius: 5px;
border: 1px solidrgba(153, 153, 153, 0.91);
height: 50px;
}

.vertical-top {
vertical-align: top;
}
.result {
color:#155724;
```

```
background-color: d4edda;
border-color: #c3e6cb;
padding:.75rem 1.25rem;
margin-bottom: 1rem;
border-radius: .25rem;
word-break: break-all;
}
.resultul {
margin-bottom:0;
}
.mandatory {
color:darkred;
}
img.thumbnail {
max-width: 250px;
}
```

5.3. PE3: table formatting

5.3.1. *Purpose*

In this workshop, we focus on creating tables using the HTML5 language.

5.3.2. *Presentation*

1) This workshop presents a simple structure of a web page with several types of format of styled tables in CSS. The web page contains the HTML structure and its associated style sheet. It covers the following concepts:

– structuring a table in HTML (table/caption/head/tbody/tfoot/etc.);

– applying a CSS style;

– presentation of an advanced table (commonly known as a datatable).

2) Referring to the following list of screenshots (see Figure 5.5), you are asked to create an HTML web page, as well as its CSS, while respecting the following indications:

– create the <header> element containing a table icon, an <h1> title;

– create a <div> element as the container;

– create a first <section> element containing the following elements: right sidebar <aside>, containing an <h2> title, two <h3> titles and two unordered lists; <article> containing an <h2> title and a paragraph and a table with its title, header, body and footer;

– create a second <section> element containing the following elements: right sidebar, containing an <h2> title, an unordered list; <article> containing an <h2> title and a paragraph and a table with its title, header, body and footer;

– create a third <section> element containing the following elements: right sidebar <aside>, containing an <h2> title and an unordered list; create an <article> containing an <h2> title and a paragraph, a <div> container of the datatable, including a <div> header of the datatable containing another <div> element with the lines of the header as a drop-down list, and then a <div> element containing a search box, after the datatable header, a datatable table with its title, header (containing search boxes and drop-down lists), body (with a subtitle for each column set) and footer and finally a <div> footer of the datatable (the datatable contains a <div> element of the results and a <div> element of the page list);

– create a CSS: "style.css";

– import the following Google fonts, icons and CSS: https://fonts. googleapis.com/css?family=Roboto (Roboto font); https://cdnjs.cloudflare. com/ajax/libs/font-awesome/5.13.0/css/all.min.css (icons); import a JavaScript code snippet to verify that HTML5 works with older versions of the IE browser: https://cdnjs.cloudflare.com/ajax/libs/html5shiv/3.7.3/html5shiv.js (JS script);

– add style properties to the HTML elements of your web page already defined according to Table 5.3.

Selector	Style
\<body>	Font: Roboto, Helvetica, Arial, Sans-serif Font size: 16 px; outer margin: 0
header-fix	Height: 85 px Width: 100% Sets the positioning to fixed Sets the screen positioning for the Y-axis Sets the screen positioning for the X-axis Background color: #eee Bottom border: 1 px solid #ddd Box shadow: 0 px 3 px 5 px 0 px rgba(0,0,0,0.75)
header class	Width: 1,024 px. Outer margin: 0
container	Width: 1,024 px. Outer margin: 84 px auto 10 px Rounded border radius: 5 px Border: 1 px solid #bbbbbb Background color: #eeeeee Inner margin: 10 px
(first div class)	Float: right Width: 25% Left outer margin: 1% Right outer margin: 0 Inner margin: 10 px Rounded border radius: 5 px Border: 1 px solid #bbbbbb Background color: white
aside (class of the aside element)	Bottom outer margin: 0 px
H3 in the aside element	Top outer margin: 10 px
ul in the aside element	Text alignment: justified
article	Width: 71% Define fixed column widths (see below) with: nth-child(x) The borders are merged into one Border: 2 px solid #597aed Background color: #3d4bff Font family: Bangers, Helvetica, Arial, Sans-Serif

Selector	Style
withStyle (table element class)	Width: 35%
table.withStyletheadth:nth-child(1) 1st child of the th element of the header of the table	Width: 20%
table.withStyletheadth:nth-child(4) 4th child of the th element of the header of the table	Width: 25%
table.withStylethead tr	Text color: white; font size: 1.5 em Text alignment: left Background image: url('../images/bg-table.jpg')
table.withStylefoot tr	Background color: #6c7aff
The tr elements of the thead and tfooter	Background color: #4659ff
table.withStylebodytr:nth-child(odd) the odd children of the tr elements of the body of the table	Text color: #f2f1ec Font size: 1.2 em
table.withStylebodytr:nth-child(even) the even children of the tr elements of the body of the text	Font size: 1.5 em Inner margin: 20 px Font style: italic Location of the caption (<caption>): bottom (caption = table title) Text color: #0041c3 Text alignment: right Letter spacing: 1 px
table.withStylebody th the th elements of the body of the table	Width: 71%
table.withStylecaption the caption element of the table	Width: 100% Display: flexible Content justification: spacing between elements Bottom outer margin: 5 px
datatable-container ID of the div of the datatable	Display: flexible inline
datatable-header ID of the div of the header of the datatable	Width: 100% Background color: #ccc Border: 1 px solid #bbb Border collapse: collapse

Selector	Style
datatable-container table theadthID of the datatable container in the th element of the header of the table	Font size: 1.15 em Font weight: bold Inner margin: 5 px Text color: #2b2b2b Text alignment: centered Background color: #ccc Top border: 1 px solid #bbb Left border: 1 px solid #bbb Right border: 1 px solid #bbb
datatable-container thead .sort_asc ID of the datatable container in the sort_asc class of the header of the table	Background image: url("../images/sort_asc.png") Cursor: pointer Background repetition: no Background position: centered to the right
datatable-container thead .no_sort ID of the datatable container in the no_sort class of the header of the table	Background image: url("../images/sort_both.png") Cursor: pointer Background repetition: no Background position: centered to the right
datatable-container table caption ID of the datatable container in the caption element of the table	Font size: 1.3 em Font weight: bold Top inner margin: 5 px Bottom inner margin: 5 px Font style: italic Location of the (<caption>) caption: top Text color: #0041c3 Text alignment: centered Letter spacing: 1 px Background color: #ccc Top border: 1 px solid #bbb Left border: 1 px solid #bbb Right border: 1 px solid #bbb
datatable-container table tbodytr ID of the datatable container in the tr element of the body of the table	Text alignment: centered
datatable-container table tbodytd ID of the datatable container in the td element of the body of the table	Font size: 1 em Top inner margin: 5 px Bottom inner margin: 5 px

Selector	Style
datatable-container table tbodytr:nth-child(odd) ID of the datatable container in the odd child element of the tr of the table	Background color: #ddd
datatable-container table tbodytr:nth-child(even) ID of the datatable container in the even child element of the tr of the table	Background color: #eee
datatable-container table tfoottdID of the datatable container in the td element of the footer of the table	Top inner margin: 5 px Bottom inner margin: 5 px
datatable-container table tfootthID of the datatable container in the th element of the footer of the table	Text alignment: right Right border: 1 px solid #bbb Right inner margin: 10 px
datatable-container table tfoottdID of the datatable container in the td element of the footer of the table	Text alignment: centered Font weight: bold Text decoration: underlined
datatable-footer ID of the div of the footer of the datatable	Width: 100% Display: flexible Content justification: spacing between elements Bottom inner margin: 5 px
datatable-footer-results ID of the div of the result of the datatable	Top outer margin: 20 px
datatable-footer-paginator ID of the div of the pagination of the datatable	Display: flexible inline
datatable-footer .paginationclass of the div of the pagination of the footer of the datatable	Display: flexible Left inner margin: 0 List style: no Rounded border radius: 25 rem Top outer margin: 15 px
datatable-footer .page:first-child .linkclass of the divof the link of the 1st child of the page in the footer of the datatable	Left outer margin: 0 Top left border radius: 5 px Bottom left border radius: 5 px

Selector	Style
datatable-footer .link:not(:disabled) :not(.disabled) class of the div of the link not disabled in the footer of the datatable	Cursor: pointer
datatable-footer .linkclass of the div of the link in the footer of the datatable	Position: relative Display: block Inner margin: 0.3 rem 0.6 rem Left outer margin: −1 px Row height: 1.25 Text color: #0041c3 Background color: #fff Border: 1 px solid #dee2e6 Text decoration: no
datatable-footer .link.disabledclass of the div of the link disabled in the footer of the datatable	Text color: #bbb
datatable-footer .link.activeclass of the div of the activated link in the footer of the datatable	Text color: white Background color: #0041c3
datatable-footer .page:last-child .linkclass of the div of the link of the last child of the page in the footer of the datatable	Top right border radius 5 px Bottom right border radius 5 px

Table 5.3. *Style properties of
the page Table.html*

NOTE.– To simplify the presentation of the content of the page *Table.html*, we have tried to break the page down into several sections. This is detailed in Figure 5.5.

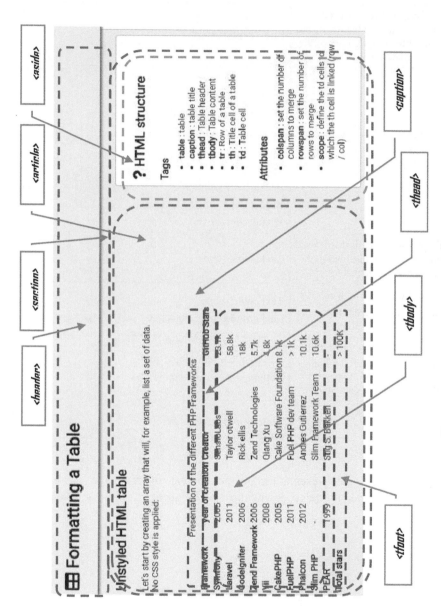

Figure 5.5A. *Screenshot of Table.html*

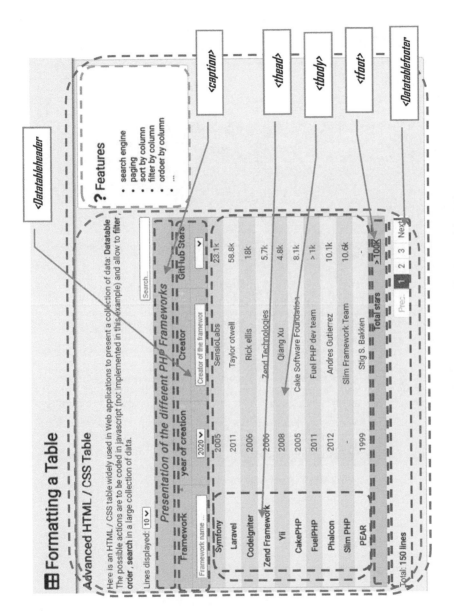

Figure 5.5B. *Screenshot of Table.html (cont.)*

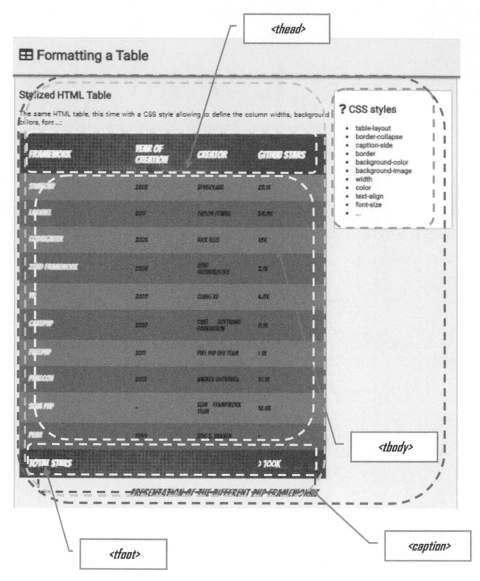

Figure 5.5C. *Screenshot of Table.html (cont.)*

5.3.3. *Solution*

Table.html

```
<!DOCTYPE html>
<html>
<head>
<meta charset="utf-8">
<title>Example 3: Table formatting</title>
<!-- Import of a Google font -->
<link href="https://fonts.googleapis.com/css?family=Roboto"
rel="stylesheet" type="text/css">
<link href='https://fonts.googleapis.com/css?family=Bangers'
rel='stylesheet' type='text/css'>
<!-- Link to CSS style sheet of HTML page -->
<link rel="stylesheet" href="sets/css/style.css">
<!-- Import of an icon library -->
<link href="https://cdnjs.cloudflare.com/ajax/libs/font-
awesome/5.13.0/css/all.min.css" rel="stylesheet" type="text/css">
<!-- Conditional structure to verify that HTML5 works with older
versions of IE browser -->
<!--[if lt IE 9]>
<script
src="https://cdnjs.cloudflare.com/ajax/libs/html5shiv/3.7.3/html5shiv.
js"></script>
<![endif]-->
</head>
<body>
<!-- Fixed Position Block -->
<header class="header-fix">
<div class="header-container">
<h1><i class="fas fa-table"></i> Formatting a Table</h1>
</div>
</header>
<!--Content of the page -->
```

```
<div class="container">
<section>
<!-- Sidebar -->
<aside>
<h2><I class="fas fa-question"></i> HTML Structure</h2>
<h3>Tags</h3>
<ul>
<li><b>table</b>: table</li>
<Li><b>table</b>: table title</li>
<li><b>thead</b>: Table header</li>
<li><b>tbody</b>: Table content</li>
<li><b>tr</b>: Row of a table</li>
<li><b>th</b>: Title cell of a table</li>
<li><b>td</b>: Cell of a table</li>
</ul>
<h3>Attributes</h3>
<ul>
<li><b>colspan</b>: defines the number of columns to be merged</li>
<li><b>rowspan</b>: defines the number of rows to be merged</li>
<li><b>scope</b>: defines the td cells to which the th cell is linked
(row / col)</li>
</ul>
</aside>
<!-- Article -->
<article>
<h2>Unstyled HTML Table</h2>
<p class="marginBot50">Let's start by creating a table that will list
a data set, for example.<br>No CSS style is applied:  </p>
<table>
<caption>Presentation of the various PHP Frameworks</caption>
<thead>
<tr>
<th scope="col">Framework</th>
<th scope="col">Year of creation</th>
```

```
<th scope="col">Creator</th>
<th scope="col">GitHub Stars</th>
</tr>
</thead>
<tbody>
<tr>
<th scope="row">Symfony</th>
<td>2005</td>
<td>SensioLabs</td>
<td>23.1k</td>
</tr>
<tr>
<th scope="row">Laravel</th>
<td>2011</td>
<td>Taylor Otwell</td>
<td>58.8k</td>
</tr>
<tr>
<th scope="row">CodeIgniter</th>
<td>2006</td>
<td>Rick Ellis</td>
<td>18k</td>
</tr>
<tr>
<th scope="row">Zend Framework</th>
<td>2006</td>
<td>Zend Technologies</td>
<td>5.7k</td>
</tr>
<tr>
<th scope="row">Yii</th>
<td>2008</td>
<td>Qiang Xu</td>
<td>4.8k</td>
</tr>
```

```
</tr>
<tr>
<th scope="row">CakePHP</th>
<td>2005</td>
<td>Cake Software Foundation</td>
<td>8.1k</td>
</tr>
<tr>
<th scope="row">FuelPHP</th>
<td>2011</td>
<td>Fuel PHP dev team</td>
<td>>1k</td>
</tr>
<tr>
<th scope="row">Phalcon</th>
<td>2012</td>
<td>Andres Gutierrez</td>
<td>10.1k</td>
</tr>
<tr>
<th scope="row">Slim PHP</th>
<td>-</td>
<td>Slim Framework Team</td>
<td>10.6k</td>
</tr>
<tr>
<th scope="row">PEAR</th>
<td>1999</td>
<td>Stig S. Bakken</td>
<td>-</td>
</tr>
</tbody>
<tfoot>
<tr>
```

```
<th scope="row" colspan="3">Total stars</th>
<td>>100K</td>
</tr>
</tfoot>
</table>
</article>
</section>
<style section="margin-top:50px;">
<!-- Sidebar -->
<aside>
<h2><i class="fas fa-question"></i>CSS Styles</h2>
<ul>
<li><b>table-layout</b></li>
<li><b>border-collapse</b></li>
<li><b>caption-side</b></li>
<li><b>border</b></li>
<li><b>background-color</b></li>
<li><b>background-image</b></li>
<li><b>width</b></li>
<li><b>color</b></li>
<li><b>text-align</b></li>
<li><b>font-size</b></li>
<li><b>...</b></li>
</ul>
</aside>
<!-- Article -->
<article>
<h2>Stylized HTML Table</h2>
<p>The same HTML table with a CSS style this time to define column
widths, background colors, font, etc.:  </p>
<table class="withStyle">
<caption>Presentation of the various PHP Frameworks</caption>
<thead>
<tr>
```

```
<th scope="col">Framework</th>
<th scope="col">Year of creation</th>
<th scope="col">Creator</th>
<th scope="col">GitHub Stars</th>
</tr>
</thead>
<tbody>
<tr>
<th scope="row">Symfony</th>
<td>2005</td>
<td>SensioLabs</td>
<td>23.1k</td>
</tr>
<tr>
<th scope="row">Laravel</th>
<td>2011</td>
<td>Taylor Otwell</td>
<td>58.8k</td>
</tr>
<tr>
<th scope="row">CodeIgniter</th>
<td>2006</td>
<td>Rick Ellis</td>
<td>18k</td>
</tr>
<tr>
<th scope="row">Zend Framework</th>
<td>2006</td>
<td>Zend Technologies</td>
<td>5.7k</td>
</tr>
<tr>
<th scope="row">Yii</th>
<td>2008</td>
```

```
<td>Qiang Xu</td>
<td>4.8k</td>
</tr>
<tr>
<th scope="row">CakePHP</th>
<td>2005</td>
<td>Cake Software Foundation</td>
<td>8.1k</td>
</tr>
<tr>
<th scope="row">FuelPHP</th>
<td>2011</td>
<td>Fuel PHP dev team</td>
<td>>1k</td>
</tr>
<tr>
<th scope="row">Phalcon</th>
<td>2012</td>
<td>Andres Gutierrez</td>
<td>10.1k</td>
</tr>
<tr>
<th scope="row">Slim PHP</th>
<td>-</td>
<td>Slim Framework Team</td>
<td>10.6k</td>
</tr>
<tr>
<th scope="row">PEAR</th>
<td>1999</td>
<td>Stig S. Bakken</td>
<td>-</td>
</tr>
</tbody>
```

```
<tfoot>
<tr>
<th scope="row" colspan="3">Total stars</th>
<td>>100K</td>
</tr>
</tfoot>
</table>
</article>
</section>
<style section="margin-top:50px;">
<!-- Sidebar -->
<aside>
<h2><i class="fas fa-question"></i>Features</h2>
<ul>
<Li><b>search engine</b></li>
<li><b>pagination</b></li>
<li><b>sort by column</b></li>
<li><b>filter by column</b></li>
<li><b>order by column</b></li>
<li><b>...</b></li>
</ul>
</aside>
<!-- Article -->
<article>
<h2>HTML Table / Advanced CSS</h2>
<p>
Here is an HTML / CSS table widely used in Web applications to present
a collection of data: <b>Datatable</b>
<br>The possible actions are to be encoded in JavaScript (not
implemented in this example) and make it possible to <b>filter</b>,
<b>order</b>, <b>search</b> in a large data collection.
</p>
<div id="datatable-container">
<div id="datatable-header">
```

```
<div id="datatable-header-lines">
Lines displayed:
<select>
<option>10</option>
<option>20</option>
<option>30</option>
<option>40</option>
<option>50</option>
</select>
</div>
<div id="datatable-header-search">
<input type="search" name="search" value="" placeholder="Search..." />
</div>
</div>
<table class="datatable">
<caption>Presentation of the various PHP Frameworks</caption>
<thead>
<tr>
<th scope="col" class="sort_asc">Framework</th>
<th scope="col" class="no_sort">Year of creation</th>
<th scope="col" class="no_sort">Creator</th>
<th scope="col" class="no_sort">GitHub Stars</th>
</tr>
<tr class="search-filter">
<th scope="col"><input type="search" name="framework"
placeholder="Framework name..." /></th>
<th scope="col">
<select name="year">
<option>2020</option>
<option>2019</option>
<option>2018</option>
<option>2017</option>
<option>...</option>
</select>
```

```
</th>
<th scope="col"><input type="search" name="creator"
placeholder="Framework creator..." /></th>
<th scope="col">
<select name="stars">
<option><10k</option>
<option>> 10k</option>
<option>> 20k</option>
<option>> 30k</option>
<option>...</option>
</select>
</th>
</tr>
</thead>
<tbody>
<tr>
<th scope="row">Symfony</th>
<td>2005</td>
<td>SensioLabs</td>
<td>23.1k</td>
</tr>
<tr>
<th scope="row">Laravel</th>
<td>2011</td>
<td>Taylor Otwell</td>
<td>58.8k</td>
</tr>
<tr>
<th scope="row">CodeIgniter</th>
<td>2006</td>
<td>Rick Ellis</td>
<td>18k</td>
</tr>
<tr>
```

```
<th scope="row">Zend Framework</th>
<td>2006</td>
<td>Zend Technologies</td>
<td>5.7k</td>
</tr>
<tr>
<th scope="row">Yii</th>
<td>2008</td>
<td>Qiang Xu</td>
<td>4.8k</td>
</tr>
<tr>
<th scope="row">CakePHP</th>
<td>2005</td>
<td>Cake Software Foundation</td>
<td>8.1k</td>
</tr>
<tr>
<th scope="row">FuelPHP</th>
<td>2011</td>
<td>Fuel PHP dev team</td>
<td>>1k</td>
</tr>
<tr>
<th scope="row">Phalcon</th>
<td>2012</td>
<td>Andres Gutierrez</td>
<td>10.1k</td>
</tr>
<tr>
<th scope="row">Slim PHP</th>
<td>-</td>
<td>Slim Framework Team</td>
<td>10.6k</td>
```

```
</tr>
<tr>
<th scope="row">PEAR</th>
<td>1999</td>
<td>Stig S. Bakken</td>
<td>-</td>
</tr>
</tbody>
<tfoot>
<tr>
<th scope="row" colspan="3">Total stars</th>
<td>>100K</td>
</tr>
</tfoot>
</table>
<div id="datatable-footer">
<div id="datatable-footer-results">
Total :<b>150 rows</b>
</div>
<div id="datatable-footer-paginator">
<ul class="pagination">
<li class="page"><aclass="link disabled" href="#">Back</a></li>
<li class="page"><aclass="link active" href="#">1</a></li>
<li class="page"><aclass="link" href="#">2</a></li>
<li class="page"><aclass="link" href="#">3</a></li>
<li class="page"><aclass="link" href="#">Forward</a></li>
</ul>
</div>
</div>
</div>
</article>
</section>
</div>
</body>
</html>
```

Style.css

```css
body {
font-family: 'Roboto', helvetica, arial, sans-serif; /* All texts will
use Google font */
font-size: 16px;
margin: 0;
}
header.header-fix {
height:85px;
width: 100%.
position:fixed; /* Sets the positioning to fixed */
top:0; /* Sets the screen positioning for the Y-axis */
Left:0; /* Sets the screen positioning for the X-axis */
background-color: #eee;
border-bottom: 1px solid #ddd;
box-shadow: 0px 3px 5px 0px rgba(0,0,0,0.75;
}
div.header-container {
width: 1024px;
margin: auto;
}
.container {
width: 1024px;
margin: 84px auto 10px;
border-radius: 5px;
border: 1px solid #bbbbbb;
background-color: #eeeeee;
padding:10px;
}
/*    CSS used for the sidebar*/
aside{
float:right;
```

```
width: 25%.
margin-right: 0;
margin-left: 1%.
padding: 10px;
background-color: white;
border-radius: 5px;
border: 1px solid #bbbbbb;
}
asideh3 {
margin-bottom:0px;
}
asideul {
margin-top: 10px;
}
/*    CSS used for the article*/
article {
text-align: justify;
}
.marginBot50 {
margin-bottom: 50px;
}
/*    CSS used for the table*/
table.withStyle {
width: 71%.
table-layout: fixed; /* enables fixed column widths to be defined (see
below with :nth-child(x) */
border-collapse: collapse; /* the borders are merged into one */
border:2px solid#597aed; /* Add a border around the table */
background-color: #3d4bff;
font-family: 'Bangers', helvetica, arial, sans-serif;;
}
table.withStyletheadth:nth-child(1) {
width: 35%.
}
```

```
table.withStyletheadth:nth-child(2) {
width: 20%.
}
table.withStyletheadth:nth-child(3) {
width: 20%.
}
table.withStyletheadth:nth-child(4) {
width: 25%.
}
table.withStyleth, table.withStyletd {
padding: 20px;
}
table.withStyletheadtr,
table.withStyletfoottr
{
color: white;
font-size: 1.5em;
text-align: left;
background-image: url('../images/bg-table.jpg');
}
table.withStyletbodytr:nth-child(odd) {
background-color: #6c7aff;
}
table.withStyletbodytr:nth-child(even) {
background-color: #4659ff;
}
table.withStyletbodyth {
color: #f2f1ec;
font-size: 1.2em;
}
table.withStylecaption {
font-size: 1.5em;
padding: 20px;
font-style: italic;
```

```
caption-side: bottom;
color: #0041c3;
text-align: right;
letter-spacing: 1px;
}
/*Datatable*/
#datatable-container {
width: 71%.
}
#datatable-header {
width: 100%.
display: flex;
justify-content: space-between;
margin-bottom: 5px;
}
#datatable-header-search {
display: inline-flex;
}
#datatable-containertable {
width: 100%.
background: #ccc;
border: 1px solid #bbb;
border-collapse: collapse;
}
#datatable-containertablecaption {
font-size: 1.3em;
font-weight: bold;
padding-top: 5px;
padding-bottom: 5px;
font-style: italic;
caption-side: top;
color: #0041c3;
text-align: center;
letter-spacing: 1px;
```

```
background: #ccc;
border-top: 1px solid #bbb;
border-left: 1px solid #bbb;
border-right: 1px solid #bbb;
}
#datatable-containertabletheadth {
font-size: 1.15em;
font-weight: bold;
padding: 5px;
color: #2b2b2b;
text-align: center;
background: #ccc;
border-bottom: 1px solid #bbb;
border-left: 1px solid #bbb;
border-right: 1px solid #bbb;
}
#datatable-containerthead .sort_asc {
background-image: url("../images/sort_asc.png");
cursor: pointer;
background-repeat: no-repeat;
background-position: center right;
}
#datatable-containerthead .no_sort {
background-image: url("../images/sort_both.png");
cursor: pointer;
background-repeat: no-repeat;
background-position: center right;
}
#datatable-containertabletbodytr{
text-align: center;
}
#datatable-containertabletbodytd{
font-size: 1em;
padding-top: 5px;
```

```
padding-bottom: 5px;
}
#datatable-containertabletbodytr:nth-child(odd){
background: #ddd;
}
#datatable-containertabletbodytr:nth-child(even){
background: #eee;
}
#datatable-containertabletfoottd{
padding-top: 5px;
padding-bottom: 5px;
}
#datatable-containertabletfootth{
text-align: right;
border-right: 1px solid #bbb;
padding-right:10px;
}
#datatable-containertabletfoottd{
text-align: center;
font-weight: bold;
text-decoration: underline;
}
#datatable-footer {
width: 100%.
display: flex;
justify-content: space-between;
margin-bottom: 5px;
}
#datatable-footer-results{margin-top:20px;}


#datatable-footer-paginator {
display: inline-flex;
}
```

```
#datatable-footer .pagination {
display: flex;
padding-left: 0;
list-style: none;
border-radius: .25rem;
margin-top:15px;
}
#datatable-footer .page:first-child .link {
margin-left: 0;
border-top-left-radius: 5px;
border-bottom-left-radius: 5px;
}
#datatable-footer .link:not(:disabled):not(.disabled) {
cursor: pointer;
}
#datatable-footer .link {
position: relative;
display: block;
padding: .3rem .6rem;
margin-left: -1px;
line-height: 1.25;
color: #0041c3;
background-color: #fff;
border: 1px solid #dee2e6;
text-decoration: none;
}
#datatable-footer .link.disabled {
color: #bbb;
}
#datatable-footer .link.active {
color: white;
background-color: #0041c3;
}
```

```
#datatable-footer .page:last-child .link {
border-top-right-radius: 5px;
border-bottom-right-radius: 5px; }
```

5.4. TP 4: media (image, video and audio)

5.4.1. *Purpose*

In this workshop, we present the principle of embedding several multimedia objects within a web page.

5.4.2. *Presentation*

1) This workshop presents examples of the embedding in HTML of non-textual content such as:

– single image;

– image with caption;

– CSS decorative image;

– vector image;

– responsive image;

– audio file;

– video file.

2) Referring to the following list of screenshots (see Figure 5.6), you are asked to create an HTML web page, as well as its CSS, while respecting the following indications:

– create the <header> element containing a table icon, an <h1> title;

– create a <div> element as the container;

– create a first <section> element containing the following elements: right sidebar <aside>, containing an <h2> title, two <h3> titles, an unordered list and two paragraphs; <article> containing an <h2> title and a paragraph and an image;

– create a second <section> element containing the following elements: right sidebar <aside>, containing an <h2> title, two <h3> titles, an unordered list and a paragraph; <article> containing an <h2> title and a paragraph and a figure;

– create a third <section> element containing the following elements: right sidebar <aside>, containing an <h2> title and an unordered list; <article> containing an <h2> title and a paragraph, and a <div> element containing a paragraph with decorative image in the background;

– create a fourth <section> element containing the following elements: <article> containing an <h2> title and a paragraph, and a <div> element containing two figures of matrix and vector images;

– create a fifth <section> element containing the following elements: right sidebar <aside>, containing an <h2> title, two <h3> titles and an unordered list; <article> containing an <h2> title and a paragraph, and a <div> element containing a responsive image;

– create a sixth <section> element containing the following elements: right sidebar <aside>, containing an <h2> title, two <h3> titles and an unordered list and a paragraph; <article> containing an <h2> title and a paragraph and a <div> element containing an audio medium;

– create a seventh <section> element containing the following elements: right sidebar <aside>, containing an <h2> title, two <h3> titles and an unordered list and a paragraph; <article> containing an <h2> title and a paragraph, and a <div> element containing a video medium;

– create an eighth <section> element containing the following elements: right sidebar <aside>, containing an <h2> title, two <h3> titles and an unordered list and a paragraph; <article> containing an <h2> title and a paragraph, and a <div> element containing an iframe;

– create a footer containing a paragraph and a hyperlink;

– create a CSS: "style.css";

– import the following Google fonts, icons and CSS: https://fonts. googleapis.com/css?family=Roboto (Roboto font); https://cdnjs.cloudflare.com/ ajax/libs/font-awesome/5.13.0/css/all.min.css (icons);

– import a JavaScript code snippet to verify that HTML5 works with older versions of the IE browser: https://cdnjs.cloudflare.com/ajax/libs/html5shiv/3.7.3/ html5shiv.js (JS script);

– add style properties to the HTML elements of your web page already defined according to Table 5.4.

Selector	Style
<body>	Font: Roboto, Helvetica, Arial, Sans-serif Font size: 16 px Outer margin: 0
header-fix (class of the header)	Height: 85 px Width: 100% Sets the positioning to fixed Sets the screen positioning for the Y-axis to 0 Sets the screen positioning for the X-axis to 0 Background color: #eee Bottom border: 1 px solid #ddd Box shadow: 0 px 3 px 5 px 0 px rgba(0,0,0,0.75).
header-container (class of the div element of the header)	Width: 1,024 px Outer margin: 0
Aside (class of the aside element)	Float: right Width: 25% Left outer margin: 1% Right outer margin: 0 Inner margin: 10 px Rounded border radius: 5 px Border: 1 px solid #bbbbbb Background color: white
container (first div class)	Width: 1,024 px Outer margin: 84 px auto 10 px Rounded border radius: 5 px Border: 1 px solid #bbbbbb Background color: #eeeeee Inner margin: 10 px
H3 in the aside element	Bottom outer margin: 0 px
ul in the aside element	Top outer margin: 10 px
asidep.aside-info class applied to paragraphs in aside	Outer margin: 0 Font size: 12 px
article	Text alignment: justified
code	Inner margin: 10 px Font size: 12 px Background color: white Text color: blue

Selector	Style
pre.pre: class applied to pre elements	Text alignment: left Background color: white Inner margin: 10 px
pre.pre code: class applied to code in pre elements	Inner margin: 0 px
div.content: class applied to the content of the div elements	Width: 72% Text alignment: centered
bg-image: class applied to background images	Inner margin: 10 px Text color: white Background image: url('../images/background-image.jpg') Background repetition: no Background size: cover
#map: map identifier	Width: 640 px Background: transparent url('../images/map/map.gif') no-repeat Top outer margin: 40 px Left outer margin: 60 px
#map div: div in map identifier	Outer margin: 0 px
#map #tooltip: tooltip identifier in map	Width: 200 px Height: 84 px Background: url("../images/map/tooltip.png") no-repeat Position: absolute Display: no Top inner margin: 5 px Text alignment: centered Left position: 150 px Text color: white

Table 5.4. *Style properties of the page Multimediaobjects.html*

NOTE.– To simplify the presentation of the content of the page *Multimediaobjects.html*, we have tried to break the page down into several sections, detailed in Figure 5.6.

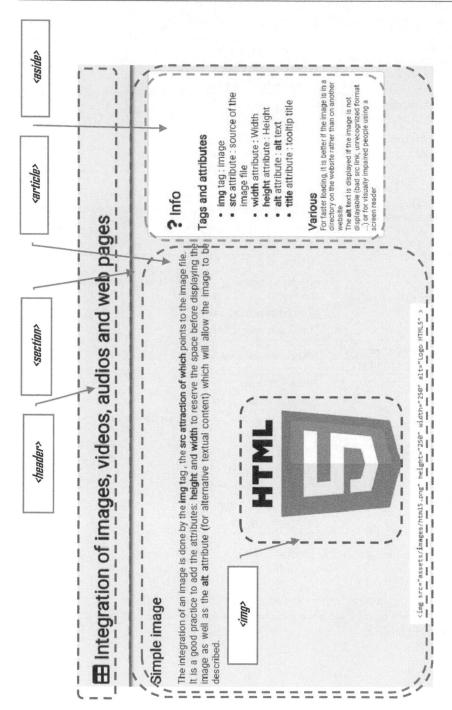

Figure 5.6A. *Screenshot of Multimediaobjects.html*

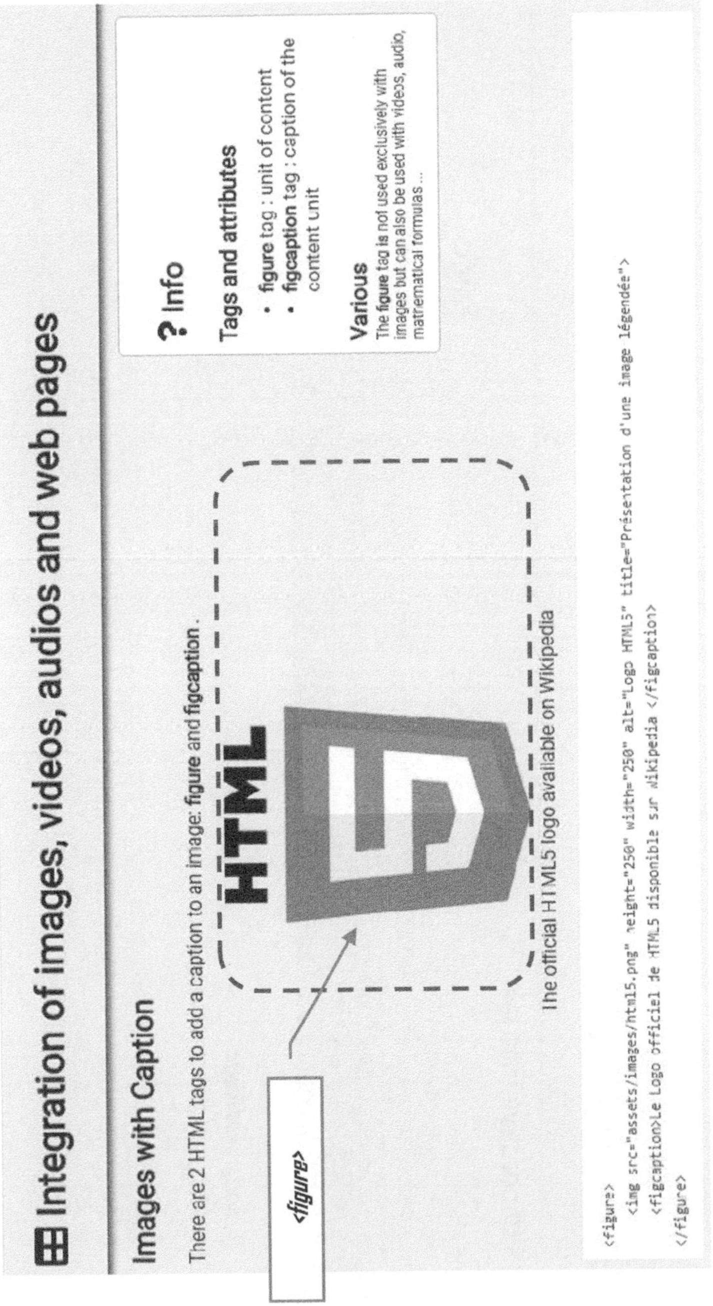

⊞ Integration of images, videos, audios and web pages

Images with Caption

There are 2 HTML tags to add a caption to an image: figure and figcaption .

‹figure›

The official HTML5 logo available on Wikipedia

```
<figure>
    <img src="assets/images/html5.png" height="250" width="250" alt="Logo HTML5" title="Présentation d'une image légendée">
    <figcaption>Le Logo officiel de HTML5 disponible sur Wikipedia </figcaption>
</figure>
```

❓ Info

Tags and attributes

- **figure** tag : unit of content
- **figcaption** tag : caption of the content unit

Various

The **figure** tag is not used exclusively with images but can also be used with videos, audio, mathematical formulas ...

Figure 5.6B. *Screenshot of Multimediaobjects.html (cont.)*

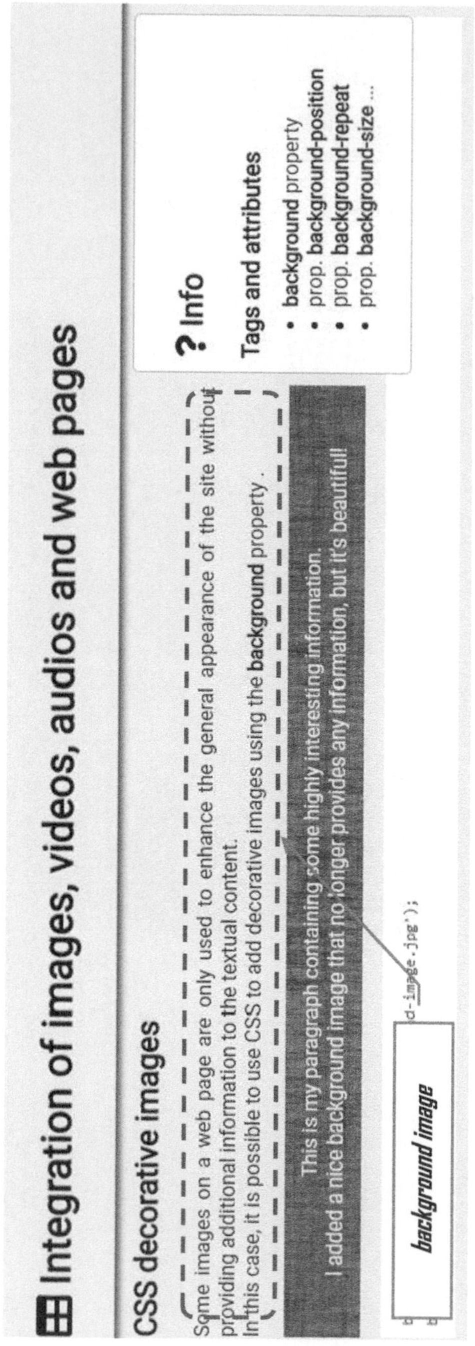

⊞ Integration of images, videos, audios and web pages

CSS decorative images

Some images on a web page are only used to enhance the general appearance of the site without providing additional information to the textual content.
In this case, it is possible to use CSS to add decorative images using the **background** property.

This is my paragraph containing some highly interesting information.
I added a nice background image that no longer provides any information, but it's beautiful!

d-image.jpg');

background image

? Info

Tags and attributes

- **background** property
- prop. **background-position**
- prop. **background-repeat**
- prop. **background-size** ...

Figure 5.6C. *Screenshot of Multimediaobjects.html (cont.)*

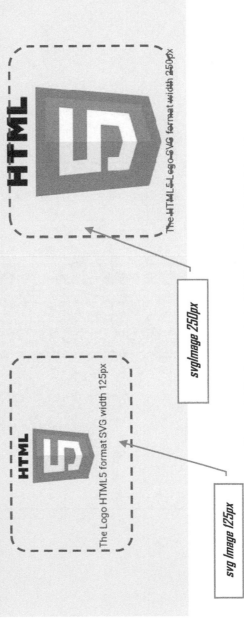

Integration of images, videos, audios and web pages

Vector images

Unlike the classic JPG, GIF, PNG ... images which are assemblies of pixels of different colors, vector images are an assemblage of lines and shapes.
This has the advantage of obtaining images that do not pixelate and can adjust to any size container. The format of this type of image is **SVG**.

The Logo HTML5 format SVG width 125px

The HTML5 Logo SVG format width 250px

svg Image 125px

svgImage 250px

Figure 5.6D. *Screenshot of Multimediaobjects.html (cont.)*

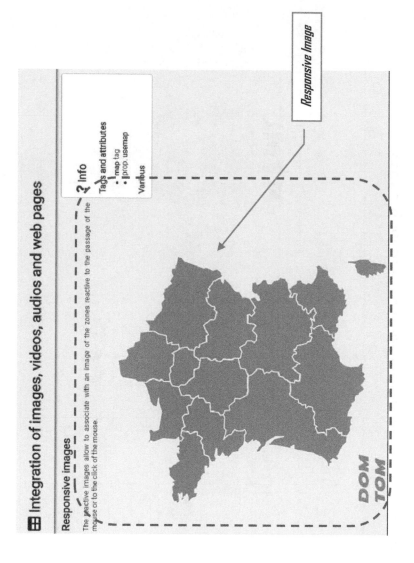

Figure 5.6E. *Screenshot of Multimediaobjects.html (cont.)*

⊞ Integration of images, videos, audios and web pages

Audio file

The insertion of an audio file is done by the **audio** tag. Similar to video, it is possible to define multiple source files in case the browser does not support the specified format

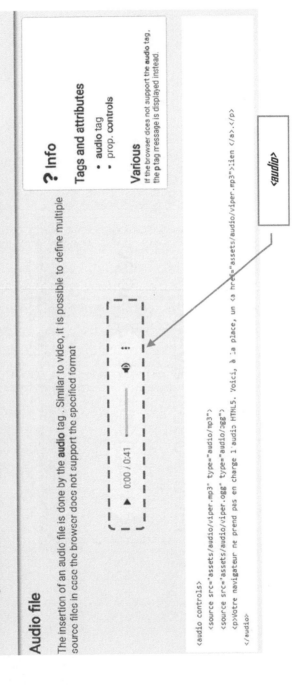

```
<audio controls>
    <source src="assets/audio/viper.mp3" type="audio/mp3">
    <source src="assets/audio/viper.ogg" type="audio/ogg">
    <p>Votre navigateur ne prend pas en charge l audio HTML5. Voici, à la place, un <a href="assets/audio/viper.mp3">lien </a>.</p>
</audio>
```

? Info

Tags and attributes

* **audio** tag
* prop. **controls**

Various

If the browser does not support the **audio** tag, the **p** tag message is displayed instead.

`<audio>`

Figure 5.6F. *Screenshot of Multimediaobjects.html (cont.)*

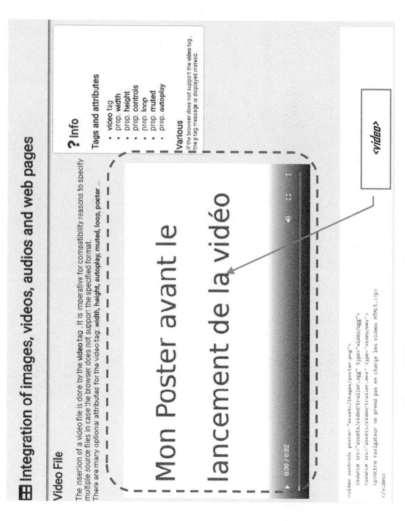

Figure 5.6G. *Screenshot of Multimediaobjects.html (cont.)*

⊞ Integration of images, videos, audios and web pages

Iframes

An Iframe makes it possible to integrate other Web pages into the HTML page: Youtube video, interactive map ...

<iframe>

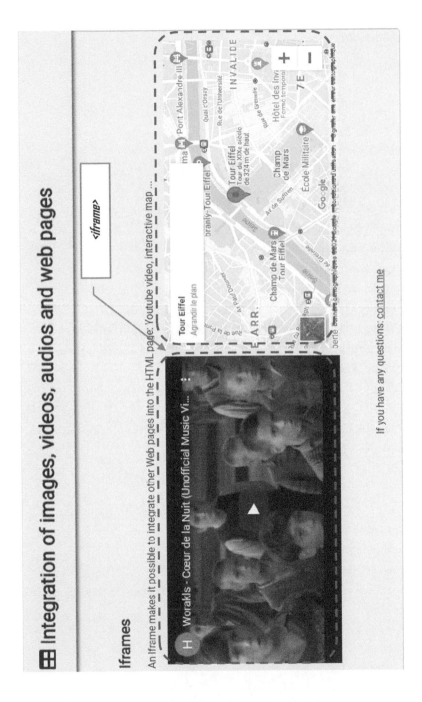

If you have any questions: contact me

Figure 5.6H. Screenshot of *Multimediaobjects.html (cont.)*

5.4.3. *Solution*

Multimediaobjects.html

```
<!DOCTYPE html>
<html>
<head>
<meta charset="utf-8">
<title>Example 5: Integration of images, videos, audios and Web
pages</title>
<!-- Import of a Google font -->
<link href="https://fonts.googleapis.com/css?family=Roboto"
rel="stylesheet" type="text/css">
<!-- Link to CSS style sheet of HTML page -->
<link rel="stylesheet" href="sets/css/style.css">
<!-- Import of an icon library -->
<link href="https://cdnjs.cloudflare.com/ajax/libs/font-
awesome/5.13.0/css/all.min.css" rel="stylesheet" type="text/css">
<!-- Conditional structure to verify that HTML5 works with older
versions of IE browser -->
<!--[if lt IE 9]>
<script
src="https://cdnjs.cloudflare.com/ajax/libs/html5shiv/3.7.3/html5shiv.
js"></script>
<![endif]-->
</head>
<body>
<!-- Fixed Position Block -->
<header class="header-fix">
<div class="header-container">
<h1><i class="fas fa-table"></I> Integration of images, videos, audios
and web pages</h1>
</div>
</header>
<!--Content of the page -->
```

```
<div class="container">
<section>
<!-- Sidebar -->
<aside>
<h2><i class="fas fa-question"></i>Info</h2>
<h3>Tags and attributes</h3>
<ul>
<li><b>img</b> tag: image</li>
<Li><b>src</b> attribute: source of image file</li>
<li><b>width</b> attribute: Width</li>
<Li><b>height</b> attribute: Height</li>
<Li><b>alt</b> attribute: alternative text</li>
<Li><b>title</b> attribute: tooltip title</li>
</ul>
<h3>Miscellaneous</h3>
<p class="aside-info">For faster loading, it is preferable for the
image to be located in a directory of the website rather than on
another Internet site</p>
<p class="aside-info">The text of <b>alt</b> is displayed if the image
cannot be displayed (wrong src link, unrecognized format, etc.) or for
visually impaired individuals using a screen reader</p>
</aside>
<!-- Article -->
<article>
<h2>Single image</h2>
<p class="marginBot50">An image is embedded using the <b>img</b> tag
whose <b>src</b> attribute points to the image file.
<br>It is good practice to add the attributes: <b>height</b> and
<b>width</b> to reserve the space before the image is displayed and
the <b>alt</b> attribute (for alternative text content) that can be
used to describe the image.
</p>
<div class="content">
<img src="assets/images/html5.png" height="250" width="250" alt="HTML5
```

```
Logo" >
<pre><code>&lt;imgsrc="assets/images/html5.png" height="250"
width="250" alt="HTML5 Logo" &gt;</code></pre>
</div>
</article>
</section>
<style section="margin-top:70px;">
<!-- Sidebar -->
<aside>
<h2><i class="fas fa-question"></i>Info</h2>
<h3>Tags and attributes</h3>
<ul>
<li>tag <b>figure</b>: content unit</li>
<li>tag <b>figcaption</b>: content unit caption</li>
</ul>
<h3>Miscellaneous</h3>
<p class="aside-info">The <b>figure</b> tag is not used exclusively
with images but can also be employed with videos, audio, mathematical
formulas, etc.</p>
</aside>
<!-- Article -->
<article>
<h2>Images with Caption</h2>
<p>2 HTML tags exist to add a caption to an image: <b>figure</b> and
<b>figcaption</b>.</p>
<div class="content">
<figure>
<img src="assets/images/html5.png" height="250" width="250" alt="HTML5
Logo" title="Presentation of a captioned image">
<figcaption>The official HTML5 Logo available on
Wikipedia</figcaption>
</figure>
</div>
```

```
<pre class="pre" style="width:
98%;"><code>&lt;figure&gt;<br>    &lt;imgsrc="asse
ts/images/html5.png" height="250" width="250" alt="HTML5 Logo"
title="Presentation of a captioned
image"&gt;<br>    &lt;figcaption&gt;The official
HTML5 Logo available on Wikipedia
&lt;/figcaption&gt;<br>&lt;/figure&gt;</code></pre>
</article>
</section>
<style section="margin-top:70px;">
<!-- Sidebar -->
<aside>
<h2><i class="fas fa-question"></i>Info</h2>
<h3>Tags and attributes</h3>
<ul>
<li>property<b>background</b></li>
<li>prop. <b>background-position</b></li>
<li>prop. <b>background-repeat</b></li>
<li>prop.
<b>background-size</b>...</li>
</ul>
</aside>
<!-- Article -->
<article>
<h2>CSS Decorative images</h2>
<p>Certain images on a web page are only used to enhance the general
look of the site without providing additional information to the text
content.<br>
                    In this case, you can use CSS to add
decorative images using the <b>background</b> property.</p>
<div class="content">
<p class="bg-image">

                    This is my paragraph containing highly
```

interesting information.
I've added a nice background image that
doesn't give more information but it looks good!
</p>
</div>
<pre class="pre" style="width: 98%;"><code>background:
url('../images/background-image.jpg');
background-repeat: no-
repeat;</code></pre>
</article>
</section>
<style section="margin-top:70px;">
<!-- Article -->
<article>
<h2>Vector Images</h2>
<p>Unlike conventional images such as JPG, GIF and PNG, which are
assemblies of pixels of different colors, vector images are an
assembly of lines and shapes.
                          This has the advantage of obtaining images
that do not pixelate and can adjust to any container size. The format
of this image type is <b>SVG</b>.</p>
<div class="content" style="width:100%;">
<div style="float: left;width:50%;">
<figure>
<img src="assets/images/HTML5_logo_and_wordmark.svg" height="125"
width="125" alt="HTML5 Logo - small">
<figcaption>The HTML5 Logo SVG format width 125px</figcaption>
</figure>
</div>
<div style="margin-left:50%;">
<figure>
<img src="assets/images/HTML5_logo_and_wordmark.svg" height="250"
width="250" alt="HTML5 Logo - large">
<figcaption>The HTML5 Logo SVG format width 250px</figcaption>
</figure>
</div>

```
</div>
</article>
</section>
<style section="margin-top:70px;">
<!-- Sidebar -->
<aside>
<h2><i class="fas fa-question"></i>Info</h2>
<h3>Tags and attributes</h3>
<ul>
<li><b>map</b> tag</li>
<li>prop. <b>usemap</b></li>
</ul>
<h3>Miscellaneous</h3>
</aside>
<!-- Article -->
<article>
<h2>Responsive images</h2>
<p>Responsive images enable an image to be associated with areas
responsive to the mouse passing over them or clicking on them.</p>
<div class="content">
<div id="map">
<div id="tooltip" style="display: none;"></div>
<div id="map_region" style="background: rgba(0, 0, 0, 0) none repeat
scroll 0% 0%;">
<map name="MapFrance" id="MapFrance">
<!-- FRANCE -->
<area onmouseover="DispReg(1); DispTooltip('Alsace - Lorraine...',
'Lorem ipsum...', event)" onmouseout="SupReg(1);" shape="poly"
coords="529,131,553,135,551,144,544,149,528,193,529,198,522,214,525,22
1,518,231,514,231,512,233,507,223,502,219,500,215,494,210,505,192,505,
187,513,179,507,175,506,166,518,151,512,145,505,146,502,141,506,135,51
4,140,524,139" href="" alt="">
<area onmouseover="DispReg(1); DispTooltip('Alsace - Lorraine...',
```

```
'Lorem ipsum...', event)" onmouseout="SupReg(1);" shape="poly"
coords="423,101,431,103,435,99,439,101,447,98,460,107,470,102,475,107,
480,106,493,122,499,119,511,126,517,122,526,122,526,128,524,136,514,13
7,507,132,498,140,502,149,509,148,514,151,503,164,505,177,506,179,502,
185,501,193,492,209,483,202,479,205,475,201,462,203,462,198,450,200,44
2,191,444,181,435,176,435,171,416,157,413,155,411,148,417,147,419,134,
413,129,416,117" href="" alt="">
<area onmouseover="DispReg(1); DispTooltip('Alsace - Lorraine...',
'Lorem ipsum...', event)" onmouseout="SupReg(1);" shape="poly"
coords="388,72,400,72,410,63,410,83,416,84,431,98,429,100,422,98,412,1
19,411,131,415,134,413,145,408,146,412,157,432,172,431,177,442,181,441
,188,441,192,449,201,441,212,441,216,436,216,430,221,418,218,413,216,4
16,209,400,192,379,201,376,198,365,199,358,184,353,182,354,177,346,172
,348,162,352,158,349,141,359,138,358,123,363,123,361,114,377,110,380,9
3,388,84" href="" alt="">
<area onmouseover="DispReg(2); DispTooltip('Aquitaine - Limousin...',
'Lorem ipsum...', event)" onmouseout="SupReg(2);" shape="poly"
coords="135,340,146,353,152,376,154,375,153,356,160,356,161,357,163,36
6,170,367,177,374,185,370,185,366,197,361,197,354,203,353,209,339,215,
336,226,342,235,355,240,355,240,361,234,365,242,376,242,386,234,401,23
3,406,227,407,222,414,222,420,215,422,214,426,218,430,217,437,209,438,
207,442,203,442,197,440,187,442,180,441,176,446,174,445,160,449,160,46
3,154,470,167,472,168,481,171,482,171,488,160,498,160,502,155,502,153,
514,139,515,134,507,113,496,110,493,106,496,101,495,106,487,101,479,94
,481,94,478,88,476,101,470,110,460,116,440,124,399,135,398,130,388,128
,384" href="" alt="">
<area onmouseover="DispReg(2); DispTooltip('Aquitaine - Limousin...',
'Lorem ipsum...', event)" onmouseout="SupReg(2);" shape="poly"
coords="224,308,244,293,255,296,286,295,288,304,301,316,300,325,290,33
0,294,335,293,341,296,345,295,351,295,360,286,363,283,371,278,375,277,
380,272,386,246,386,246,374,238,367,243,360,244,351,235,351,228,338,22
0,334,232,322" href="" alt="">
<area onmouseover="DispReg(2); DispTooltip('Aquitaine - Limousin...',
'Lorem ipsum...', event)" onmouseout="SupReg(2);" shape="poly"
```

```
coords="151,243,166,247,171,242,195,243,199,240,208,243,208,254,218,25
3,229,265,235,267,235,276,240,292,230,299,220,309,228,321,214,334,208,
337,201,350,196,351,194,358,183,364,178,371,173,365,165,364,166,356,16
0,353,152,353,141,334,132,331,130,326,120,318,120,314,126,317,134,324,
144,315,143,308,147,306,138,293,141,289,156,289,160,293,168,289,166,28
3,165,268,169,265,158,255,158,250" href="" alt="">
<area onmouseover="DispReg(3); DispTooltip('Auvergne - Rhone Alpes',
'Lorem ipsum...', event)" onmouseout="SupReg(3);" shape="poly"
coords="289,296,303,289,305,277,323,273,326,277,343,281,350,277,356,28
8,363,291,365,301,361,307,358,307,354,322,349,328,352,334,352,342,359,
357,359,367,373,366,374,371,379,371,382,377,381,383,377,383,376,389,37
3,389,372,394,354,402,348,399,348,395,343,395,341,400,339,399,336,394,
332,390,321,395,316,406,316,402,311,401,305,392,290,408,278,407,280,39
9,275,394,280,380,286,373,287,367,297,362,297,352,301,346,295,340,298,
336,294,331,304,326,303,312" href="" alt="">
<area onmouseover="DispReg(3); DispTooltip('Auvergne - Rhone Alpes',
'Lorem ipsum...', event)" onmouseout="SupReg(3);" shape="poly"
coords="359,308,361,308,365,314,379,314,388,306,400,312,404,306,407,29
4,423,294,420,299,430,309,433,306,440,311,459,300,464,306,456,315,456,
321,471,313,472,307,479,303,494,303,496,309,491,313,496,324,502,325,50
2,334,492,338,493,345,498,350,501,360,508,365,506,368,506,377,500,377,
496,382,485,381,473,386,465,386,463,393,470,396,470,402,462,400,451,40
3,443,413,437,413,434,418,437,421,437,423,428,425,424,430,429,433,434,
436,438,441,433,442,428,445,422,438,416,439,419,433,403,436,397,432,38
5,434,384,431,378,430,373,434,368,431,367,426,362,422,357,404,374,397,
376,392,379,390,379,385,384,385,387,377,382,367,376,367,374,364,361,36
5,362,358,355,340,355,334,352,329,358,322" href="" alt="">
<area onmouseover="DispReg(4); DispTooltip('Lower - Upper Normandy',
'Lorem ipsum...', event)" onmouseout="SupReg(4);" shape="poly"
coords="136,74,163,73,161,84,166,95,204,102,220,97,225,111,223,126,232
,129,241,147,241,161,236,166,234,171,223,165,223,159,218,155,203,158,2
02,152,195,146,173,151,168,146,153,143,149,148,142,144,142,141,154,140
,146,133,148,101" href="" alt="">
<area onmouseover="DispReg(4); DispTooltip('Lower - Upper Normandy',
```

```
'Lorem ipsum...', event)" onmouseout="SupReg(4);" shape="poly"
coords="218,87,231,75,271,61,277,80,273,95,276,100,272,118,263,123,260
,137,242,144,234,128,226,126,228,108,223,95,238,93" href="" alt="">
<area onmouseover="DispReg(5); DispTooltip('Burgundy - Free...',
'Lorem ipsum...', event)" onmouseout="SupReg(5);" shape="poly"
coordinates="324,184,332,175,346,175,350,178,349,184,356,186,362,200,3
72,201,381,206,399,196,413,208,412,218,419,221,433,227,429,231,431,239
,430,246,418,265,422,271,416,273,422,281,422,291,404,291,402,303,398,3
08,388,301,378,311,369,312,364,307,366,303,367,291,361,286,350,274,342
,278,327,274,328,263,324,257,324,237,321,230,323,222,326,220,323,210,3
27,202,327,185" href="" alt="">
<area onmouseover="DispReg(5); DispTooltip('Burgundy - Free...',
'Lorem ipsum...', event)" onmouseout="SupReg(5);" shape="poly"
coordinates="422,301,429,307,435,304,442,307,461,296,464,287,463,279,4
75,271,476,264,504,240,502,238,494,238,495,235,499,233,503,232,504,225
,499,220,499,216,493,213,483,205,479,210,474,203,464,205,462,201,451,2
03,443,212,444,219,438,221,436,219,434,223,438,227,431,235,434,244,421
,265,427,272,421,276,426,284,425,293,427,295" href="" alt="">
<area onmouseover="DispReg(6); DispTooltip('Brittany', 'Lorem
ipsum...', event)" onmouseout="SupReg(6);" shape="poly"
coordinates="10,164,25,180,28,175,35,176,37,180,50,182,56,189,61,189,6
9,194,69,203,75,197,86,198,87,203,81,203,85,207,104,208,111,195,119,19
6,123,192,134,192,140,187,147,190,153,180,159,179,157,164,161,160,162,
146,155,146,148,152,140,147,139,141,132,141,130,136,126,141,113,140,11
4,135,97,141,82,122,82,117,75,119,64,119,51,130,50,127,45,131,40,126,2
5,128,22,125,8,131,4,138,24,139,23,143,28,145,18,150,11,146,12,151,24,
157" href=" alt="""">
<area onmouseover="DispReg(7); DispTooltip('Center - Loire Valley',
'Lorem ipsum...', event)" onmouseout="SupReg(7);" shape="poly"
coords="244,146,261,140,265,145,265,153,273,160,282,174,298,174,303,18
4,325,188,325,197,320,211,323,218,319,224,318,233,322,239,321,258,324,
263,324,270,303,275,300,287,287,293,244,290,237,274,237,264,230,262,22
1,249,211,252,211,243,201,237,201,233,208,226,209,212,228,210,230,202,
239,194,240,185,246,182,237,173,239,168,246,164" href="" alt="">
```

```
<area onmouseover="DispReg(8); DispTooltip('Corsica', 'Lorem
ipsum...', event)" onmouseout="SupReg(8);" shape="poly"
coords="540,534,543,519,546,517,547,534,550,542,549,563,543,570,539,59
6,535,602,527,597,521,596,521,593,518,590,524,584,523,582,515,581,517,
576,516,573,512,573,517,565,511,564,511,557,513,556,513,550,519,539,52
9,537,535,534" href="" alt="">
<area onmouseover="DispReg(9); DispTooltip('Ile de France', 'Lorem
ipsum...', event)" onmouseout="SupReg(9);" shape="poly"
coords="263,138,265,126,279,120,290,119,296,123,302,120,308,127,334,13
0,337,128,347,144,347,156,345,161,343,171,331,172,320,184,304,182,301,
172,284,172,276,158,269,153,267,143" href="" alt="">
<area onmouseover="DispReg(10); DispTooltip('Languedoc Roussillon...',
'Lorem ipsum...', event)" onmouseout="SupReg(10);" shape="poly"
coords="252,544,258,552,269,549,280,557,288,553,294,556,299,549,312,54
9,314,552,316,549,309,543,307,528,312,508,321,500,332,498,343,494,352,
484,363,481,369,486,372,485,374,481,382,481,380,476,388,472,389,463,39
9,456,393,441,393,436,381,437,380,433,377,433,375,437,364,432,365,428,
360,426,353,404,346,400,345,398,342,402,337,403,335,397,330,393,322,39
7,317,411,321,420,322,438,331,440,330,446,335,451,332,455,331,460,324,
467,319,465,315,475,311,474,304,479,299,478,293,479,297,487,290,492,27
7,489,276,492,266,489,262,491,258,488,256,493,251,492,250,499,261,508,
260,521,256,525,258,529,263,529,268,534,260,541" href="" alt="">
<area onmouseover="DispReg(10); DispTooltip('Languedoc Roussillon...',
'Lorem ipsum...', event)" onmouseout="SupReg(10);" shape="poly"
coords="161,469,163,464,163,451,173,448,174,451,176,450,180,445,189,44
5,196,441,205,446,210,443,210,440,220,440,223,430,219,426,226,424,225,
414,230,409,236,407,237,402,246,388,272,389,271,396,276,400,274,410,29
2,412,304,397,309,404,312,404,314,413,318,421,319,439,328,443,327,449,
332,453,329,454,328,461,322,463,319,462,312,471,308,474,302,477,299,47
3,290,479,294,486,286,489,276,485,273,488,266,484,261,487,256,485,253,
486,253,490,248,490,248,502,258,510,258,519,252,525,256,529,263,532,26
4,535,250,543,246,541,246,535,233,533,228,524,220,527,207,518,198,517,
197,527,188,525,182,527,176,523,165,524,156,515,157,506,163,506,164,50
0,174,490,176,480,171,477,170,469,167,470" href="" alt="">
```

```
<area onmouseover="DispReg(11); DispTooltip('Nord Pas de Calais...',
'Lorem ipsum...', event)" onmouseout="SupReg(11);" shape="poly"
coords="277,42,282,13,287,8,319,4,322,17,331,25,344,21,350,38,360,39,3
64,49,382,53,385,69,380,73,374,67,363,70,356,67,345,70,341,64,316,60,3
17,54,302,53,295,45" href="" alt="">
<area onmouseover="DispReg(11); DispTooltip('Nord Pas de Calais...',
'Lorem ipsum...', event)" onmouseout="SupReg(11);" shape="poly"
coords="276,43,272,61,281,82,275,96,280,100,274,119,290,117,296,120,30
2,118,308,123,333,128,335,122,347,137,354,137,356,121,358,121,355,114,
374,108,385,82,385,73,379,76,373,70,360,72,353,71,345,75,340,67,314,63
,313,57,301,55,293,48" href="" alt="">
<area onmouseover="DispReg(12); DispTooltip('P.A.C.A', 'Lorem
ipsum...', event)" onmouseout="SupReg(12);" shape="poly"
coords="376,487,375,484,382,483,384,478,390,475,392,465,403,457,396,44
1,397,437,404,439,414,437,411,443,419,442,427,448,433,444,438,445,440,
441,437,434,429,429,430,427,440,425,442,422,438,417,441,416,445,415,45
0,406,461,402,469,405,473,404,473,396,467,391,475,390,483,385,495,403,
502,403,502,412,494,415,493,422,494,427,495,436,508,444,522,448,532,44
7,536,453,529,458,524,473,513,473,504,484,500,484,492,494,485,494,481,
500,481,502,486,503,480,507,471,506,470,511,460,509,459,513,449,510,44
9,515,436,506,423,505,423,498,418,494,406,495,405,490,399,489,395,494,
387,493,383,488" href="" alt="">
<area onmouseover="DispReg(13); DispTooltip('Pays de la Loire', 'Lorem
ipsum...', event)" onmouseout="SupReg(13);" shape="poly"
coords="165,148,174,154,194,149,198,155,202,163,216,158,220,161,220,16
6,238,180,237,183,236,193,228,198,225,208,208,208,203,227,198,230,198,
238,195,240,168,239,164,244,144,239,153,249,155,256,165,265,162,271,16
2,283,166,286,160,289,157,286,141,285,135,284,124,272,119,273,115,256,
107,249,110,247,109,245,117,238,107,229,113,225,127,225,111,219,100,22
1,95,219,96,214,105,208,110,208,111,197,122,198,126,196,134,196,139,19
0,146,195,155,185,154,182,164,181,160,166,164,160" href="" alt="">
<!-- Overseas Departments And Territories -->
<area onmouseover="DispReg(14); DispTooltip('Overseas Departments',
```

```
'Lorem ipsum...', event)" onmouseout="SupReg(14);" shape="rect"
coords="0,540,118,570" href="" alt="">
<area onmouseover="DispReg(15); DispTooltip('Overseas Territories',
'Lorem ipsum...', event)" onmouseout="SupReg(15);" shape="rect"
coords="0,577,108,604" href="" alt="">
</map>
<img usemap="#MapFrance" src="assets/images/map/map_empty.png" alt=""
width="557" height="606">
</div>
</div>
</div>
</article>
</section>
<style section="margin-top:70px;">
<!-- Sidebar -->
<aside>
<h2><i class="fas fa-question"></i>Info</h2>
<h3>Tags and attributes</h3>
<ul>
<li><b>audio</b> tag</li>
<li>prop. <b>controls</b></li>
</ul>
<h3>Miscellaneous</h3>
<p class="aside-info">If the browser does not support the <b>audio</b>
tag, the <b>p</b> tag message is displayed instead.</p>
</aside>
<!-- Article -->
<article>
<h2>Audio File</h2>
<p>An audio file is inserted using the <b>audio</b> tag. In the same
way as video, multiple source files can be defined should the browser
not support the specified format</p>
<div class="content marginBot50 marginTop50" style="padding-
bottom:10px;">
```

```
<audio controls>
<source src="assets/audio/viper.mp3" type="audio/mp3">
<source src="assets/audio/viper.ogg" type="audio/ogg">
<p>Your browser does not support HTML5 audio. Here instead is a <a
href="sets/audio/viper.mp3">link to the audio</a>.</p>
</audio>
</div>
<pre class="pre" style="width:
98%;"><code>&lt;audiocontrols&gt;<br>    &lt;sourc
esrc="assets/audio/viper.mp3"
type="audio/mp3"&gt;<br>    &lt;sourcesrc="assets/
audio/viper.ogg"
type="audio/ogg"&gt;<br>    &lt;p>Your browser
does not support HTML5 audio. Here instead is a &lt;a
href="assets/audio/viper.mp3"&gt;link
&lt;/a&gt;.&lt;/p&gt;<br>&lt;/audio&gt;</code></pre>
</article>
</section>
<style section="margin-top:70px;">
<!-- Sidebar -->
<aside>
<h2><I class="fas fa-question"></i>Info</h2>
<h3>Tags and attributes</h3>
<ul>
<li>tag<b>video</b></li>
<li>prop. <b>width</b></li>
<li>prop. <b>height</b></li>
<li>prop. <b>controls</b></li>
<li>prop. <b>loop</b></li>
<li>prop. <b>muted</b></li>
<li>prop. <b>autoplay</b></li>
</ul>
<h3>Miscellaneous</h3>
<p class="aside-info">If the browser does not support the <b>video</b>
```

tag, the <b>p</b> tag message is displayed instead.</p>

</aside>

<!-- Article -->

<article>

<h2>Video File</h2>

<p>A video file is inserted using the <b>video</b> tag. It is imperative for compatibility reasons to specify multiple source files in case the browser does not support the specified format.
There are numerous optional attributes for the video tag: <b>width, height, autoplay, muted, loop, poster</b>...</p>

<div class="content marginBot50 marginTop50" style="padding-bottom:10px;">

<video controls poster="assets/images/poster.png">

<source src="assets/video/trailer.ogg" type="video/ogg">

<source src="assets/video/trailer.m4v" type="video/m4v">

<p>Your browser does not support HTML5 videos.</p>

</video>

</div>

<pre class="pre" style="width: 98%;"><code><video controls poster="assets/images/poster.png">
    <source src="assets/video/trailer.ogg" type="video/ogg">
    <sourcesrc="assets/video/trailer.m4v" type="video/m4v">
    <p>Your browser does not support HTML5 videos.</p>
</video></code></pre>

</article>

</section>

<style section="margin-top:70px;">

<!-- Article -->

<article>

<h2>Iframes</h2>

<p>An Iframe enables other Web pages to be integrated into the HTML

```
page: YouTube video, interactive map, etc. </p>
<div class="content" style="width:100%;">
<div style="float: left;width:50%;">
<iframe width="500" height="281"
src="https://www.youtube.com/embed/Wyj6Cl9IizM" frameborder="0"
allow="accelerometer; autoplay; encrypted-media; gyroscope; picture-
in-picture" allowfullscreen></iframe>
</div>
<div style="margin-left:50%;">
<iframe
src="https://www.google.com/maps/embed?pb=!1m14!1m8!1m3!1d10499.966498
430253!2d2.2944813!3d48.8583701!3m2!1i1024!2i768!4f13.1!3m3!1m2!1s0x0%
3A0x8ddca9ee380ef7e0!2sTour%20Eiffel!5e0!3m2!1sfr!2sfr!4v1589040077932
!5m2!1sfr!2sfr" width="500" height="281" frameborder="0"
style="border:0;" allowfullscreen="" aria-hidden="false"
tabindex="0"></iframe>
</div>
</div>
</article>
</section>
<!-- Footer -->
<footer class="marginTop50">
<p class="align-center">If you have any questions: <a
href="https://antoinechedebois.com" title="My CV online">contact
me</a><br>
<p class="align-center">
       If you have any questions: <a
href="https://antoinechedebois.com" title="My CV online">contact
me</a><br> Credits: HTML5 Logo <a
href="https://fr.wikipedia.org/">wikipedia</a> - Decorative background
image <a
href="https://torange.biz/">https://www.solidbackgrounds.com/</a> -
Audio Files <a href="https://developer.mozilla.org">Mozilla
Development Network</a><br>- Video Files (c) copyright Blender
```

```
Foundation |
<a href="http://www.bigbuckbunny.org">www.bigbuckbunny.org</a>
</p>
</p>
</footer>
</div>
<!-- Loading of JS files at end of HTML flow just before body is
closed -->
<script src="assets/js/map.js"></script>
</body>
</html>
```

Style.css

```css
/* Style applied directly to the body of the HTML page */
body {
font-family: 'Roboto', helvetica, arial, sans-serif; /* All texts will
use Google font */
font-size: 16px;
margin: 0;
}
header.header-fix {
height:85px;
width: 100%.
position:fixed; /* Sets the positioning to fixed */
top:0; /* Sets the screen positioning for the Y-axis */
Left:0; /* Sets the screen positioning for the X-axis */
background-color: #eee;
border-bottom: 1px solid #ddd;

box-shadow: 0px 3px 5px 0px rgba(0,0,0,0.75;
}
div.header-container {
width: 1024px;
margin: auto;
```

```
}
.container {
width: 1024px;
margin: 84px auto 10px;
border-radius: 5px;
border: 1px solid #bbbbbb;
background-color: #eeeeee;
padding:10px;
}
/* CSS used for the sidebar*/
aside{
float:right;
width: 25%.
margin-right: 0;
margin-left: 1%.
padding: 10px;
background-color: white;
border-radius: 5px;
border: 1px solid #bbbbbb;
}
asideh3 {
margin-bottom:0px;
}
asideul {
margin-top: 10px;
}
asidep.aside-info{
margin: 0;

font-size: 12px;
}
/*CSS used for the article*/
article {
text-align: justify;
```

```
}
.marginBot50 {
margin-bottom: 50px;
}
.marginTop50 {
margin-top: 50px;
}
.align-center{
text-align: center;
}
code {
padding: 10px;
font-size: 12px;
background-color: white;
color: blue;
}
pre.pre {
text-align: left;
background-color: white;
padding: 10px;
}
pre.precode{
padding: 0;
}
div.content {
width: 72%.
text-align: center;
}

.bg-image {
padding: 10px;
color: white;
background-image: url('../images/background-image.jpg');
background-repeat: no-repeat;
```

```
background-size: cover;
}
#map {
width: 640px;
background: transparent url('../images/map/map.gif') no-repeat;
margin-top: 40px;
margin-left: 60px;
}
#map #tooltip {
width: 200px;
height: 84px;
background: url("../images/map/tooltip.png") no-repeat;
position: absolute;
display: none;
padding-top: 5px;
text-align: center;
left: 150px;
color: white;
}
#mapdiv {
margin: 0;
}
```

5.5. PE: element positioning

5.5.1. *Purpose*

In this workshop, we present the different methods of positioning HTML elements within a web page.

5.5.2. *Presentation*

1) This workshop presents the methods of positioning HTML elements in relation to each other, namely:

– margin and spacing;

– vertical and horizontal centering;

– display property;

– floating object;

– relative, absolute and fixed positioning.

2) Referring to the following list of screenshots (see Figure 5.7), you are asked to create an HTML web page, as well as its CSS, while respecting the following indications:

– create the <header> element containing a CSS3 icon, an <h1> title;

– create a <div> element as the container;

– create a <section> element containing the following: a paragraph and a list; <article> containing an <h2> title and a paragraph and two <div> elements; <article> containing an <h2> title (a <h3> title, a paragraph and two <div> elements) twice; <article> containing an <h2> title, a paragraph, an <h3> title, a <p> paragraph, a <nav> and two <div> elements and then an <h3> title, a paragraph and two <div> elements; <article> containing an <h2> title (an <h3> title, a paragraph and two <div> elements) three times; <article> containing an <h2> title, a paragraph and two <div> elements;

– create a <footer> containing a paragraph and a hyperlink;

– create a CSS: "style.css";

– import the following Google fonts, icons and CSS: https://fonts. googleapis.com/css?family=Roboto (Roboto font); https://cdnjs.cloudflare.com/ajax/ libs/font-awesome/5.13.0/css/all.min.css (icons);

– add style properties to the HTML elements of your web page already defined according to Table 5.5.

NOTE.– To simplify the presentation of the content of the page *Positioning.html*, we have tried to break the page down into several sections, detailed in Figure 5.7.

Selector	Style
<body>	Font: Roboto, Helvetica, Arial, Sans-serif Font size: 16 px Outer margin: 0
header-fix (class of the header)	Height: 85 px Width: 100% Sets the positioning to fixed Sets the screen positioning for the Y-axis to 0 Sets the screen positioning for the X-axis to 0 Background color: #eee Bottom border: 1 px solid #ddd Box shadow: 0 px 3 px 5 px 0 px rgba(0,0,0,0.75) Z-index: 100
header-container (class of the div element of the header)	Width: 1,024 px Outer margin: automatic
aside (class of the aside element)	Float: right Width: 25% Left outer margin: 1% Right outer margin: 0 Inner margin: 10 px Rounded border radius: 5 px Border: 1 px solid #bbbbbb Background color: white
container (class of the first div)	Width: 1,024 px Outer margin: 84 px auto 10 px Rounded border radius: 5 px Border: 1 px solid #bbbbbb Background color: #eeeeee Inner margin: 10 px
H3 in the aside element	Bottom outer margin: 0 px
ul in the aside element	Top outer margin: 10 px
asidep.aside-info: class applied to paragraphs in aside	Outer margin: 0 Font size: 12 px
article	Text alignment: justified

Selector	Style
code	Inner margin: 10 px Font size: 12 px Background color: white Text color: blue
pre.pre: class applied to pre elements	Text alignment: left Background color: white Inner margin: 10 px
pre.pre code: class applied to codes in pre elements	Inner margin: 0 px
div.content: class applied to the content of the div elements	Width: 72% Text alignment: centered
nav	Width: 100% Text alignment: right
menu class in the ul element	Inner margin: 0 px Outer margin: 0 px List bullet style: none
li element of the menu class in the ul element	Left outer margin: 20 px Text alignment: centered
a element in an li element in the menu class in the ul element	Display: block * by default an a link is displayed inline */ Float left positioning Width: 100 px Inner margin: 5 px Rounded border radius: 5 px Border: 1 px solid white Background color: #597aed Color: white Text decoration: none /* to prevent the a tag from displaying an underline under the text */
a element hovered over in an li element in the menu class in the ul element	Background color: #1226ed Color: white
footer element	Font size: 0.8 rem

Table 5.5. *Style properties of the page Positioning.html*

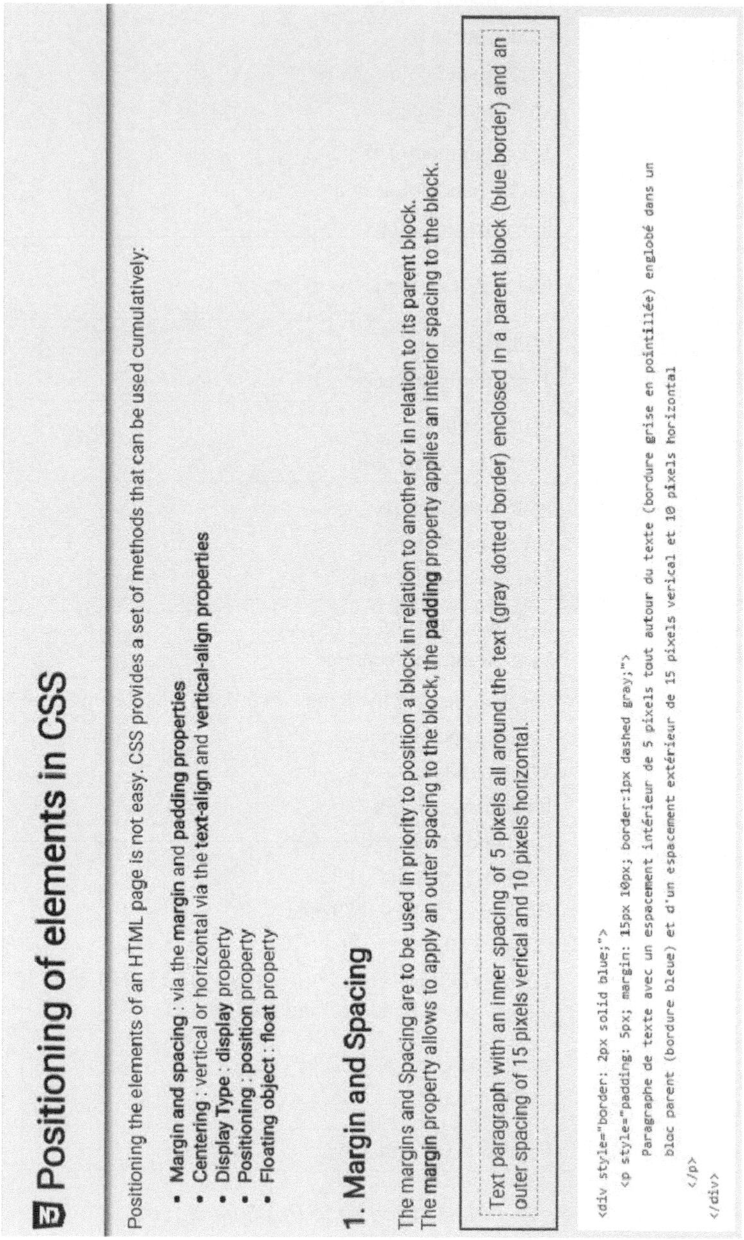

Positioning of elements in CSS

Positioning the elements of an HTML page is not easy. CSS provides a set of methods that can be used cumulatively:

- **Margin and spacing** : via the **margin** and **padding properties**
- **Centering** : vertical or horizontal via the **text-align** and **vertical-align properties**
- **Display Type** : **display** property
- **Positioning** : **position** property
- **Floating object** : **float** property

1. Margin and Spacing

The margins and Spacing are to be used in priority to position a block in relation to another or in relation to its parent block. The **margin** property allows to apply an outer spacing to the block, the **padding** property applies an interior spacing to the block.

Text paragraph with an inner spacing of 5 pixels all around the text (gray dotted border) enclosed in a parent block (blue border) and an outer spacing of 15 pixels verical and 10 pixels horizontal.

```
<div style="border: 2px solid blue;">
    <p style="padding: 5px; margin: 15px 10px; border:1px dashed gray;">
        Paragraphe de texte avec un espacement intérieur de 5 pixels tout autour du texte (bordure grise en pointillée) englobé dans un
        bloc parent (bordure bleue) et d'un espacement extérieur de 15 pixels verical et 10 pixels horizontal
    </p>
</div>
```

Figure 5.7A. *Screenshot of page Positioning.html*

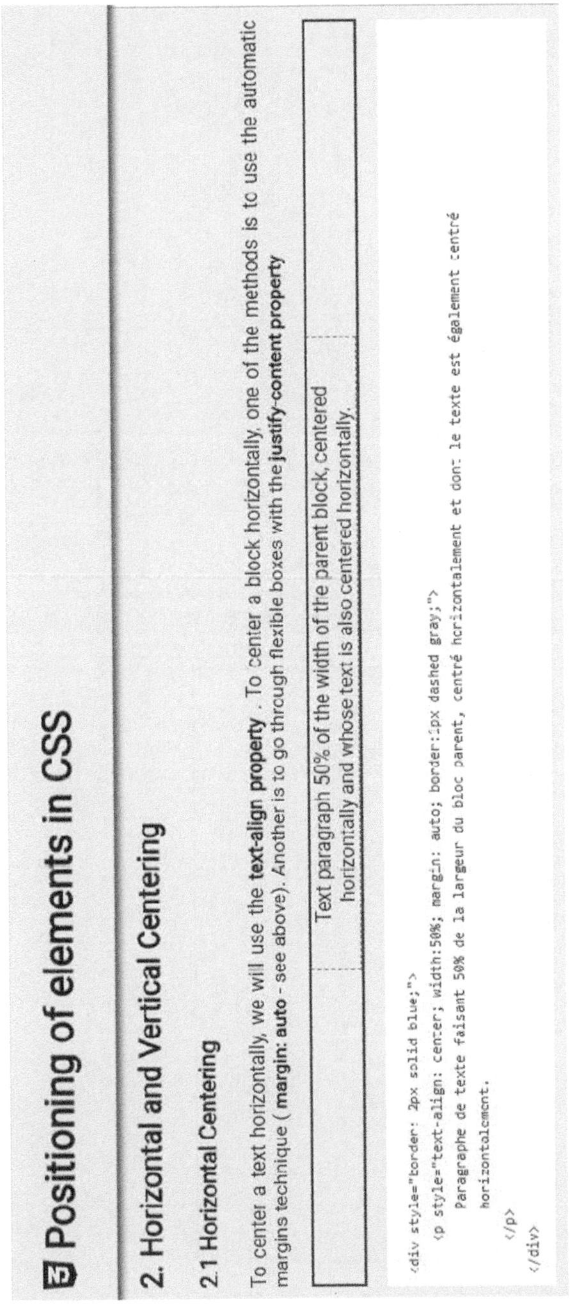

⊟ **Positioning of elements in CSS**

2. Horizontal and Vertical Centering

2.1 Horizontal Centering

To center a text horizontally, we will use the **text-align property** . To center a block horizontally, one of the methods is to use the automatic margins technique (**margin: auto** - see above). Another is to go through flexible boxes with the **justify-content property**.

> Text paragraph 50% of the width of the parent block, centered horizontally and whose text is also centered horizontally.

```
<div style="border: 2px solid blue;">
    <p style="text-align: center; width:50%; margin: auto; border:1px dashed gray;">
        Paragraphe de texte faisant 50% de la largeur du bloc parent, centré horizontalement et dont le texte est également centré
        horizontalement.
    </p>
</div>
```

Figure 5.7B. *Screenshot of page Positioning.html (cont.)*

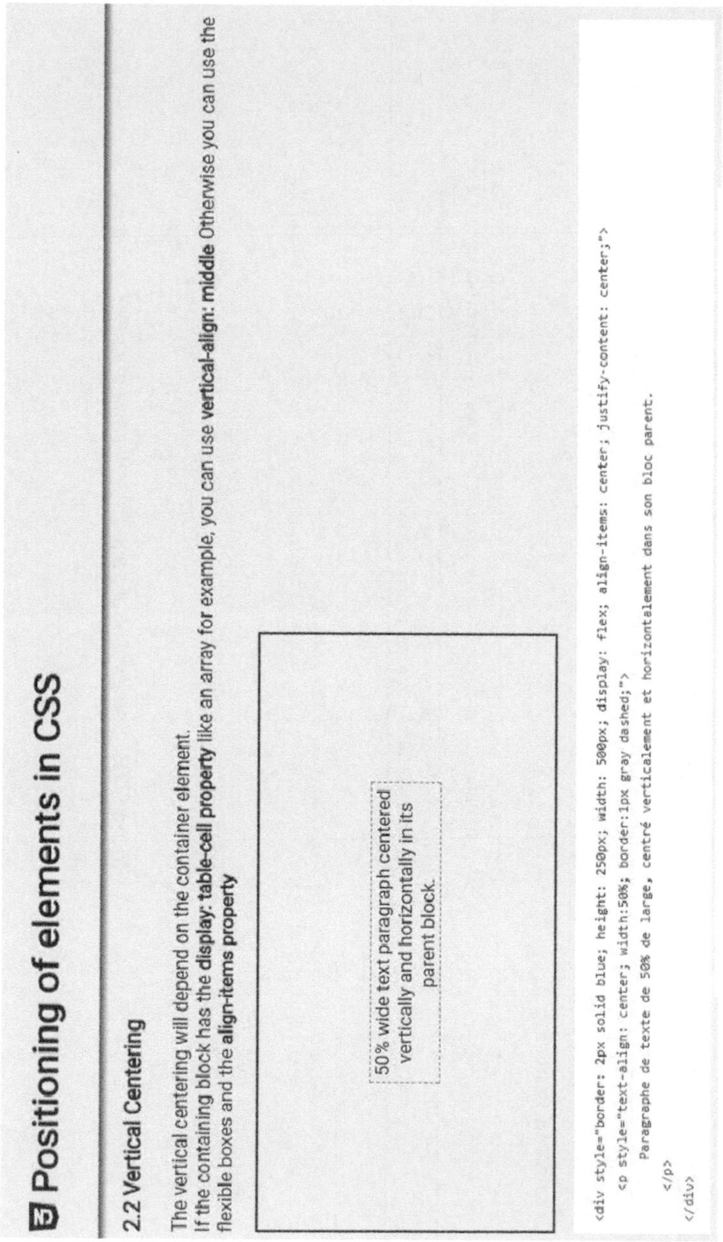

Positioning of elements in CSS

2.2 Vertical Centering

The vertical centering will depend on the container element.
If the containing block has the **display: table-cell** property like an array for example, you can use the flexible boxes and the **align-items property**

Otherwise you can use the **vertical-align: middle**

> 50% wide text paragraph centered vertically and horizontally in its parent block.

```
<div style="border: 2px solid blue; height: 250px; width: 500px; display: flex; align-items: center; justify-content: center;">
   <p style="text-align: center; width:50%; border:1px gray dashed;">
      Paragraphe de texte de 50% de large, centré verticalement et horizontalement dans son bloc parent.
   </p>
</div>
```

Figure 5.7C. *Screenshot of page Positioning.html (cont.)*

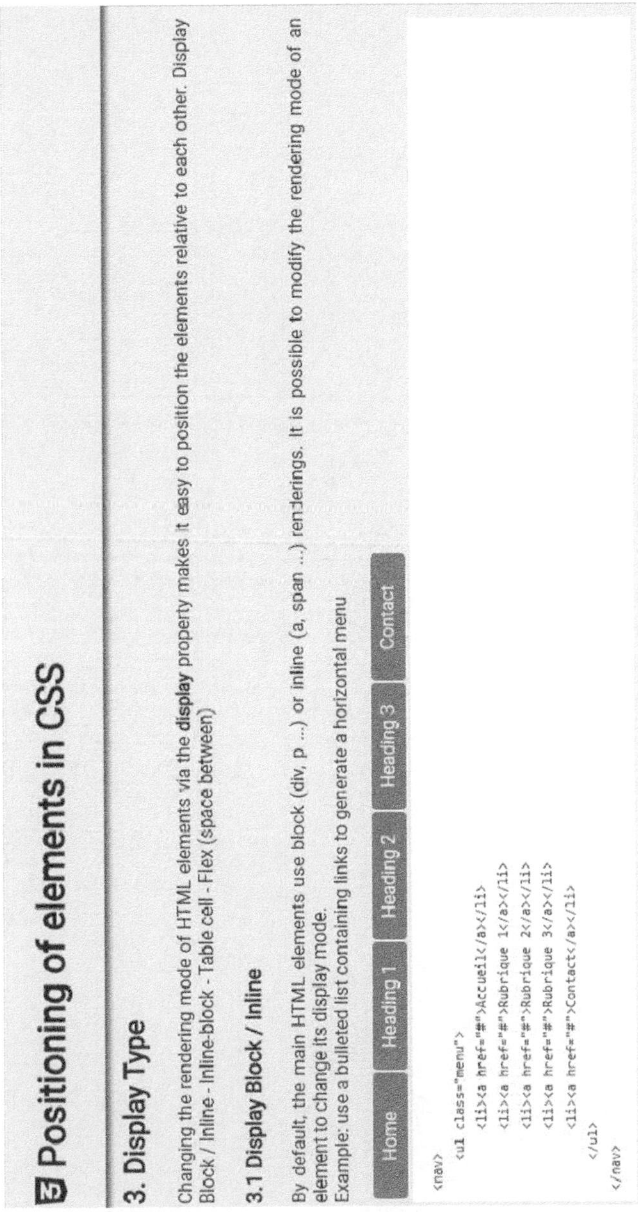

Positioning of elements in CSS

3. Display Type

Changing the rendering mode of HTML elements via the **display** property makes it easy to position the elements relative to each other. Display Block / Inline - Inline-block - Table cell - Flex (space between)

3.1 Display Block / Inline

By default, the main HTML elements use block (div, p ....) or inline (a, span ...) renderings. It is possible to modify the rendering mode of an element to change its display mode.
Example: use a bulleted list containing links to generate a horizontal menu

| Home | Heading 1 | Heading 2 | Heading 3 | Contact |

```
<nav>
    <ul class="menu">
        <li><a href="#">Accueil</a></li>
        <li><a href="#">Rubrique 1</a></li>
        <li><a href="#">Rubrique 2</a></li>
        <li><a href="#">Rubrique 3</a></li>
        <li><a href="#">Contact</a></li>
    </ul>
</nav>
```

Figure 5.7D. *Screenshot of page Positioning.html (cont.)*

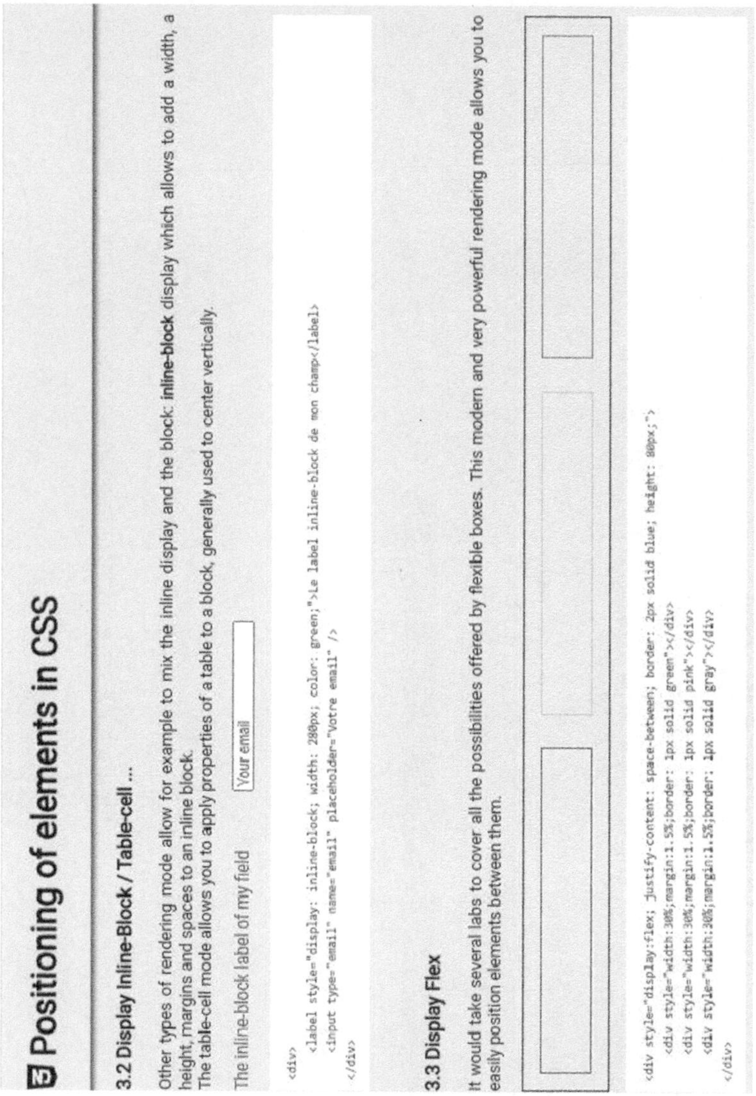

🔟 Positioning of elements in CSS

3.2 Display Inline-Block / Table-cell ...

Other types of rendering mode allow for example to mix the inline display and the block: **inline-block** display which allows to add a width, a height, margins and spaces to an inline block.
The table-cell mode allows you to apply properties of a table to a block, generally used to center vertically.

The inline-block label of my field   [Your email   ]

```
<div>
  <label style="display: inline-block; width: 288px; color: green;">Le label inline-block de mon champ</label>
  <input type="email" name="email" placeholder="Votre email" />
</div>
```

3.3 Display Flex

It would take several labs to cover all the possibilities offered by flexible boxes. This modern and very powerful rendering mode allows you to easily position elements between them.

```
<div style="display:flex; justify-content: space-between; border: 2px solid blue; height: 80px;">
  <div style="width:30%;margin:1.5%;border: 1px solid green"></div>
  <div style="width:30%;margin:1.5%;border: 1px solid pink"></div>
  <div style="width:30%;margin:1.5%;border: 1px solid gray"></div>
</div>
```

Figure 5.7E. *Screenshot of page Positioning.html (cont.)*

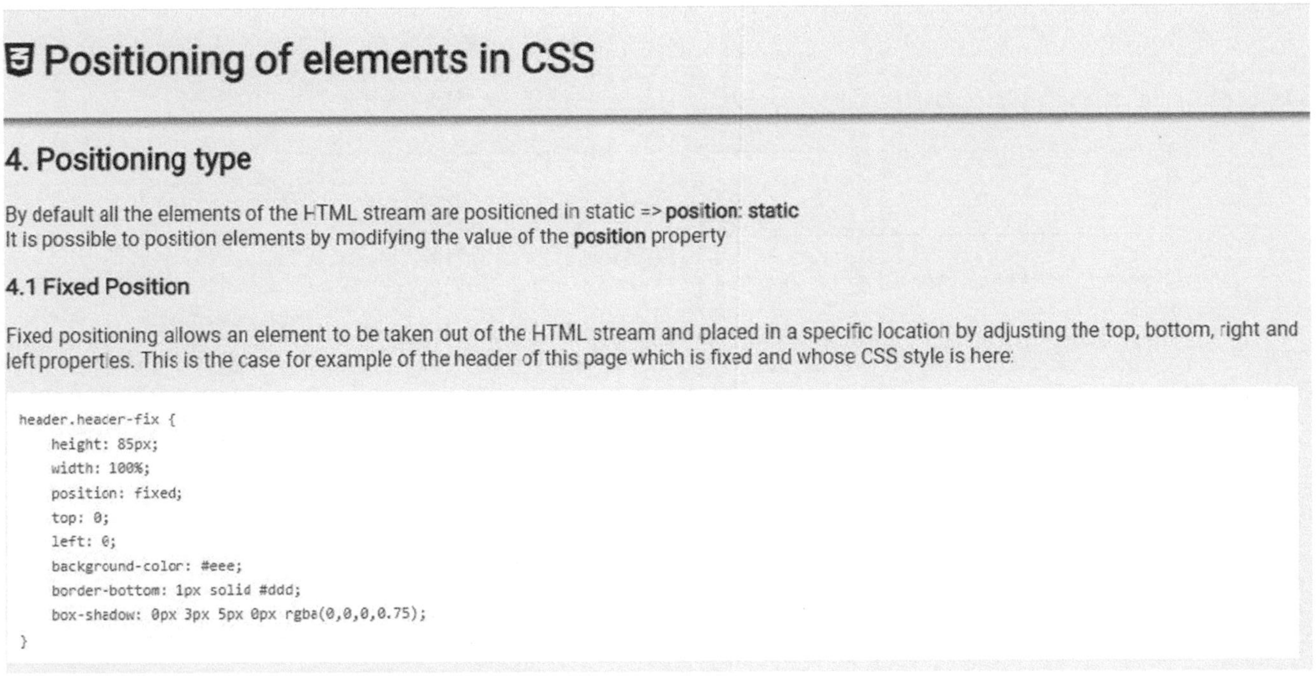

Positioning of elements in CSS

4. Positioning type

By default all the elements of the HTML stream are positioned in static => **position**: **static**
It is possible to position elements by modifying the value of the **position** property

4.1 Fixed Position

Fixed positioning allows an element to be taken out of the HTML stream and placed in a specific location by adjusting the top, bottom, right and
left properties. This is the case for example of the header of this page which is fixed and whose CSS style is here:

```
header.header-fix {
    height: 85px;
    width: 100%;
    position: fixed;
    top: 0;
    left: 0;
    background-color: #eee;
    border-bottom: 1px solid #ddd;
    box-shadow: 0px 3px 5px 0px rgba(0,0,0,0.75);
}
```

Figure 5.7F. *Screenshot of page Positioning.html (cont.)*

Positioning of elements in CSS

4.2 Relative Position

Relative positioning keeps the element in the flow but allows it to be offset from its initial position via the left, right, top and bottom properties.

This block is shifted 10 pixels down and to the right

```
<div style="display:flex; justify-content: space-between; border: 2px solid blue; height: 80px;">
  <div style="width:30%;margin:1.5%;border: 1px solid green"></div>
  <div style="width:30%;margin:1.5%;border: 1px solid pink;position: relative; top: 10px; left:10px;">Ce bloc est décalé de 10 pixels
  vers le bas et la droite</div>
  <div style="width:30%;margin:1.5%;border: 1px solid gray"></div>
</div>
```

4.3 Absolute Position

Absolute positioning takes the HTML element out of the steam and positions it relative to the enclosing block (having the relative positioning property) according to the values provided by top, left, right and / or bottom

This block is shifted 10 pixels down and to the right from the parent block

```
<div style="display:flex; justify-content: space-between; border: 2px solid blue; height: 80px; position: relative;">
  <div style="width:30%;margin:1.5%;border: 1px solid green"></div>
  <div style="width:30%;margin:1.5%;border: 1px solid pink;position: relative; top: 10px; left:10px;">Ce bloc est décalé de 10 pixels
  vers le bas et la droite par rapport au bloc parent</div>
  <div style="width:30%;margin:1.5%;border: 1px solid gray"></div>
</div>
```

Figure 5.7G. *Screenshot of page Positioning.html (cont.)*

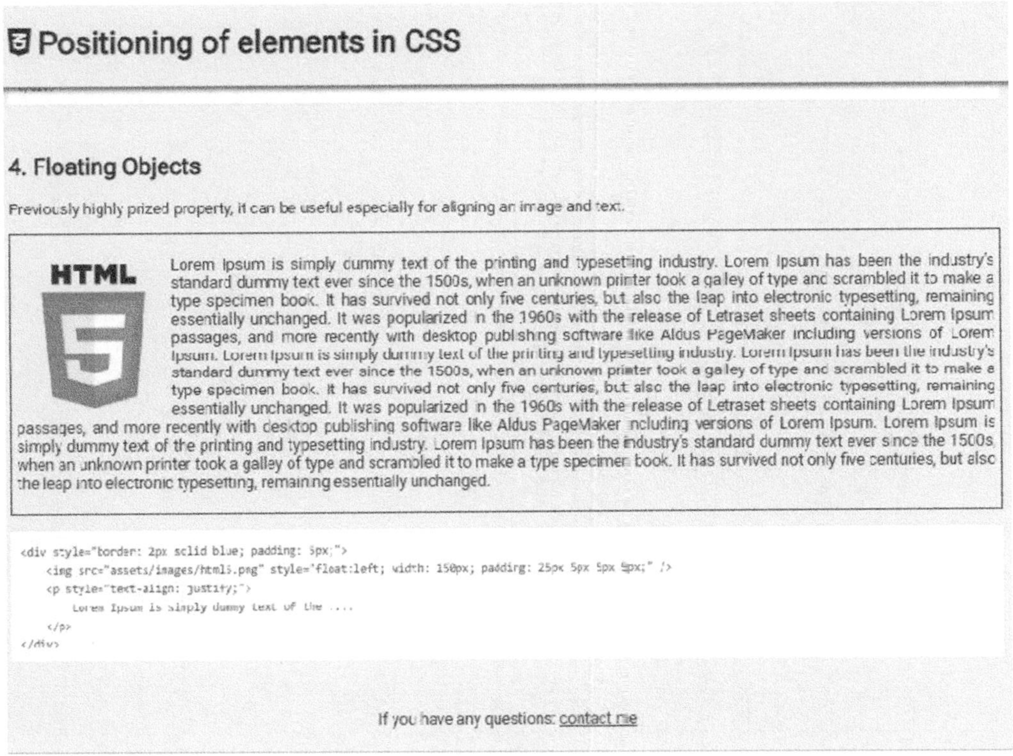

Positioning of elements in CSS

4. Floating Objects

Previously highly prized property, it can be useful especially for aligning an image and text.

Lorem Ipsum is simply dummy text of the printing and typesetting industry. Lorem Ipsum has been the industry's standard dummy text ever since the 1500s, when an unknown printer took a galley of type and scrambled it to make a type specimen book. It has survived not only five centuries, but also the leap into electronic typesetting, remaining essentially unchanged. It was popularized in the 1960s with the release of Letraset sheets containing Lorem Ipsum passages, and more recently with desktop publishing software like Aldus PageMaker including versions of Lorem Ipsum. Lorem Ipsum is simply dummy text of the printing and typesetting industry. Lorem Ipsum has been the industry's standard dummy text ever since the 1500s, when an unknown printer took a galley of type and scrambled it to make a type specimen book. It has survived not only five centuries, but also the leap into electronic typesetting, remaining essentially unchanged. It was popularized in the 1960s with the release of Letraset sheets containing Lorem Ipsum

passages, and more recently with desktop publishing software like Aldus PageMaker including versions of Lorem Ipsum is simply dummy text of the printing and typesetting industry. Lorem Ipsum has been the industry's standard dummy text ever since the 1500s, when an unknown printer took a galley of type and scrambled it to make a type specimen book. It has survived not only five centuries, but also the leap into electronic typesetting, remaining essentially unchanged.

```
<div style="border: 2px solid blue; padding: 5px;">
  <img src="assets/images/html5.png" style="float:left; width: 150px; padding: 25px 5px 5px 5px;" />
  <p style="text-align: justify;">
    Lorem Ipsum is simply dummy text of the ....
  </p>
</div>
```

If you have any questions: contact me

Figure 5.7H. *Screenshot of page Positioning.html (cont.)*

5.5.3. *Solution*

Positioning.html

```
<!DOCTYPE html>
<html>
<head>
<meta charset="utf-8">
<title>Example 5: CSS positioning of HTML elements</title>
<!-- Import of a Google font -->
<link href="https://fonts.googleapis.com/css?family=Roboto"
rel="stylesheet" type="text/css">
<!-- Link to CSS style sheet of HTML page -->
<link rel="stylesheet" href="sets/css/style.css">
<!-- Import of an icon library -->
<link href="https://cdnjs.cloudflare.com/ajax/libs/font-
awesome/5.13.0/css/all.min.css" rel="stylesheet" type="text/css">
<!-- Conditional structure to verify that HTML5 works with older
versions of IE browser -->
<!--[if lt IE 9]>
<script
src="https://cdnjs.cloudflare.com/ajax/libs/html5shiv/3.7.3/html5shiv.
js"></script>
<![endif]-->
</head>
<body>
<!-- Fixed Position Block -->
<header class="header-fix">
<div class="header-container">
<h1><i class="fab fa-css3-alt"></i> Positioning of elements in
CSS</h1>
</div>
</header>
<!--Content of the page -->
<div class="container">
```

```
<section>
<p>
                    Positioning the elements of an HTML page is no
easy feat. CSS provides a set of methods that can be used
cumulatively:
</p>
<ul>
<li><b>Margin and spacing</b>: via the <b>margin</b> and
<b>padding</b> properties</li>
<li><b>Centering</b>: vertical or horizontal via the <b>text-align</b>
and <b>vertical-align</b></li> properties
<li><b>Display Type</b>: <b>display</b> property </li>
<li><b>Positioning</b>: <b>position</b> property </li>
<li><b>Floating Object</b>: <b>float</b> property </li>
</ul>
<!-- Article -->
<article class="marginTop50">
<h2>1. Margin and Spacing</h2>
<p class="marginBot20">
                    Margins and Spacing are used as a priority to
position a block with respect to another block or with respect to its
parent block.<br>
                    The <b>margin</b> property is used to apply
outer spacing to the block and the <b>padding</b> property applies
inner spacing to the block.
</p>
<div style="border: 2px solidblue;">
<p style="padding: 5px; margin: 15px 10px; border:1px gray dashed;">
A paragraph of text with an inner spacing of 5 pixels all around the
text (gray dotted border) wrapped in a parent block (blue border) and
vertical outer spacing of 15 pixels and horizontal outer spacing of 10
pixels.
</p>
</div>
```

```
<div>
<pre class="pre" style="width: 98%;"><code>&lt;div style="border: 2px
solidblue;"&gt;<br>    &lt;p style="padding: 5px;
margin: 15px 10px; border:1px dashed
gray;"&gt;<br>        Paragrap
h of text with an inner spacing of 5 pixels all around the text (gray
dotted border) wrapped in a
<br>        parent block (blue
border) and vertical outer spacing of 15 pixels and horizontal outer
spacing of 10
pixels<br>    &lt;/p&gt;<br>&lt;/div&gt;</code></p
re>
</div>
</article>
<!-- Article -->
<article class="marginTop50">
<h2>2. Horizontal and Vertical centering</h2>
<h3>2.1 Horizontal Centering</h3>
<p class="marginBot20">
                    To center a text horizontally, the <b>text-
align</b> property will be used.
                    To center a block horizontally, one method is
to use the automatic margins technique (<b>margin: auto</b> - cf.
above. Another is to make use of flexible boxes with the <b>justify-
content</b> property
</p>
<div style="border: 2px solidblue;">
<p style="text-align: center; width:50%; margin: auto; border:1px gray
dashed;">
A paragraph of text with a width of 50% that of the parent block,
centered horizontally, and whose text is also centered horizontally.
</p>
</div>
<div>
```

```
<pre class="pre" style="width: 98%;"><code>&lt;div style="border: 2px
solidblue;"&gt;<br>    &lt;p style="text-align:
center; width:50%; margin: auto; border:1px dashed
gray;"&gt;<br>        A
paragraph of text with a width of 50% that of the parent block,
centered horizontally, and whose text is also centered
horizontally<br>        horizo
ntalement.<br>    &lt;/p&gt;<br>&lt;/div&gt;</code
></pre>
</div>
<h3>2.2 Vertical Centering</h3>
<p class="marginBot20">
                    Vertical centering will depend on
the container element.<br>
                    If the container block has the <b>display:
table-cell</b> property, such as a table for example, you can use
<b>vertical-align: middle</b>
                    Otherwise you can use the flexible boxes and
the <b>align-items</b> property
</p>
<div style="border: 2px solidblue; height: 250px; width: 500px;
display: flex; align-items: center; justify-content: center;">
<p style="text-align: center; width:50%; border:1px gray dashed;">
Text paragraph 50% wide, centered vertically and horizontally in its
parent block.
</p>
</div>
<div>
<pre class="pre" style="width: 98%;"><code>&lt;div style="border: 2px
solidblue; height: 250px; width: 500px; display: flex; align-items:
center; justify-content: center;"&gt;<br>    &lt;p
style="text-align: center; width:50%; border:1px gray
dashed;"&gt;<br>        Text
paragraph 50% wide, centered vertically and horizontally in its parent
```

```
block.<br>    &lt;/p&gt;<br>&lt;/div&gt;</code></p
re>
</div>
</article>
<article class="marginTop50">
<h2>3. Display Type</h2>
<p class="marginBot20">
```

Changing the rendering mode of HTML elements
via the `<b>display</b>` property enables easy positioning of the
elements relative to one another.
Display Block / Inline - Inline-block - Table cell - Flex
(spacebetween)

```
</p>
<h3>3.1 Display Block / Inline</h3>
<p class="marginBot20">
```

By default, the main HTML elements use the
block (div, p...) or inline (a, span...) renderings.
It is possible to modify the rendering mode of
an element to change its display mode.`<br>`
Example: use a bullet list containing links to
generate a horizontal menu

```
</p>
<nav>
<ul class="menu">
<li><a href="#">Home</a></li>
<li><a href="#">Section 1</a></li>
<li><a href="#">Section 2</a></li>
<li><a href="#">Section 3</a></li>
<li><a href="#">Contact</a></li>
</ul>
</nav>
<div class="marginTop50">
<pre class="pre" style="width:
98%;"><code>&lt;nav&gt;<br>    &lt;ul
```

```
class="menu"&gt;<br>        &l
t;li&gt;&lt;a
href="#">Home&lt;/a&gt;&lt;/li&gt;<br>     &n
bsp; &lt;li&gt;&lt;a href="#">Section
1&lt;/a&gt;&lt;/li&gt;<br>       &n
bsp;&lt;li&gt;&lt;a href="#">Section
2&lt;/a&gt;&lt;/li&gt;<br>       &n
bsp;&lt;li&gt;&lt;a href="#">Section
3&lt;/a&gt;&lt;/li&gt;<br>       &n
bsp;&lt;li&gt;&lt;a
href="#">Contact&lt;/a&gt;&lt;/li&gt;<br>    &lt;/
ul&gt;<br>&lt;/nav&gt;</code></pre>
</div>
<h3 class="marginTop50">3.2 Display Inline-Block / Table-cell...</h3>
<p class="marginBot20">
                        Other types of rendering modes allow, for
example, inline and block display to be mixed: <b>inline-block</b>
which allows a width, a height, margins and spacing to be added to an
inline block.<br>
                        Table-cell mode allows table properties to be
applied to a block, generally used to center vertically.
</p>
<div>
<label style="display: inline-block; width: 280px; color: green;">The
inline-block label in my field</label>
<input type="email" name="email" placeholder="Your email" />
</div>
<div>
<pre class="pre" style="width:
98%;"><code>&lt;div&gt;<br>    &lt;labelstyle="dis
play: inline-block; width: 280px; color: green;"&gt;The inline-block
label in my field&lt;/label&gt;<br>    &lt;input
type="email" name="email" placeholder="Your email"
/&gt;<br>&lt;/div&gt;</code></pre>
```

```
</div>
<h3 class="marginTop50">3.3 Display Flex</h3>
<p>It would take several PEs to cover all the possibilities presented
by flexible boxes. This modern and very powerful rendering mode makes
it possible to easily position elements relative to each other.</p>
<div style="display:flex; justify-content: space-between; border: 2px
solidblue; height: 80px;">
<div style="width:30%;margin:1.5%;border: 1px solid green"></div>
<div style="width:30%;margin:1.5%;border: 1px solidpink"></div>
<div style="width:30%;margin:1.5%;border: 1px solid gray"></div>
</div>
<div>
<pre class="pre" style="width: 98%;"><code>&lt;div
style="display:flex; justify-content: space-between; border: 2px
solidblue; height: 80px;"&gt;<br>    &lt;div
style="width:30%;margin:1.5%;border: 1px
solidgreen"&gt;&lt;/div&gt;<br>    &lt;div
style="width:30%;margin:1.5%;border: 1px
solidpink"&gt;&lt;/div&gt;<br>    &lt;div
style="width:30%;margin:1.5%;border: 1px
solidgray"&gt;&lt;/div&gt;<br>&lt;/div&gt;</code></pre>
</div>
</article>
<article class="marginTop50">
<h2>4. Positioning Type</h2>
<p>
                    By default, all elements in the HTML flow are
positioned statically =><b>position:static</b><br>
                    It is possible to position elements by
changing the value of the <b>position</b> property
</p>
<h3>4.1 Fixed Position</h3>
<p class="marginBot20">
                    Fixed positioning allows an element to be
```

taken out of the HTML flow and placed in a specific location by adjusting the top, bottom, right and left properties.
                         This is the case, for example, of the header of this page, which is fixed and which has the following CSS style:
```
</p>
<div>
<pre class="pre" style="width: 98%;"><code>header.header-fix
{<br>    height:
85px;<br>    width:
100%;<br>    position:
fixed;<br>    top:
0;<br>    left:
0;<br>    background-color:
#eee;<br>    border-bottom: 1px solid
#ddd;<br>    box-shadow: 0px 3px 5px 0px
rgba(0,0,0,0.75);<br>}</code></pre>
</div>
<h3 class="marginTop50">4.2 Relative Position</h3>
<p class="marginBot20">
```
                         Relative positioning keeps the element in the flow but allows it to be offset from its initial position via the left, right, top, and bottom properties.

```
</p>
<div style="display:flex; justify-content: space-between; border: 2px
solidblue; height: 80px;">
<div style="width:30%;margin:1.5%;border: 1px solid green"></div>
<div style="width:30%;margin:1.5%;border: 1px solidpink;position:
relative; top: 10px; left:10px;">This block is offset by 10 pixels
down and to the right</div>
<div style="width:30%;margin:1.5%;border: 1px solid gray"></div>
</div>
<div>
<pre class="pre" style="width: 98%;"><code>&lt;div
style="display:flex; justify-content: space-between; border: 2px
```

```
solidblue; height: 80px;"&gt;<br>    &lt;div
style="width:30%;margin:1.5%;border: 1px
solidgreen"&gt;&lt;/div&gt;<br>    &lt;div
style="width:30%;margin:1.5%;border: 1px solidpink;position: relative;
top: 10px; left:10px;"&gt;This block is offset by 10
pixels<br>     down and to the
right&lt;/div&gt;<br>    &lt;div
style="width:30%;margin:1.5%;border: 1px
solidgray"&gt;&lt;/div&gt;<br>&lt;/div&gt;</code></pre>
</div>
<h3 class="marginTop50">4.3 Absolute Position</h3>
<p class="marginBot20">
                        Absolute positioning takes the HTML element
out of the flow and positions it relative to the wrapping block
(having the relative positioning property) according to the values
provided by top, left, right and / or bottom.<br>
</p>
<div style="display:flex; justify-content: space-between; border: 2px
solidblue; height: 80px; position: relative;">
<div style="width:30%;margin:1.5%;border: 1px solid green"></div>
<div style="width:30%;margin:1.5%;border: 1px solidpink;position:
absolute; top: 10px; left:10px;">this block is offset by 10 pixels
down and to the right with respect to the parent block</div>
<div style="width:30%;margin:1.5%;border: 1px solid gray"></div>
</div>
<div>
<pre class="pre" style="width: 98%;"><code>&lt;div
style="display:flex; justify-content: space-between; border: 2px
solidblue; height: 80px; position:
relative;"&gt;<br>    &lt;div
style="width:30%;margin:1.5%;border: 1px
solidgreen"&gt;&lt;/div&gt;<br>    &lt;div
style="width:30%;margin:1.5%;border: 1px solidpink;position: relative;
top: 10px; left:10px;"&gt;This block is offset by 10
```

```
pixels<br>     down and to the right with respect
to the parent block&lt;/div&gt;<br>    &lt;div
style="width:30%;margin:1.5%;border: 1px
solidgray"&gt;&lt;/div&gt;<br>&lt;/div&gt;</code></pre>
</div>
</article>
<!-- Article -->
<article class="marginTop50">
<h2>4. FloatingObjects</h2>
<p class="marginBot20">
```

This property, which was very popular in the past, can be useful particularly for aligning an image and text.

```
</p>
<div style="border: 2px solidblue; padding: 5px;">
<img src="assets/images/html5.png" style="float:left; width: 150px;
padding: 25px 5px 5px5px;" />
<p style="text-align: justify;">
```

Lorem Ipsum is simply dummy text of the printing and typesetting industry. Lorem Ipsum has been the industry's standard dummy text ever since the 1500s, when an unknown printer took a galley of type and scrambled it to make a type specimen book. It has overcome not only five centuries, but also the leap into electronic typesetting, remaining essentially unchanged. It was popularized in the 1960s with the release of Letraset sheets containing Lorem Ipsum passages, and more recently with desktop publishing software like AldusPageMaker including versions of Lorem Ipsum.

Lorem Ipsum is simply dummy text of the printing and typesetting industry. Lorem Ipsum has been the industry's standard dummy text ever since the 1500s, when an unknown printer took a galley of type and scrambled it to make a type specimen book. It has overcome not only five centuries, but also the leap into electronic typesetting, remaining essentially unchanged. It was popularized in the 1960s with the release of Letraset sheets containing Lorem Ipsum passages, and more recently with desktop publishing software like

AldusPageMaker including versions of Lorem Ipsum.

Lorem Ipsum is simply dummy text of the printing and typesetting industry. Lorem Ipsum has been the industry's standard dummy text ever since the 1500s, when an unknown printer took a galley of type and scrambled it to make a type specimen book. It has overcome not only five centuries, but also the leap into electronic typesetting, remaining essentially unchanged. It was popularized in the 1960s with the release of Letraset sheets containing Lorem Ipsum passages, and more recently with desktop publishing software like AldusPageMaker including versions of Lorem Ipsum.

```
</p>
</div>
<div>
<pre class="pre" style="width: 98%;"><code>&lt;div style="border: 2px
solidblue; padding:
5px;"&gt;<br>    &lt;imgsrc="assets/images/html5.p
ng" style="float:left; width: 150px; padding: 25px 5px 5px5px;"
/&gt;<br>    &lt;p style="text-align:
justify;"&gt;<br>        Lorem
Ipsum is simply dummy text of the
....<br>    &lt;/p&gt;<br>&lt;/div&gt;</code></pre
>
</div>
</article>
</section>
<!-- Footer -->
<footer class="marginTop50">
<p class="align-center">If you have any questions: <a
href="https://antoinechedebois.com" title="My CV online">contact
me</a> - Credits: HTML5 logo <a
href="https://fr.wikipedia.org/">wikipedia</a></p>
</footer>
</div>
</body>
</html>
```

Style.css

```css
/* Style applied directly to the body of the HTML page */
body {
font-family: 'Roboto', helvetica, arial, sans-serif; /* All texts will
use Google font */
font-size: 16px;
margin:0;
}
header.header-fix {
height:85px;
width:100%;
position:fixed; /* Sets the positioning to fixed */
top:0; /* Sets the screen positioning for the Y-axis */
Left:0; /* Sets the screen positioning for the X-axis */
background-color: #eee;
border-bottom: 1px solid#ddd;
box-shadow: 0px 3px 5px 0px rgba(0,0,0,0.75;
z-index: 100;
}
div.header-container {
width:1024px;
margin: auto;
}
.container {
width:1024px;
margin:84px auto 10px;
border-radius: 5px;
border:1px solid#bbbbbb;
background-color: #eeeeee;
padding:10px;
}
/*CSS used for the sidebar*/
```

```
aside{
float:right;
width:25%;
margin-right: 0;
margin-left: 1%.
padding:10px;
background-color: white;
border-radius: 5px;
border:1px solid#bbbbbb;
}
asideh3 {
margin-bottom:0px;
}
asideul {
margin-top: 10px;
}
asidep.aside-info{
margin:0;
font-size: 12px;
}
/*CSS used for the article*/
article {
text-align: justify;
}
.marginBot50 {
margin-bottom: 50px;
}
.marginTop50 {
margin-top: 50px;
}
.align-center{
text-align: center;
}
code {
```

```
padding:10px;
font-size: 12px;
background-color: white;
color:blue;
}
pre.pre {
text-align: left;
background-color: white;
padding:10px;
}
pre.precode{
padding:0;
}
nav {
width:100%;
text-align: right;
}
/*CSS used for the menu*/
ul.menu {
padding:0;
margin:0;
list-style-type: none; /* To remove the bullet in front of the LI text
*/
}
ul.menuli {
margin-left: 2px;
text-align: center;
}

ul.menulia {
display: block; /* By default an a link is displayed inline */
float:left; /* Float left positioning */
width:100px;
padding:5px;
```

```
border-radius: 5px;

border:1px solid white;

background-color: #597aed; /* A color can be designated by its

hexadecimal code */

color: white; /* A color can be designated by its shortcut */

text-decoration: none; /* to avoid the a tag displaying an underline

under the text */

}

ul.menulia:hover {

background-color: #1226ed;

color:white;

}

footer {

font-size: 0.8rem;

}
```

5.6. PE6: creating a template model

5.6.1. *Purpose*

In this workshop, we present the creation of an HTML5 interface that refers to an administration panel, or a monitoring panel for an application or website.

5.6.2. *Presentation*

1) This workshop presents a web page that corresponds to an administration or supervision panel and its associated style sheet. It covers the following concepts:

– positioning via CSS Grid;

– positioning via Flexible;

– responsive design.

2) Referring to the following screenshot (see Figure 5.8), you are asked to create an HTML web page, as well as its CSS, while respecting the following indications:

– create a <div> element as the grid container;

– create the <header> element containing a collapse menu icon, a search box with a submit button and a profile icon;

– create the <aside> element containing the title of the navigation menu and the list of items with icons;

– create the <main> element containing the following <div> elements: main header <div>, containing mini-card<div> elements; <div> main content, containing card <div> elements in each, an <h2> title and a paragraph;

– create the <footer> element containing a <div> element with the footer text;

– create a CSS: "style.css";

– import the following Google fonts, icons and CSS: https://fonts. googleapis.com/css?family=Roboto (Roboto font); https://cdnjs.cloudflare.com/ajax/ libs/font-awesome/5.13.0/css/all.min.css (icons);

– add style properties to the HTML elements of your web page already defined according to Table 5.6.

Selector	Style
<body>	Font: Roboto Font size: 16 px Outer margin: 0
grid-container (class of the first div)	Display: display in CSS Grid mode Grid column template: two columns: one 260 px wide, the other of the rest (fraction) Grid row template: three rows: 60 px in height for the header, 42 px in height for the footer Grid element template: "aside header"; "aside main"; "aside footer" (layout of the various elements) Height: the entire viewport
aside (class of the aside element)	Grid element: aside
main (class of the main element)	Display: flexbox positioning

Selector	Style
footer (class of the footer element)	Grid element: footer Display: flexbox positioning Placement: flexible Direction: right-to-left row Item alignment: vertical centering of the content of the child elements Inner margin: 0.8 px; text color: #ddd Background color: #466f8a
header-collapse (class of the element of the menu icon)	Text color: #ddd
header-profile (class of the element of the profile icon)	Text color: #ddd Display: align text vertically with a FontAwesome icon Font size: 2 em Vertical alignment: middle Left inner margin: 10 px
i tag in the header-profile class	Font size: 2 em Vertical alignment: middle /* to vertically align the FontAwesome icon regardless of its font size */ Left inner margin: 10 px
header-profile when hovered over with the mouse	Cursor: pointer
aside-logo class of the div element of the logo	Display: flexible /* alternative method of vertical alignment of a text with its FontAwesome icon */ Item alignment: centered /* vertical alignment of content */ Outer margin: 0 Left inner margin: 30 px Color: white Font size: 2 em Font weight: bold Height: 60 px

Selector	Style
aside-logo class of the *i* element of the logo	Right inner margin: 10 px
aside-links class of the div element of the links	Inner margin: 0 Top outer margin: 54 px List style type: none
aside-links-item class of the div element of the link items	Inner margin: 20 px 20 px 20 px 30 px Text color: #ddd
i element in the aside-links-item class	Right inner margin: 10 px
the aside-links-item class with active link	Background color: #466f8a Text color: #ddd
the aside-links-item class with non-active but hovered-over link	Background color: rgba(255, 255, 255, 0.3) Cursor: pointer
aside-links-item-title class of the div element of the titles of the link items	Inner margin: 20 px 20 px 10 px 30 px Text color: #ddd Font weight: bold Text transformation: text to uppercase
item-subtitle class of the div elements of the subtitles	Inner margin: 20 px 20 px 20 px 40 px
main-header class of the div element of the main header	Display: grid/* definition of a container with Grid positioning */ Template for grids in columns: *responsive design*: dynamically defines the width of a column, the limit being 250 px Grid automatic rowsg: 100 px /* defines the size of a grid row: 100 px in height*/ Vertical and horizontal spacing between grid elements: 20 px Outer margin: 20 px
mini-card class of the div element of the mini-card	Positioning: flexible Item alignment: centered (vertical centering) Horizontal spacing: max Inner margin: 20 px Background color: rgba(89, 122, 237, 0.2) Text color: #102b4a

Selector	Style
mini-card-info class of the div info element of the mini-card div	Font size: 3 em Text shadow: 1 px 1 px 2 px black
main-content class of the div element of the main content	Number of columns: 2 Vertical and horizontal spacing between grid elements: 20 px Outer margin: 20 px
card class of the div element of the card	Flexible box positioning Flexible column direction Item alignment: centered Width: 100% Background color: rgba(89, 122, 237, 0.2) Inner margin: 20 px Bottom outer margin: 20 px Box format: border-box Text color: #102b4a
<p> in card class of the card div element	Overflow-y: auto Outer margin: 0
1st child of the card class	Height: 695 px
2nd child of the card class	Height: 200 px
3rd child of the card class	Height: 250 px

Table 5.6. *Style properties of the page webadmin.html*

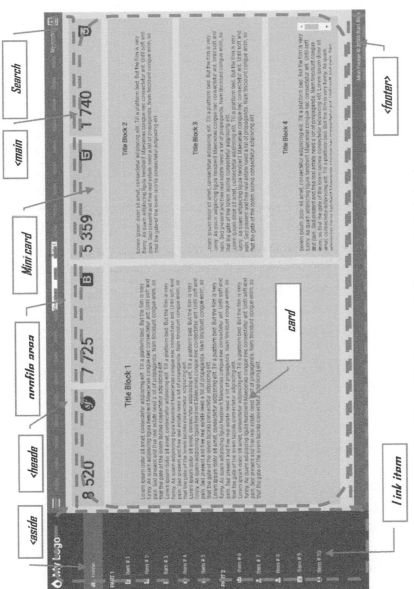

Figure 5.8. *Screenshot of page webadmin.html*

5.6.3. *Solution*

Webadmin.html

```html
<!DOCTYPE html>
<html>
<head>
<meta charset="utf-8">
<title>Title of my Dashboard</title>
<!-- Import of a Google font -->
<link href="https://fonts.googleapis.com/css?family=Roboto"
rel="stylesheet" type="text/css">
<!-- Link to CSS style sheet of HTML page -->
<link rel="stylesheet" href="assets/css/style.css">
<!-- Import of an icon library -->
<link href="https://cdnjs.cloudflare.com/ajax/libs/font-
awesome/5.13.0/css/all.min.css" rel="stylesheet" type="text/css">
</head>
<body>
<div class="grid-container">
<!-- Header -->
<header class="header">
<div class="header-collapse">
<i class="fas fa-bars fa-2x"></i>
</div>
<div class="header-search">
<form>
<input type="search" name="q" placeholder="Search">
<input type="submit" value="Go!">
</form>
</div>
<div class="header-profile">
                    My Profile
<i class="far fa-id-badge"></i>
</div>
```

```
</header>
<!-- Aside -->
<aside class="aside">
<h1 class="aside-logo">
<i class="fas fa-burn"></i> My Logo
</h1>
<ul class="aside-links">
<li class="aside-links-item active">
<i class="fa fa-home"></i>Home
</li>
<li class="aside-links-item-title">
Part #1
</li>
<li class="aside-links-item item-subtitle">
<i class="fas fa-address-book"></i>Section #1
</li>
<li class="aside-links-item item-subtitle">
<i class="fas fa-archive"></i>Section #2
</li>
<li class="aside-links-item item-subtitle">
<i class="fas fa-atlas"></i>Section #3
</li>
<li class="aside-links-item item-subtitle">
<i class="fas fa-briefcase"></i>Section #4
</li>
<li class="aside-links-item item-subtitle">
<i class="fas fa-bug"></i>Section #5
</li>
<li class="aside-links-item-title">
Part #2
</li>
<li class="aside-links-item item-subtitle">
<i class="fas fa-users"></i>Section #6
</li>
```

```
<li class="aside-links-item item-subtitle">
<i class="fas fa-user-md"></i>Section #7
</li>
<li class="aside-links-item item-subtitle">
<i class="fas fa-user-alt"></i>Section #8
</li>
<li class="aside-links-item item-subtitle">
<i class="fas fa-id-card-alt"></i>Section #9
</li>
<li class="aside-links-item item-subtitle">
<i class="fas fa-user-circle"></i>Section #10
</li>
</ul>
</aside>
<!-- Main Content -->
<mainclass="main">
<div class="main-header">
<div class="mini-card">
<div class="mini-card-info">8 520</div>
<div class="mini-card-icon"><i class="fab fa-symfony fa-
3x"></i></div>
</div>
<div class="mini-card">
<div class="mini-card-info">7 725</div>
<div class="mini-card-icon"><i class="fab fa-bootstrap fa-
3x"></i></div>
</div>
<div class="mini-card">
<div class="mini-card-info">5 359</div>
<div class="mini-card-icon"><i class="fab fa-html5 fa-3x"></i></div>
</div>
<div class="mini-card">
<div class="mini-card-info">1 740</div>
<div class="mini-card-icon"><i class="fab fa-css3-alt fa-
```

```
3x"></i></div>
</div>
</div>
<div class="main-content">
<div class="card">
<h2>Block 1 Title</h2>
<p>
                    Lorem ipsum dolor sit amet,
consecteturadipisicingelit. Donec a diam lectus. Set sitamet ipsum
mauris. Maecenascongueligula as quamviverra nec
consecteturanthendrerit. Donec et mollis dolor. Praesent et diam eget
libero egestasmattissitamet vitae augue. Nam tinciduntcongueenim, ut
porta loremlaciniaconsectetur.
<br>Lorem ipsum dolor sit amet, consecteturadipisicingelit. Donec a
diam lectus. Set sitamet ipsum mauris. Maecenascongueligula as
quamviverra nec consecteturanthendrerit. Donec et mollis dolor.
Praesent et diam eget libero egestasmattissitamet vitae augue. Nam
tinciduntcongueenim, ut porta loremlaciniaconsectetur.
<br>Lorem ipsum dolor sit amet, consecteturadipisicingelit. Donec a
diam lectus. Set sitamet ipsum mauris. Maecenascongueligula as
quamviverra nec consecteturanthendrerit. Donec et mollis dolor.
Praesent et diam eget libero egestasmattissitamet vitae augue. Nam
tinciduntcongueenim, ut porta loremlaciniaconsectetur.
<br>Lorem ipsum dolor sit amet, consecteturadipisicingelit. Donec a
diam lectus. Set sitamet ipsum mauris. Maecenascongueligula as
quamviverra nec consecteturanthendrerit. Donec et mollis dolor.
Praesent et diam eget libero egestasmattissitamet vitae augue. Nam
tinciduntcongueenim, ut porta loremlaciniaconsectetur.
<br>Lorem ipsum dolor sit amet, consecteturadipisicingelit. Donec a
diam lectus. Set sitamet ipsum mauris. Maecenascongueligula as
quamviverra nec consecteturanthendrerit. Donec et mollis dolor.
Praesent et diam eget libero egestasmattissitamet vitae augue. Nam
tinciduntcongueenim, ut porta loremlaciniaconsectetur.
</p>
```

```
</div>
<div class="card">
<h3>Block 2 Title</h3>
<p>Lorem ipsum dolor sit amet, consecteturadipisicingelit. Donec a
diam lectus. Set sitamet ipsum mauris. Maecenascongueligula as
quamviverra nec consecteturanthendrerit. Donec et mollis dolor.
Praesent et diam eget libero egestasmattissitamet vitae augue. Nam
tinciduntcongueenim, ut porta loremlaciniaconsectetur.</p>
</div>
<div class="card">
<h3>Block 3 Title</h3>
<p>
                              Lorem ipsum dolor sit amet,
consecteturadipisicingelit. Donec a diam lectus. Set sitamet ipsum
mauris. Maecenascongueligula as quamviverra nec
consecteturanthendrerit. Donec et mollis dolor. Praesent et diam eget
libero egestasmattissitamet vitae augue. Nam tinciduntcongueenim, ut
porta loremlaciniaconsectetur.
<br>Lorem ipsum dolor sit amet, consecteturadipisicingelit. Donec a
diam lectus. Set sitamet ipsum mauris. Maecenascongueligula as
quamviverra nec consecteturanthendrerit. Donec et mollis dolor.
Praesent et diam eget libero egestasmattissitamet vitae augue. Nam
tinciduntcongueenim, ut porta loremlaciniaconsectetur.
</p>
</div>
<div class="card">
<h3>Block 4 Title</h3>
<p>
                              Lorem ipsum dolor sit amet,
consecteturadipisicingelit. Donec a diam lectus. Set sitamet ipsum
mauris. Maecenascongueligula as quamviverra nec
consecteturanthendrerit. Donec et mollis dolor. Praesent et diam eget
libero egestasmattissitamet vitae augue. Nam tinciduntcongueenim, ut
porta loremlaciniaconsectetur.
```

Lorem ipsum dolor sit amet, consecteturadipisicingelit. Donec a diam lectus. Set sitamet ipsum mauris. Maecenascongueligula as quamviverra nec consecteturanthendrerit. Donec et mollis dolor. Praesent et diam eget libero egestasmattissitamet vitae augue. Nam tinciduntcongueenim, ut porta loremlaciniaconsectetur.

```
</p>
</div>
</div>
</main>
<!-- Footer -->
<footerclass="footer">
<div>Mon Footer &copy; 2020 Blah Blah - Credit: <a
href="https://mcdium.com/better-programming/build-a-responsive-
modern-dashboard-layout-with-css-grid-and-flexbox-bd343776a97e">Matt
Holland - build a rooponoive modern dashboard</a></div>
</footer>
</div>
</body>
</html>
```

Style.css

```
body {
font-family: 'Roboto'; /* All texts will uoc Google fonl */
font-size: 16px;
margin:0; /* Default margins are canceled so that the site
 takes up the full width and height of the screen */
}
/* CSS Grid: General definition of positioning on the page */
.grid-container {
display:grid; /* display in CSS Grid mode */
grid-template-columns: 260px 1fr; /* 2 columns: 1 of 260 pixels
wide, the other of the rest (fraction) */
grid-template-rows: 60px 1fr 42px; /* 3 rows: 60px in height for
the header, 42px in height for the footer */
```

```
grid-template-areas:
"aside header"
"aside main"
"asidefooter";/* Layout of the different elements */
height:100vh; /* height: the entire viewport */
}
/* CSS Grid: Definition of grid areas */
.header {
grid-area: header;
}
.aside {
grid-area: aside;
}
.main {
grid-area: main;
}
.footer {
grid-area: footer;
}
/*Header*/
.header {
display: flex; /* Flexible positioning */
align-items: center; /* vertical centering of child elements */
justify-content: space-between; /* sets the space between
child elements: the first element aligned to the left, the last to the
right */
padding: 016px;
background-color: #466f8a;
}
.header-collapse{
color: #ddd;
}
.header-collapse:hover{
cursor: pointer;
```

```
}
.header-profile {
color: #ddd;
display:inline-block; /* To align text vertically with a FontAwesome
icon */
}
.header-profili{
font-size: 2em;
Vertical-align: middle; /* To align the FontAwesome icon vertically
regardless of its font size */
padding-left: 10px;
}
.header-profilc:hover{
cursor: pointer;
}
/*Aside */
.aside {
display: flex; /* Flexible box positioning */
flex-direction: column; /* Positioning of elements in columns */
background-color: #394263;
}
.aside-logo {
display:flex; /* Alternative method of vertical alignment of a text
with its FontAwesome icon */
Align-items: center; /* Vertical alignment of content */
margin: 0;
padding-left: 30px;
color: white;
font-size: 2em;
font-weight: bold;
height: 60px;
}
.aside-logoi {
```

```css
padding-right: 10px;
}
.aside-links {
padding: 0;
margin-top: 54px;
list-style-type: none;
}
.aside-links-item {
padding: 20px 20px20px30px;
color: #ddd;
}
.aside-links-itemi {
padding-right: 10px;
}
.aside-links-item.active {
background-color: #466f8a;
color: #ddd;
}
.aside-links-item:not(.active):hover { /* :not() enables a filter to
be applied to the .aside-links-item selector */
background-color: rgba(255, 255, 255, 0.3;
cursor: pointer;
}
.aside-links-item-title {
padding: 20px 10px 30px;
color: #ddd;
font-weight: bold;
text-transform: uppercase; /* Whatever the HTML text, it will be
displayed in uppercase */
}
.item-subtitle {
padding: 20px 20px20px40px;
}
/*Footer*/
```

```
.footer {
display: flex; /* Flexible box positioning*/
flex-direction: row-reverse; /* Direction: right-to
-left row */
align-items: center; /* vertical centering of the content of child
elements */
padding: 08px;
color: #ddd;
background-color: #466f8a;
}
/*Main*/
.main {
background-color: #ddd;
}
.main-header {
display:grid; /* Definition of a container with Grid positioning */
grid-template-columns: repeat(auto-fit, minmax(250px, 1fr)); /*
Responsive design: dynamically sets the width of a column, the limit
being 250 pixels */
grid-auto-rows: 100px; /* Sets the size of a grid row: 100px in height
*/
grid gap: 20px; /* Vertical and horizontal spacing between grid
elements: 20px */
margin: 20px;
}
.mini-card {
display: flex; /* Flexible Positioning */
align-items: center; /* Vertical centering */
justify-content: space-between; /* Max. horizontal spacing */
padding: 20px;
background-color: rgba(89, 122, 237, 0.2);
color: #102b4a;
}
.mini-card-info{
```

```
font-size: 3em;
text-shadow: 1px 1px2px black;
}
.main-content {
column-count: 2; /* No. of columns: here 2 */
column-gap: 20Ppx; /* Vertical and horizontal spacing between grid
elements: 20px */
margin: 20px;
}
.card {
display: flex; /* Flexible box positioning*/
flex-direction: column; /* Column direction */
align-items: center;
width: 100%.
background-color: rgba(89, 122, 237, 0.2);
padding: 20px;
margin-bottom: 20px;
box-sizing: border-box;
color: #102b4a;
}
.cardp {
overflow-y: auto;
margin: 0;
}
/* Forces the height of the different blocks */
.card:first-child {
height: 695px;
}
.card:nth-child(2) {
height: 200px;
}
.card:nth-child(3) {
height: 250px;
}
```

```
.card:nth-child(4) {

height: 205px;

}
```

5.7. PE7: creating a website from A to Z

In this workshop, we discuss all of the steps necessary to create a professional website.

5.7.1. *Step 0: purpose of the site*

The first task is, of course, knowing what to do; that is, defining a theme, a purpose for your website or web application.

In our example (based on a concrete case), our purpose is to create a site for connecting athletes who practice running.

5.7.2. *Step 1: functional scope*

This step consists of listing all of the features expected by the project in order to have a comprehensive view of what the web platform will do.

This collection of features is called a specification or *backlog*. Of course, other features may emerge during the other phases of the project and should be integrated into the backlog.

A backlog is composed of *user stories*, all of which are normally independent of each other and present a functional requirement.

NOTE.– User story is a simple description of a user-expressed need or expectation used in the field of software development and new product design to determine the functions to be developed.

Here is what the initial backlog of our running platform could look like:

– as a visitor, I should be able to read the general information of the site (members, ads, routes, events, etc.), but not interact with them;

– as a visitor, I should be able to register on the platform to become a member;

– as a member, I should be able to log in and access my personalized home page (see members close to where I live, upcoming outings, ads, etc.);

– as a member, I should be able to access my profile and change the login information (password, email and browsing preferences);

– as a member, I should be able to access and edit my runner profile information (photo, geographic area, description, level, performance, etc.);

– as a member, I should be able to see members who have viewed my profile (my visits);

– as a member, I should be able to send recommendations to other runners and receive recommendations;

– as a member, I should be able to view the runner records of other members of the site and perform advanced searches (by geographical area, level, etc.);

– as a member, I should be able to exchange with other members by sending and receiving messages;

– as a member, I should be able to chat with other members online;

– as a member, I should be able to suggest running, racing and jogging outings to other members;

– as a member, I should have my own blog that allows me to communicate about my running activity;

– as a member, I should be able to submit running ads (material for sale, teacher giving classes, etc.) and receive responses from other members to my ads;

– as a member, I should be able to announce a race that I will be participating in to find other members who wish to run it with me;

– as a member, I should be able to upload GPS traces that I have run or download GPS traces of other members' running outings;

– as a member and as a visitor, I should be able to consult the advice given by the coaches on the site in the form of categorized articles (physical and mental preparation, etc.);

– etc.

Of course, this backlog will need to be fine-tuned and detailed to achieve a sufficient level of granularity, in order to be exploitable by a team of developers.

NOTE. In what is known as "agile" methodology, this collection of features is called a *backlog*, while in the V-model project method it is referred to as *specifications*.

5.7.3. *Step 2: site mockup*

5.7.3.1. *Site tree*

From the features identified in the previous step, it is now possible to gather the various features into large sections that will define the site's page tree. For our example, the site tree could be organized as follows:

1) Profile management:

   - login credentials;

   - my runner profile;

   - my preferences;

   - my blog;

   - my internal messages;

   - my visits;

   - my recommendations.

2) Member directories:

   - multi-criteria search;

   - paginated list of members;

   - outing suggestion;

   - submitting an outing suggestion;

   - paginated list of outings and multi-criteria searches;

   - detail of an outing and opportunity to participate.

3) Ad submission:

   - submitting an ad;

   - paginated list of ads and multi-criteria search;

   - detail of an ad and opportunity to reply.

4) Race organization:

   - submitting a race;

   - paginated list of races and multi-criteria search;

   - detail of a race and opportunity to participate.

5) Route directory:

- submitting a route;

- route mapping;

- detail of a route with the opportunity to download it;

- coaching articles;

- list of articles and multi-criteria search.

5.7.3.2. *Creating wireframes*

We have defined a fairly complete list of the pages of the site. We now need to try to organize the presentation of all of this information as ergonomically as possible.

From the list of pages, it can be noted that the profile management section will only be available to registered, identified members, unlike the others. From this observation, it can be inferred that the main menu of the site is accessible to all visitors. It might consist of:

Members	Outings	Ads	Races	Routes	Coaching

The secondary menu (displayed after the member is identified) might consist of:

My profile	My messages	My blog	My preferences	Logout (redirection page)

It now remains to create a model of the website, i.e. define the site's pages for each target platform (*smartphone*, *tablet* and *computer*) in the form of wired blocks, otherwise known as mockups, wireframes, etc.

The tool used in our example to create these wireframes, very widespread in the world of web design, is called: Balsamiq[1].

For example, see Figure 5.9 for the mockup of the home page in computer version, accessible to all visitors, on which the main menu is viewed. See Figure 5.10 for the mockup of the home page once the member has been identified (still in computer version) on which the secondary menu, accessible to members only, is viewed.

---

1 Balsamiq is a wireframe editing tool: https://balsamiq.com/.

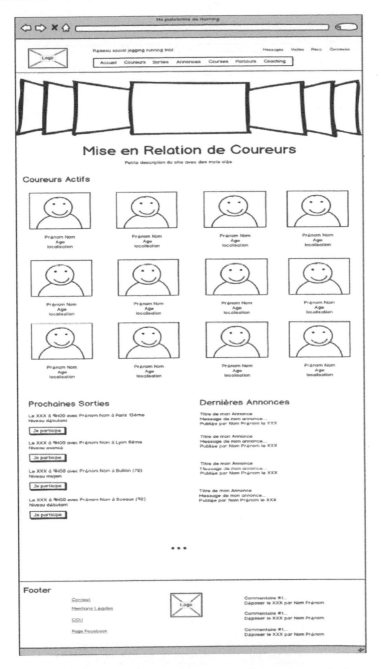

Figure 5.9. *Mockup of the home page (computer version) of the envie2courir.fr site: visitor scenario*

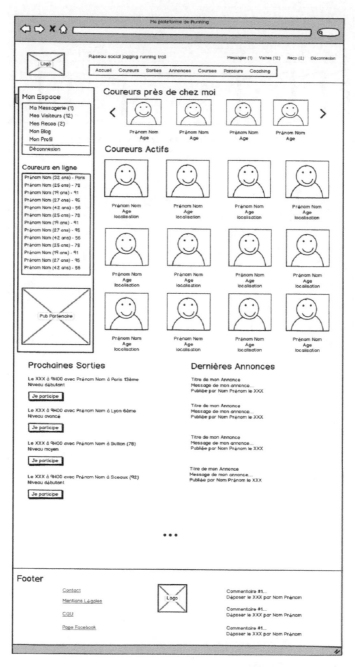

Figure 5.10. *Mockup of the home page (computer version) of the envie2courir.fr site: member scenario*

5.7.4. *Step 3: choosing/defining the graphic charter*

The project is beginning to take shape, but before starting to code the website, a very important last step needs to be performed: defining the site's graphic charter.

From the list of features, the site domain, the target audience, etc., the main guidelines need to be chosen. For our example, here is what this could look like:

– simple and refined, with neutral colors (*the least aggressive possible*) to please a maximum number of people (*of all ages*): white background, black and gray text and green color for certain links, buttons and specific areas;

– in order to be correctly displayed on all types of devices (tablets, smartphones and desktop computers), the site will use *responsive design*: adaptive design (the general look and the different HTML blocks of the site will be displayed differently depending on the resolution of the device displaying it);

– *mobile first* (web design optimized for mobile): the site is created primarily for mobile devices. The pages of the site are first created for display on smartphones, then tablets and finally desktop computers. This stems from an increase witnessed since 2017: the majority of website searches and visits are from smartphones rather than from computers.

NOTE.–

– Because Google represents the majority of searches on the Net, the site has been optimized for this search engine. Points 2 and 3 are important for referencing the site with Google.

– If we had a team of web designers for this project, we could fully define the graphic charter of the website by drawing up graphic mockups of the pages and of all of the components of the site (buttons, forms, tables, etc.) following the guidelines set out above.

Moreover, it should be noted that creating a fully responsive site with many different pages is extremely time-consuming and requires solid web design skills.

Rather than spending a lot of time creating the container, it is preferable to use an HTML/CSS theme, allowing focus to be placed on the content.

To do so, there are many web platforms offering HTML/CSS website templates. These templates already use *responsive design*; they are composed of numerous generic pages (*login page, contact page, lost password, shopping cart, paginated list*, etc.) that simply need to be customized as needed. For our running website, the theme used will be Atropos[2].

NOTE.– It is important to check the technologies used before choosing a theme. Indeed, each theme is based on:

– a CSS framework (Bootstrap or Material being the two most commonly used at present);

– a JavaScript library (JQuery) or JavaScript framework (ReactJS, Angular, Ember, etc.);

– external components (slider, carousel, fonts, graphics, etc.).

You need to know and ideally master these technologies, or you may have to spend a lot of time getting up to speed.

5.7.5. *Step 4: creating HTML/CSS mockups of the main pages*

This step consists of creating non-functional mockups of the future website. That is to say, developing the main pages of the site in HTML/CSS by using the site template (found on the web) and adapting it to match our graphic charter: changing the color codes of the backgrounds, links, fonts, images, etc.

In addition, the use of a CSS framework such as Bootstrap[3] saves a very significant amount of time in the creation of HTML/CSS pages.

Bootstrap is the most widely used CSS framework in the world; the CSS link simply needs to be included in the HTML page header and the JavaScript just before closing the </body> tag to take advantage of extended HTML/CSS features:

– responsive design grid system;

– multitude of web components (carousels, buttons, badges, menus, panels, modals, jumbotron, popovers, etc.);

– CSS Helper classes (colors, display, flexbox, position, sizing, etc.).

Bootstrap has been used for this project in version 3. At the time of writing of this book, version 5 has just been released in alpha version.

---

2 See: https://wrapbootstrap.com/theme/atropos-responsive-website-template-WB05SR527.
3 Bootstrap is a CSS framework: https://getbootstrap.com/.

NOTE.–

– The home page is a very important page on a website.

– It is the starting point for the visitor, who will quickly notice if it is not sufficiently eye-catching.

– In addition, it is very important for referencing, so significant work needs to go into its content, keywords, links, etc.

5.7.6. *Step 5: developing the site from mockups*

This step consists of:

– rendering the HTML mockups previously created so that they are functional (for a contact form page, it is a matter of coding the sending of an email on the server side, for example, or accessing a database to dynamically display data on the HTML page);

– linking the pages of the site together;

– testing your site from end to end, adding error pages, checking the *robots.txt* file, the *sitemap*, etc.

It is also recommended to use tools such as Google Search Console to optimize your site for better referencing. This includes image optimization and HTML optimizations of the site.

NOTE.–

– The *robots.txt*[4] file is used to indicate which parts of the site need to be indexed to the indexing robots that are going to register your site in their search engine.

– The *sitemap*[5] of a website lists the pages and indicates their hierarchy to the index search engines to facilitate referencing.

Once the development step is completed, the final rendering of the site[6] can be seen in Figure 5.11.

---

4 Robots.txt: https://en.wikipedia.org/wiki/Robots_exclusion_standard.
5 Sitemap: https://en.wikipedia.org/wiki/Site_map.
6 See: www.envie2courir.fr.

Figure 5.11. *Final result of the home page of the envie2courir.fr site*

References

Aubry, C. (2019a). *HTML5 et CSS3 : faites évoluer le design de vos sites web*, 4th edition. ENI, Saint-Herblain.

Aubry, C. (2019b). *HTML5 et CSS3 : maîtrisez les standards de la création de sites web*. ENI, Saint-Herblain.

Draillard, F. (2019). *Premiers pas en CSS3 et HTML5*, 8th edition. Eyrolles, Paris.

Engels, J. (2012). *HTML5 et CSS3 : cours et exercices corrigés*. Eyrolles, Paris.

Keith, J. and Andrew, R. (2016). *HTML5 pour les web designers*, 2nd edition. Eyrolles, Paris.

Martin, M. (2013). *HTML5 et CSS3 : l'essentiel des pratiques actuelles*, 2nd edition. Eyrolles, Paris.

Nebra, M. (2017). *Réalisez votre site web avec HTML5 et CSS3*, 2nd edition. Eyrolles, Paris.

Rimelé, R. (2017). *HTML5 : une référence pour le développeur web*. Eyrolles, Paris.

Van Lancker, L. (2013). *HTML5 et CSS3 : maîtrisez les standards des applications Web*, 2nd edition. ENI, Saint-Herblain.

Index

Other titles from

in

Information Systems, Web and Pervasive Computing

GAUCHEREL Cédric, GOUYON Pierre-Henri, DESSALLES Jean-Louis
Information, The Hidden Side of Life

GEORGE Éric
*Digitalization of Society and Socio-political Issues 1: Digital,
Communication and Culture*

GHLALA Riadh
Analytic SQL in SQL Server 2014/2016

JANIER Mathilde, SAINT-DIZIER Patrick
Argument Mining: Linguistic Foundations

SOURIS Marc
*Epidemiology and Geography: Principles, Methods and Tools of Spatial
Analysis*

TOUNSI Wiem
*Cyber-Vigilance and Digital Trust: Cyber Security in the Era of Cloud
Computing and IoT*

2018

ARDUIN Pierre-Emmanuel
*Insider Threats
(Advances in Information Systems Set – Volume 10)*

CARMÈS Maryse
*Digital Organizations Manufacturing: Scripts, Performativity and
Semiopolitics
(Intellectual Technologies Set – Volume 5)*

CARRÉ Dominique, VIDAL Geneviève
*Hyperconnectivity: Economical, Social and Environmental Challenges
(Computing and Connected Society Set – Volume 3)*

CHAMOUX Jean-Pierre
The Digital Era 1: Big Data Stakes

SAUVAGNARGUES Sophie
Decision-making in Crisis Situations: Research and Innovation for Optimal Training

SEDKAOUI Soraya
Data Analytics and Big Data

SZONIECKY Samuel
Ecosystems Knowledge: Modeling and Analysis Method for Information and Communication
(Digital Tools and Uses Set – Volume 6)

2017

BOUHAÏ Nasreddine, SALEH Imad
Internet of Things: Evolutions and Innovations
(Digital Tools and Uses Set – Volume 4)

DUONG Véronique
Baidu SEO: Challenges and Intricacies of Marketing in China

LESAS Anne-Marie, MIRANDA Serge
The Art and Science of NFC Programming
(Intellectual Technologies Set – Volume 3)

LIEM André
Prospective Ergonomics
(Human-Machine Interaction Set – Volume 4)

MARSAULT Xavier
Eco-generative Design for Early Stages of Architecture
(Architecture and Computer Science Set – Volume 1)

REYES-GARCIA Everardo
The Image-Interface: Graphical Supports for Visual Information
(Digital Tools and Uses Set – Volume 3)

REYES-GARCIA Everardo, BOUHAÏ Nasreddine
Designing Interactive Hypermedia Systems
(Digital Tools and Uses Set – Volume 2)

SAÏD Karim, BAHRI KORBI Fadia
Asymmetric Alliances and Information Systems:Issues and Prospects
(Advances in Information Systems Set – Volume 7)

SZONIECKY Samuel, BOUHAÏ Nasreddine
Collective Intelligence and Digital Archives: Towards Knowledge
Ecosystems
(Digital Tools and Uses Set – Volume 1)

2016

BEN CHOUIKHA Mona
Organizational Design for Knowledge Management

BERTOLO David
Interactions on Digital Tablets in the Context of 3D Geometry Learning
(Human-Machine Interaction Set – Volume 2)

BOUVARD Patricia, SUZANNE Hervé
Collective Intelligence Development in Business

EL FALLAH SEGHROUCHNI Amal, ISHIKAWA Fuyuki, HÉRAULT Laurent,
TOKUDA Hideyuki
Enablers for Smart Cities

FABRE Renaud, in collaboration with MESSERSCHMIDT-MARIET Quentin,
HOLVOET Margot
New Challenges for Knowledge

GAUDIELLO Ilaria, ZIBETTI Elisabetta
Learning Robotics, with Robotics, by Robotics
(Human-Machine Interaction Set – Volume 3)

HENROTIN Joseph
The Art of War in the Network Age
(Intellectual Technologies Set – Volume 1)

KITAJIMA Munéo
Memory and Action Selection in Human–Machine Interaction
(Human–Machine Interaction Set – Volume 1)

LAGRAÑA Fernando
E-mail and Behavioral Changes: Uses and Misuses of Electronic Communications

LEIGNEL Jean-Louis, UNGARO Thierry, STAAR Adrien
Digital Transformation
(Advances in Information Systems Set – Volume 6)

NOYER Jean-Max
Transformation of Collective Intelligences
(Intellectual Technologies Set – Volume 2)

VENTRE Daniel
Information Warfare – 2ⁿᵈ edition

VITALIS André
The Uncertain Digital Revolution
(Computing and Connected Society Set – Volume 1)

2015

ARDUIN Pierre-Emmanuel, GRUNDSTEIN Michel, ROSENTHAL-SABROUX Camille
Information and Knowledge System
(Advances in Information Systems Set – Volume 2)

BÉRANGER Jérôme
Medical Information Systems Ethics

BRONNER Gérald
Belief and Misbelief Asymmetry on the Internet

IAFRATE Fernando
From Big Data to Smart Data
(Advances in Information Systems Set – Volume 1)

KRICHEN Saoussen, BEN JOUIDA Sihem
Supply Chain Management and its Applications in Computer Science

NEGRE Elsa
Information and Recommender Systems
(Advances in Information Systems Set – Volume 4)

SALLABERRY Christian
Geographical Information Retrieval in Textual Corpora

2012

BUCHER Bénédicte, LE BER Florence
Innovative Software Development in GIS

GAUSSIER Eric, YVON François
Textual Information Access

STOCKINGER Peter
Audiovisual Archives: Digital Text and Discourse Analysis

VENTRE Daniel
Cyber Conflict

2011

BANOS Arnaud, THÉVENIN Thomas
Geographical Information and Urban Transport Systems

DAUPHINÉ André
Fractal Geography

LEMBERGER Pirmin, MOREL Mederic
Managing Complexity of Information Systems

STOCKINGER Peter
Introduction to Audiovisual Archives

STOCKINGER Peter
Digital Audiovisual Archives

VENTRE Daniel
Cyberwar and Information Warfare

2010

BONNET Pierre
Enterprise Data Governance

GUERMOND Yves
Modeling Process in Geography

KANEVSKI Michael
Advanced Mapping of Environmental Data

MANOUVRIER Bernard, LAURENT Ménard
Application Integration: EAI, B2B, BPM and SOA

PAPY Fabrice
Digital Libraries

2007

DOBESCH Hartwig, DUMOLARD Pierre, DYRAS Izabela
Spatial Interpolation for Climate Data

SANDERS Lena
Models in Spatial Analysis

2006

CLIQUET Gérard
Geomarketing

CORNIOU Jean-Pierre
Looking Back and Going Forward in IT

DEVILLERS Rodolphe, JEANSOULIN Robert
Fundamentals of Spatial Data Quality

Printed and bound by CPI Group (UK) Ltd, Croydon, CR0 4YY